Ford In The Thirties
AF592993

CONTENTS

AUTHOR'S PREFACE 4

INTRODUCTION 5

I THE RISE AND FALL OF THE MODEL A 6

Phasing Out Fours:1928-31
Model A Against Competition
Melancholy Times

II EIGHT-CYLINDER GENIUS 16

Timing the Move:1931-32
The Mechanics of Inspiration
Colossal Commitment
Developmental Difficulties

III LOSING THE LOW-PRICE LEADERSHIP 26

Here it Comes:1932
V-8 Sensation Vs. Depression
Trouble: Expressed and Implied
Discount Discourse
A Loss in Spite of Itself

IV FORD AT HOME AND ABROAD 38

He Preferred Short Strokes
Shook-Up by Streamlining
Model 40's Advantages
Models for Milestones:1933

V COMING OF AGE IN ENGINEERING 48

"Hot" Car for 1934
Most for the Money

COVER: Illustrator Shusei Nagaoka was selected to produce the front cover of *Ford in the Thirties* because of his abilities to depict real-life objects in fanciful settings. The car is his rendering of an early 1932 Ford Deluxe Roadster liberally accessory-bedecked. The symbolic V-8 engine design was used during the era of the Thirties in Ford Factory Service Bulletins. Cover design by Dick Fischer, after a color transparency by Jay Storer.

FORD IN THE THIRTIES

Editor
SPENCE MURRAY
Associate Editor
JIM NORRIS
Art Director
DICK FISCHER
Artist, Design
GEORGE FUKUDA
Editorial Assistant
ANGIE ULLRICH

SPECIALTY PUBLICATIONS DIVISION

Erwin M. Rosen/Executive Editor
Spencer Murray/Editor
Al Hall/Managing Editor
Jay Storer/Feature Editor
Jim Norris/Associate Editor
Richard L. Busenkell/Associate Editor
Eric Rickman/Special Assignments
Dick Fischer/Art Director
George Fukuda/Artist, Design
Angie Ullrich/Editorial Assistant

By Paul R. Woudenberg Ph.D. Edited by Spence Murray with Managing Editor Jim Norris, of the Specialty Publications Division.

Library of Congress Catalog Card No. 76-5982

ISBN 0-8227-0644-X

VI GROWING PAINS AND GOOD RESULTS — **54**
Experimenting with Care
"Bird Wings Are Transverse"
Sheldrick's Solution
Styling Credit:1935

VII WIND OF THE ZEPHYR — **68**
Springing for Trouble
Blossoms of 1936
Blossoms Can Wither, Too

VIII STYLING DRAWS BATTLE LINES — **78**
Splendid Isolation
Struggling to Improve
Bugged with Similarity
1937: A Question of Convention

IX THE RECOVERY OF PROPORTIONS — **88**
Up and Down Advances
Winners from Dagenham
Designing the '37's
A Sudden Recession

X MR. FORD, EDSEL, AND MERCURY — **98**
Mercury: The Messenger
Rumble Seats Are out in the Cold
Competition Stiffens:1938

XI NEW AGE STIRRING—OLD AGE DYING — **108**
Smokers and Stabilizers
Ahead yet Behind:1939

XII TRUCKS AND FORD — **118**
Banner Years:1928-40
Cab-Over-Engine Models

XIII FORD JOINS THE RANKS: 1941 — **128**

XIV A MAN WHO WAS THERE
Looking Back with Emil Zoerlein — **132**

XV FORD CAR MODEL SPECIFICATIONS — **136**

ACKNOWLEDGMENTS

Some books cannot be prepared for print without the special expertise of people outside the ranks of staff members, and this is one of them. For extensive effort, then, in helping make this book possible, considerable credit is due: Gordon Chamberlin, Windom Estes, Phil Hill, Lorin Sorenson; Jim Edwards of Harrah's Automobile Collection; Henry Edmunds, Director, Ford Archives, Greenfield Village, Dearborn; and James Bradley, Automotive Historical Collection, Detroit Public Library, Detroit.

Further thanks are particularly due the following for assistance in amassing the thousands of illustrations from which those used in this book were selected: Bill Honda, Charles Seims, Elmer Ryan, W. Everett Miller, Bob Wingate, Gene Trindl, *Old Motor* Magazine; Automotive Classics, Santa Monica, Calif.; Ford Motor Co. News Department, Dearborn; Petersen Publishing Co. Research Library; Ford of England, Dagenham, Essex; and David R. Crippen, Research Archivist, Ford Archives, Greenfield Village, Dearborn.

AUTHOR'S PREFACE

The most popular enthusiast's and collector's cars in the world today are the Model A and early Ford V-8. Prices for some Fords have reached astronomical levels, far above contemporary luxury and classic makes. But this popularity is not simply a question of the sheer weight of sales because, between 1930 and 1940, Ford was outsold by Chevrolet in all but two years. There is clearly a mystique about the Ford which has transcended all other mass-produced cars.

This mystique derives from the remarkable individuality of the Ford in the Thirties, a car which was quite unlike all its competitors. The Ford had stamina and speed, an engine of unusual merit, and bodies that were not only lighter in weight but of a greater variety than Chevrolet and Plymouth. The Ford was the last major automobile which resisted corporate conformity and retained the clear stamp of its founder. Mr. Ford's ideas and design philosophies persisted in the face of massive changes that occurred throughout the industry from 1930 to 1940. The Ford remained a spirited and responsive pony of a car with excitement and driving rewards.

The paradox that this book attempts to describe is that the very qualities of the Ford car which make it so beloved today are the same that brought about the gradual commercial decline of the company and its products in the Thirties. In 1930, two out of every five cars sold in America were Fords. In 1940, Ford was fighting to hold second place against a superb challenge from Plymouth, a challenge which very nearly succeeded on the eve of World War II.

The decade can be said to have begun auspiciously with the introduction of the Ford V-8 in 1932. It was to be the last major engineering achievement of Mr. Ford. The beginnings of the V-8 were marked by delay, erratic development, and profound manufacturing problems, and some of the solutions were forecasts of the troubles of later years. The undeniably brilliant result and the recovery of sales momentum in 1934, culminating in the great success of 1935, confirmed Mr. Ford's conservatism which would act like a brake upon all innovation in the last half of the decade. Ford Engineering erupted now and then with sometimes bizarre but often genuinely fruitful ideas, yet the company was clearly on the defensive after 1935.

The conversion to hydraulic brakes was virtually completed throughout the industry by 1936 at the moment when Ford was about to take what today is conceded to be a backward step in mechanical braking. The independent front suspension was technically victorious by 1934 though it took some years before the principle makes had fully converted. Ford soldiered on with the transverse springs and solid front axle; and by the end of the decade they had become a serious problem, not only for salesmen but for engineers. The cooling troubles of the Ford were attacked time and again, with only modest success. The competition was not slow in taking advantage of every weakness and Ford dealers pleaded for change.

In truth, Mr. Ford was growing old. The central development work on the 1932 V-8 engine was done in his 68th year. His health was particularly poor in his 75th year, 1938, which really marks his significant withdrawal from engineering. It is remarkable enough that he could continue to lead his company through the decade with such energy and power and yet the steady stream of his vetoes upon technical change in the mid-Thirties must be seen in the context of his aging.

The lack of corporate administrative structure was to prove more serious as Mr. Ford declined. His son Edsel never achieved the rightful independence of leadership in the decade at a time when the Ford car could have profited immensely from his vision. His attention moved to Lincoln and Mercury, areas of greater freedom. Internal squabbles seriously hurt the company as the decade drew to a close and dealer morale was further affected.

The car grew old with Mr. Ford for it was so totally in his image that every attempt to change it was viewed by its founder as a personal assault. This is why the 1940 Ford, the last of the "small" Fords, was so much like its progenitors, going all the way back to 1932.

Thus the virtues and vices of the early V-8's were uniquely preserved throughout the decade which explains in some measure why the cars have retained their popularity in our time. The buying public of the Thirties must be pardoned for forgetting the virtues and concentrating on the vices as Chevrolet and Plymouth forged ahead with automobiles so new in 1940 as to throw Ford's conservatism into stark relief.

History appears to be vindicating Mr. Ford. His unique car with its uncompromising quality and technical eccentricities is the one mass-produced car of that turbulent decade which arouses the loyalties and passions of devoted followers 40 years later. Perhaps it is because we still see the man so clearly in the car.

Carmel, California
April 1976

Paul R. Woudenberg, Ph.D.

INTRODUCTION

It seems appropriate as the Ford Motor Co. draws close to the assembly of its hundred-millionth passenger car—an event projected to occur in late 1977—that we take a backward look at the decade of the Thirties when many current engineering trends were little more than drawing board scribbles. The milestone car will be another in a long series of memorable achievements dating back to the firm's founding in 1903. Mass-vehicle production was unkown then, but Henry Ford would yet bring personal transportation to the masses at prices thought to be unattainable by contemporary manufacturers. *Ford in the Thirties* author Paul R. Woudenberg, Ph. D., has been a student of automotive lore since his earliest days. Now an ordained minister, he continues to seek the little-known about cars, trucks, and the men and companies who designed and built them. His ever-changing stable of collectable cars ranges from early English Bentleys to several pristine Fords of various age. He lectures at the University of California at Los Angeles (UCLA) on the finer points of restoration and on early car values as investment potential, covering not only American products but European counterparts as well. He attends, his schedule permitting, an endless array of car auctions, shows, the large annual swap meets, and Concours d'Elegance events where he is often the chief judge and arbiter, and the final authority on the awarding of points and trophies.

While Paul Woudenberg's automotive interests are sufficiently broad to include virtually everything self-propelled and on wheels, Ford is his favorite, particularly when put into perspective against the industry as a whole.

Ford, the car as well as the man, may be measured by many standards which can be interpreted according to the individual's own value judgments. If one, for example, gauges car design by virtue of year-end sales, then the number one spot might be hypothesized as belonging to the car with the superior styling. But by the same token, the sales winner might have sold well only due to its price advantage, so the first postulation is not necessarily true. Obviously, it is a matter of pure judgment through hindsight. *Ford in the Thirties* is Paul Woudenberg's studied interpretation of the swath that the mighty Ford Motor Co. cut during one of its more significant decades.

To further authenticate several Ford facts, as well as to obtain witness to the inner sanctums at Ford Engineering during the Thirties, the editors sought out Mr. Emil Zoerlein, corporate head of electrical development with the responsibility of designing and perfecting Ford's ignition systems, and who is now retired. Mr. Zoerlein's role in the development of the first Ford V-8 engine, and a few further challenges under the directives of Mr. Ford, are brought out in this book where appropriate. But a final chapter has been added to the Woudenberg manuscript in which excerpts of the actual interview, conducted at the Zoerlein home in November 1975, are transcribed from tapes made at the time. It was felt this precedent-setting addition would shed valuable light on both certain truths and certain myths perpetuated around Mr. Ford himself. We are deeply grateful to Mr. Zoerlein for his time and patience, and for reliving some of his moments of 40 years ago.

Though a full decade of industrial power can, by itself, usually signify a firm's strength and scope, it is inadequate testimony in the case of Ford, whose sprawling empire was equalled by no other company in its time. It is beyond the scope of this book to take the broad overview of Ford and compress its now-73 years between a single set of covers. But the reader should put this single decade into perspective by realizing what a thin slice of automotive history our 10 years of the Thirties represents.

SPENCER MURRAY

THE RISE AND FALL OF THE MODEL A

Model T was born Oct. 1, 1908; when the last of more than 15 million was built 19 years later, it had become the most famous car in history. Despite the T's proven durability, it would lend little to Model A.

No recent decade, apart from the opening years of this century, has had more automotive technological change in America than that of the Thirties. The typical car of 1940 was vastly superior to its counterpart of 1930 in terms of performance, durability, appointments, engineering, and general quality. Performance was, perhaps, the most appreciated change. Whereas in 1930 only the great luxury cars could cruise steadily at 60 or 70 mph, by 1940 such speeds were the normal capacity of almost all cars except perhaps Willys and the Ford V-8 60. And the capacity for these speeds was matched by a reliability which made American cars the envy of the world. The ritual of decarbonization, the regular pull-up of bearings, and the relentless adjustment of valves and points had been all but forgotten. High performance was matched in most cars by synchromesh gear boxes, hydraulic brakes, and (apart from Ford, Willys, and Crosley) independent front suspensions. In addition, there were a host of minor improvements, such as automatic spark advance and generator regulators, which freed the average driver from some of the irritating demands made upon him 10 years before.

It is fashionable in some circles to decry the loss of quality of the automobile during the Thirties. It is true that the great classics at the end of the decade had all but disappeared, perhaps Lincoln being the last producer in 1940 of a car built to 1930 standards. It is true that the Cadillacs had cheapened, even the great 16. And with the end of the Senior Series in 1939, the classic Packard was no more. The issue is seen more fairly when comparing, say, a 1940 with a 1930 Chevrolet. The finish and quality of the 1940 Chevrolet was solid in all aspects. In 10 years weight had risen some 400 lbs., price only $100. There can be no comparison

Ford's first 1928 Model A, a Tudor Sedan brother to this popular Phaeton, was assembled on Oct. 20, 1927; the last Model T on May 28th. While the A introduced 4-wheel brakes, a 3-speed selective transmission, and other innovations, these were not new to the industry. Its 200.5-cu.-in. Four was obsolete, but in four years the car sold 4.8 million units.

Open cars were, and would continue to be, Ford's strong point; and models similar to this 1928 Roadster helped return some of the market penetration that had been severely lost to rival Chevrolet in 1927.

The famous T engine—here a well-used veteran in unrestored guise—was an advanced design in its early years, but was outmoded by the late Twenties.

in terms of ride, comfort, speed, and appointments. And the Chevrolet of 1930, a notorious axle-breaker, could not begin to show the high, trouble-free mileages delivered 10 years later.

The 1930's also produced dramatic changes in body design. The typical car of 1930 was entirely recognizable in terms of concepts developed 10 years earlier. Perpendicular lines, clearly defined fenders, free-standing headlamps, naked flat radiators, exposed spare tires, fabric roofs, flat running boards, vertical door lines, and squared windows were normative. By 1940 these features were all gone. The great rounded curving lines so typical of American cars had added strength, if not classic beauty. There can be no denying that the transition from the old to new brought an awkward period in the mid-Thirties in terms of body design, but by the end of the decade, General Motors and Chrysler Corp. had certainly found a new integration of successful styling ideas.

In 1930 the Ford Model A was not much different in appearance from its principal competitors. The restyled Model A had lost the spidery look of the initial design, and the new higher radiator followed the proportions established by Chevrolet in 1928. But underneath that high and shiny hood was an engine that was conservative, if not anachronistic.

The 4-cylinder engine was generally abandoned by American manufacturers in the Twenties. When Ford began production of Model A in late 1927, there were some half dozen 4-cylinder cars on the market, including such respected names as Dodge, Chrysler, and Chevrolet. But most of the 4-cylinder engines were nearing the end of a long production life, and time had already run out for Oldsmobile's Four in 1923 and for Buick, Nash, and Hupmobile in 1924. The mighty KLDH Stutz with dimensions of 4.375 ins. x 6 ins. was still offered in 1924 with few takers. The Duesenberg engine with dimensions almost as large as the Stutz was

THE RISE AND FALL OF THE MODEL A

Plymouth made substantial sales gains for 1929 against the Model A with 84,969 units sold; yet this trickle was hardly an inroad against the industrial giant. Styling and mechanical refinements were precursors of a trend, as was the heavier body and boxier concept to a status-hungry public.

The 1930 Model A frontal view shows the acceptance of the Chevrolet and Plymouth styling patterns for 1929. Radiator and hoodline are raised to allow a direct flow of lines, without the disparate elements.

Cadillac for 1929 can hardly be likened to the basics that epitomized Model A, yet there is a marked similarity evident in the comparison above. Model A for 1930 (left) wore a bright, similar grille surround.

offered in the Roamer lineup for 1925, but its price was higher than the Roamer Six or Eight, which suggests that old stock was being hopefully moved out under the "built to order" category. The Stearns Knight Model B was catalogued until 1926, and Elcar continued their 4-55 into 1927 as did Auburn their 4-44, both with a Lycoming CF engine of 5-in. stroke. In every case these remaining 4-cylinder engines were at the end of long careers, and these companies were moving resolutely toward Sixes and Eights in hopes of capturing the middle and upper class markets where four cylinders were no longer acceptable.

PHASING OUT FOURS

Of the viable majors only Dodge, Chrysler, Chevrolet, Willys, and Durant were active in 4-cylinder production when Ford introduced Model A. The great old Dodge Four would survive only through the 1928 model year as would the Chrysler in the final Model 52, developed from the previous Model 58, in turn developed from the Maxwell Model 25. The Chrysler engine would soon see new life in the forthcoming Plymouth. The Durant was using the reliable Continental W5 in its Star while the Whippet used an engine whose dimensions, 3.125 ins. x 4.375 ins., were to become world famous in the chassis of the Willys Jeep.

An analysis of 4-cylinder design in the late Twenties suggests strongly that engineers had largely abandoned development of the 4-cylinder engine in favor of Sixes and Eights, with the possible exception of the Chrysler Corp. Outputs and technology reflect engineering ideas of perhaps a decade earlier. Power outputs were understandably low. As late as 1928 the Chrysler 52 offered but 28 bhp with a 186-cu.-in. displacement, not representative of Chrysler engineering but primarily the result of continuing with the old Maxwell design. The Dodge Four introduced five main bearings in 1928 to cope with an increase of bhp from 35 to 40 at but 2000 rpm, and this from 212 cu. ins.! The Dodge engine was about as long in the tooth as its 4.5-in. stroke. The smaller companies usually extracted more horsepower from their fours, the Continental W5 coming up with 30 bhp in 1927 from 152 cu. ins. in the Star. Whippet did even better with 32 bhp from 134 cu. ins., and this at a respectable 2800 rpm in 1927. The 1927 Chevrolet Four with 171 cu. ins. produced 26 bhp at 2000 rpm, raised in the following final year to 35 bhp at 2200 rpm.

All of these horsepower figures emphasize the incredibly low power output of Ford's Model T in its last year; namely, 20 bhp from 176 cu. ins. at only 1600 rpm. The Model T was very likely the only car in U.S. production in the Twenties whose brake horsepower was exceeded by its taxable rating of 22.5, certainly the clearest indication of design ancestry traceable back to 1907-1908. That such an engine could be even remotely competitive says a great deal about Ford's tenacious grip on the low-cost market.

Thus when the Model A was introduced with 40 bhp from 200.5 cu. ins., it was a tremendous improvement over the Model T. Yet in comparison with its direct competitors, it barely caught up and was technically obsolete even as it went into production. This may be easily demonstrated by comparing power output per cubic inch. Of the 4-cylinder engines in production in 1928, only Chrysler and Dodge had output figures lower than Ford. This is all the more remarkable because Ford's design was new, and both Chrysler and Dodge Fours were in their final year of production after long and honorable careers. An accompanying chart compares horsepower per cubic inch in 1928 Fours.

It will be remembered that Model A output remained static throughout most of this time. When Model B output was raised to 50 bhp at 2600 rpm in 1932, the bhp per cubic inch was still but .249, even at that the lowest among the few remaining Fours.

Power outputs were rising rapidly toward the close of the Twenties, principally because of increased crankshaft speeds. The 6-cylinder engines in 1928 which were smaller than the Model A's were developing maximum power around 3000 rpm while some of the really hot engines, such as the little 160-cu.-in. Essex of 1929, developed no less than 55 bhp at 3600 rpm for a very respectable .343 hp per cubic inch. (None of these could begin to compare with the Duesenberg J's 265 bhp at 4200 rpm for an astounding .65 hp per cubic inch.)

In this context, Model A's 40 hp in 1928 obtained

Ford brought forth the Model A engine even as the industry was by and large advancing to the Sixes and Eights. It did compare favorably to Chrysler and Dodge Fours then, but these were in their last year.

New for the 1929 Chevrolet was the much-touted Six, but its initial success was obscured by the phenomenal sales of the 1929 Ford. Yet this powerplant was a design of the Thirties; the Ford's of the Twenties.

THE RISE AND FALL OF THE MODEL A

ABOVE: This 1929 DeSoto is recognizable to the 1923 Dodge, by virtue of freestanding head lamps, vertical windshield and door lines, and the big rear-mounted spare.

LEFT: The first Plymouth arrived in 1928. It was plainly a Chrysler product in terms of overall configuration, and was considered stodgy by some. But by 1931 the marque had risen to third in the annual sales race.

RIGHT: This 1929 Buick weighed 3630 lbs. Its engine power increase from 1928's 63 hp to 74 hp was not enough to give it any performance superiority over the Model A, especially in initial acceleration.

from 200.5 cu. ins. was exceptionally conservative. Lacking a counterweighted crank, using pressure lubrication, and hampered by small diameter bearings, Model A crank speeds were severely limited. There was little danger in over-revving because the breathing, though greatly improved over the Model T, was still asthmatic.

The undeniably bright performance of the Model A was really the result of superior torque, and Mr. Ford's constant attention to reducing weight throughout the whole car. The Model A engine was substantially larger in displacement than all of its competitors, except the Dodge Four which had the same bore and a ¼-in. longer stroke. But the Dodge, for all of its virtues of slogging power, weighed 500 lbs. more than Model A. And in 1928 the Dodge, in almost all aspects, was regarded as a very outmoded design, 4-wheel brakes having been fitted only for the first time in that year. Walter Chrysler was working as fast as possible to improve the whole concept.

MODEL A AGAINST COMPETITION

A more direct comparison should be made with Chevrolet as well as with some of the contemporary small Sixes, which despite superior engine development were burdened with much heavier bodies. The much-vaunted new Chryslers, in their smallest 6-cylinder version, were compelled to haul sedan weights of 2900 lbs. with only 54 bhp. The smallest 1928 Buick had but 63 bhp to handle a sedan of 3400 lbs. Ford's 40 bhp for a 2400-lb. sedan gave it a decided power-to-weight advantage over most other cars.

Chevrolet's new Six of 1929 might have helped reduce Ford's advantage in performance, but this was

The 1929 AC Chevrolet was the competition that triggered the decision at Ford to push development of the V-8. The success of the AC precluded a Ford Six because Mr. Ford prided himself on not copying competition. After all, the make had dethroned his beloved Model T,.

not the case. The original Chevrolet Six produced 46 bhp, raised to 50 in 1930 and 60 in 1932. But all-up weights were rising faster than Ford's, and Chevrolet was never able to reach the power/weight ratios which Ford enjoyed in 1928. This is the principal reason why Ford's reputation in the Thirties rested on speed, beginning even before the V-8 annihilated all low-priced opposition (in fact, almost all opposition at any price level) on a performance basis. Ford's low body weights, along with rapid development of the V-8 power in 1933 and 1934, gave the car an unmatched reputation for speed, perhaps challenged only by the Essex. Alas, Essex engine outputs, though always high, seemed to slightly outstrip Hudson's design ability to lubricate bearings, and by 1933 the Essex name had been sufficiently tarnished to force its withdrawal.

Though the Model A with which Ford entered the Thirties was indeed conservative, if not outmoded, it was a superbly honest car. It had virtues of strength and durability, not only because of the quality of materials, but because it was not overworked. Apart from the flimsy crankshaft with its 1.625-in. main bearings, almost every other part of the car was immensely robust. Even the crankshaft would give little trouble if revs were kept down. Certainly the public received the new Ford gladly, and in 1929 Ford boasted 1,310,147 new car registrations—33.75% of the market. This exceeded 1926, the last big year of Model T, by 121,000 units and almost equalled Ford's 36% market penetration of that year. By 1929 Mr. Ford could thus reflect with some contentment that he had regained the ground lost in 1927 and 1928 when in both years Chevrolet had beaten him by over a quarter of a million units. Model A production had very nearly tripled in 1929 from the previous year, and Model A's swept all before them. He was again king of the mountain.

What was not noticed was that in 1929, even in the face of Ford's massive recovery and mighty production, Chevrolet managed to make a small gain. The new 6-cylinder AC International represented the thinking of the Thirties, whereas Model A was the final flowering of the Twenties. Even Plymouth registrations jumped from 29,231 to 84,969 in 1929, a remarkable achievement for a brand-new car fighting against Ford's domination. Clearly both Chevrolet and Plymouth were offering something new in smooth and comfortable motoring which was of sufficient importance to offset Ford's inherent quality, speed, and low price. Both the Chevrolet and Plymouth in 1929 were more refined cars than the Ford, beginning with engines that did not have the high-speed vibrations common to Ford. Suspensions were just starting to show advances in light cars, of which both Chevrolet's and Plymouth's longer wheelbases and superior springing were but the beginning of fresh chassis development.

Thus, at the beginning of the Thirties, Ford's competitors were on the move, and it will be shown that the development of both Chevrolet and Plymouth continued throughout the decade at a relatively steady rate. Ford had development, too, but in the first two years of the decade virtually nothing happened to answer the growing competition of Chevrolet and Plymouth. The V-8 engine of 1932 was a spectacular achievement which kept Ford competitive for some years. Likewise, the new synchromesh transmission of 1932, which was virtually unchanged through 1938, compared favorably with the designs used by Chevrolet and Plymouth.

However, other innovations came late to Ford, such as hydraulic brakes and the column shift. The 1940 Ford was a strong automobile, perhaps resembling its 1932 counterpart more than Chevrolet or Plymouth. Though conservative in almost every way, the Ford performance and reliability were outstanding through the decade, a tribute to the 1932 car and the design team behind it. It is not unfair to suggest that Mr. Ford's creative energy found its final great expression in the development of the V-8, but by the end of the decade he no longer was able to provide the vision necessary for the competitive leadership of the company. Yet he still exercised a veto upon those subordinates who might have moved the company into fresh ground, and that veto power was to stifle needed change time and time again.

In essence, then, the decade brought to Ford great changes, but they occurred principally in the beginning years. Ford lapsed into a defensive stance in the late Thirties which brought the company to a position which was increasingly non-competitive. This is particularly noticeable in the years 1938 to 1940 during which

Ford dealerships had a hard time in the early Thirties. The owner of this attractive 1929 agency faced a 17.5% discount on his cars in 1930—the lowest in the industry. With the discount raised to 20% for 1931, car sales were still weak. It was a melancholy time to be in the car selling business.

time Ford body shapes were little changed, while both Chevrolet and Plymouth were undergoing major engineering and design transformations.

MELANCHOLY TIMES

To understand the decade of the Thirties, yet another factor in the automotive industry must be considered; namely, the Depression. No one could foresee that the sudden decline of the New York Stock Market culminating on Oct. 29, 1929, would bring year after year of economic disaster. Sad it was that most observers, including Mr. Ford, had anticipated a quick recovery in the manner of 1922. For, flushed with the success of the 1929 model year, Ford reduced the dealer discount to 17.5% at almost the very moment of the market crash and simultaneously ordered a ruthless, if not ruinous, increase of dealerships. Price cuts for 1930 were not fully absorbed by the company, and dealer profits were further eroded. In March 1930 Fred Rockelman, General Sales Manager, resigned in dismay at these policies and soon was to be the head of the Plymouth Division of the Chrysler Corp.

Ford sales for 1930 began auspiciously, in some measure due to introduction of the restyled Model A. But as 1930 unfolded the automobile market became increasingly stagnant, in part because of a mighty glut of used cars left over from the big push of the 1929 season. Also, the growing Depression drove buyers into the low-cost segment of the market, which benefited Ford, at first. It should be remembered that at the end of 1930 there were 4,330,000 Model T's on the road, still able to provide minimum transportation for virtually no initial cost at all. Ford's success in 1930 rested on the dramatic move of buyers away from the economically vulnerable medium-priced field. The weaker dealers faded first and with them the hopes of the independents. Names such as Elcar, Moon and Windsor, Stearns, Gardner, Locomobile, Jordan, Kissel, and later Marmon and Durant, disappeared. Sturdier independents managed to hang on, such as Nash and Hudson, and Studebaker survived even though in receivership. In 1930 Chrysler's profits were reduced to a minuscule $771,000. Ford managed to earn $40,000,000 by selling 1,055,097 units, a figure which

By 1930, the Franklin air-cooled engine had been refined to produce respectable horsepower; this one offered 95 hp at 3100 rpm from 274 cu. ins. An honorable history and undeniable quality couldn't save it.

ABOVE: The final flowering of Model A came for the 1931 model year, and this Cabriolet was among the prettier body styles of the lot. Yet behind the scenes at Dearborn, Mr. Ford was almost ready to unleash a near-miracle on an altogether unsuspecting world.

ABOVE RIGHT: Automotive competition took many forms in the early Thirties, as witness this solid, well-integrated Studebaker Commander Eight.

RIGHT: Franklin could hardly imagine the abyss into which they would fall when they marketed this handsome dual cowl phaeton for 1930. Even so, the marque would outlive many other independents which had failed by 1932.

exceeded the total GM output of 905,427. Such was the mighty momentum of the Ford empire.

Mr. Ford did not foresee the dramatic downturn of 1931. He actually expanded his branch plants in 1930 and further raised his minimum wage to $7 per day. But as the early weeks of 1931 passed by, the truth was soon clear. Ford sales were off drastically, and nothing seemed to help. Ford dealers in particular were suffering under the low discount rates, which further reduced profits, and the policy of adding dealerships in 1930 had produced chaos in orderly sales programs. One-sixth of 8275 dealers dropped their franchises even in 1930 to be replaced by a greater number of new hopefuls recruited from the ranks of yet weaker dealers who had switched, in many cases, from failing independents.

No amount of sales pressure could change the fundamental fact that Plymouth and Chevrolet were making a far better market penetration in the low-priced field. At the bottom of it all was simply because the Model A had fallen further behind in the technological race. In particular, the new Plymouth PA, introduced in June 1931 with a 109-in. wheelbase, set new standards for the low-priced field. It featured a synchromesh transmission, double drop frame, hydraulic brakes, free wheeling, a temperature gauge on the dash, and the floating power suspension. Walter P. Chrysler was proud of this car to the extent that he reportedly took

LEFT: The 1930 Hudson Super Eight roadster was truly a car without a market. Those able to pay such a price in the face of the growing Depression would either move up, or would buy the cheaper Model A.

RIGHT: The body type ahead of its time, Chevrolet's handsome 1931 Landau Phaeton was not copied by Ford, an unusual fact since Ford in the Thirties dominated the convertible market. Ford's A-400 had a similar layout, but the window frame rails were fixed. Rival Chevrolet had this true collapsible, and it was more stylish, too.

BELOW: A last-ditch effort to keep up the styling pace of 1931 was made on some Model A body styles. Note the windshield's rear slant on the Victoria.

the third one off the production line and drove it over to Dearborn, where he took Mr. Ford and Edsel on a demonstration ride. He then presented the car to the Fords and went home in a taxicab. Chrysler's optimism was justified, for in 1931 Plymouth sales actually rose to 94,289, up from 1930's 64,301. In four short years Walter Chrysler had moved Plymouth into third place within the entire industry.

It was obvious that Plymouth and Chevrolet were eating drastically into Ford's market. Plymouth's advances had captured a 5% increase of the market, and Chevrolet, despite a decline in sales, had reached a 30.6% penetration, an all-time high. Ford, meanwhile, was watching its penetration sink to 27.7%. Doomsayers wondered if Ford's conservative policies were going to kill the company. But a surprise was soon to rock the industry, as the seemingly intransigent Mr. Ford roused himself to produce his last major revolutionary design, a genius stroke that would transcend itself.

COMPARED HP PER CU. IN. FOR 1928 4'S	
Chrysler	.164 hp at 2200 rpm
Dodge	.189 hp at 2200 rpm
Ford	.199 hp at 2200 rpm
Chevrolet	.205 hp at 2200 rpm
Star	.230 hp at 2400 rpm
Durant	.236 hp at 2400 rpm
Whippet	.238 hp at 2800 rpm
COMPARED HP PER CU. IN. FOR POST-1928 4'S	
1929 Plymouth	.2642 hp at 2800 rpm
1929 Whippet	.2745 hp at 2800 rpm
1932 Plymouth PA	.2850 hp at 2800 rpm
1933 Willys 77	.3576 hp at 3200 rpm

This 1931 Model A reveals its painted grille shell insert which readily distinguishes it from the 1930 models. Restorers today look for more subtle changes, as one-piece runningboard aprons and fuel lines.

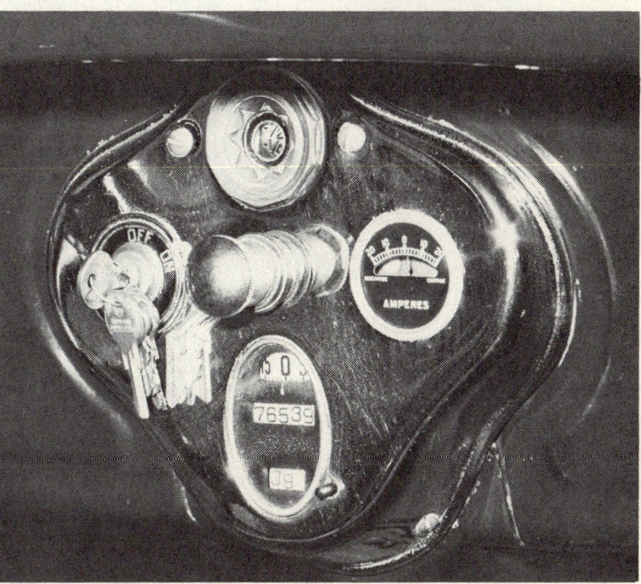

Model A instrument panel told the driver very little as compared to the range of dials and indicators of the competition. Fuel level, amps, speedometer and odometer comprised the limit of the A's telltales.

EIGHT-CYLINDER GENIUS

The final evolvement of Model A showed Ford's priorities in open-car styling, but the engine was long outmoded. Few knew at this car's unveiling that behind the scenes an engine was being spawned that would in one leap move Ford far ahead of his competition.

Deep in a hidden laboratory in Greenfield Village, Carl Schultz and Ray Laird began the layout of the V-8 engine in the spring of 1930. Mr. Ford had reconstructed Edison's Fort Myers Laboratory in time for the opening of the Edison Institute in October 1929, and its isolation within the walls of Greenfield Village made it well suited for research. The order for development of the V-8 was made in late 1929, soon after the introduction of the Chevrolet Six. It has been commonly held that the V-8 was developed only after the Model A had been clearly judged obsolete; that is, in 1931. The truth is that the decision for the V-8 development was made at the very zenith of Model A's success and was not a defensive measure at all. However, Mr. Ford's moves in 1930 suggest that he had no intention of abandoning Model A in the foreseeable future, and, as a consequence, the development of the V-8 moved leisurely. It is true that the V-8 project took on a new intensity in late 1931 when the end of Model A was obvious, but then the project was two years old.

The reason for Ford's choice of the V-8 must primarily be seen in his antipathy to the Six and particularly the challenge of Chevrolet's new AC Model. According to historian Allan Nevins, Ford approached engineering assistant Fred Thoms in 1929 with these words, "We are going from a Four to an Eight because Chevrolet is going to a Six. Now, you try to get all the 8-cyl. engines that you can."

Mr. Ford's dislike of the Six was certainly of long standing, perhaps rooted in his experiences with Model K in 1906. Throughout the Thirties he would persistently fight the Six, even when good experimental units were brought to him occasionally by his engineers.

Although it is generally conceded that Mr. Ford thought that an inline 6-cyl. engine was fundamentally unbalanced, Ford engineer Emil Zoerlein in a recent interview stated differently. He reported that Mr. Ford abhored the "wasted power" caused by the piston stroke overlap necessitated by the 60° spacing between the crankpins. The engineers persevered, however, and a 226-cu.-in., 90-hp, 6-cyl. engine was finally announced for the 1941 model year and it became publically available by June. Cars equipped with the Six were priced $15 lower than comparable V-8's.

Evidently, Mr. Ford's dislike of the 6-cyl. configuration led to early 1930's experiments with an inline 5-cyl. engine. If anything was to drive his engineers to near-madness, it was the thought of producing such an inherently unbalanced engine as one of five cylinders. But on Mr. Ford's insistence, a running 150-cu.-in. prototype was built, tested on a dynamometer, and it produced horsepower figures of between 50 and 60. The project, fortunately, was permanently shelved. That prototype exists today at Greenfield Village.

The V-8 arrangement must have commended itself to Mr. Ford for several good reasons, the most important of which was the production of the Model L Lincoln V-8 in his own plant. The Lincoln engine, with its 180° crank and 60° Vee angles, hardly regulated Ford engine design, but the family influence was present in the same manner that Lincoln details in body and chassis design found echoes in the Ford car.

Furthermore, Mr. Ford could not have forgotten that Henry Leland had taken the Cadillac from a Four to a V-8 in one jump back in 1914 with resounding success. The compactness of the V-8 design, when compared to the lengthy straight Eights of Packard and others, commended itself to the small-car concept. Moreover, the trend in 1930 was to Vee-type engines. Cadillac opened the decade with a magnificent new 16, followed in 1931 by Marmon's 16. A new generation of V-12's was in preparation, too, Cadillac once more leading the way in 1931 to be followed a year later by Packard, Lincoln, Franklin, Pierce Arrow, and Auburn. The Vee-engine climate in the luxury market must have appealed to Ford's sense of the dramatic as he surveyed the low-priced field.

TIMING THE MOVE

That sense of the dramatic was still a powerful motive in Mr. Ford's thinking, for he sought a radical repeat of his earlier success with Model T which would capture the imagination of the public. This explains the abortive experiments with the X-8 engine beginning in

Chevrolet for 1929 had seemingly anticipated Ford's 1930 styling with high roof and unbroken belt line. The fenders are especially stylish when compared to the following year's Ford. Shown is Chevrolet's 1930 offering with its two-year-old 6-cyl. engine that stirred Mr. Ford to his greatest feat.

It is popularly conceded that Mr. Ford abhored the 6-cyl. engine design through the unsuccessful marketing of his Model K, shown here. But whether this is fact or fiction can never be decided. He just detested 6's due to wasted power in the fundamental design.

When, through Edsel's urging, a Ford 6-cyl. engine did emerge, it debuted for the 1941 model year and was probably inspired by the younger Ford's study of the Studebaker engine. This rather rare, unrestored 1941 example shows its out-of-place look in a Ford.

1922. With a displacement of 288 cu. ins., the engine was built both in water- and air-cooled forms, and Mr. Ford pursued its development as late as 1926. Flawed by a high crankshaft position, oiling troubles, and complexity, the engine was never seriously considered for production, and no one in Ford engineering could forget that the Model A was an emergency answer to the company's failure to produce a more creative line of development. Dramatic as the introduction of the A had been, it remained a car of conservative design whose limitations were becoming more apparent as competitors moved ahead.

Model A's 40 bhp from 200.5 cu. ins. at a leisurely 2200 rpm was well-behind both Chevrolet and Plymouth, who were pushing crank speeds up toward 3000 rpm with resultant gains in horsepower. As noted previously, development along these lines for Model A was limited by the flimsy crankshaft with its 1.625-in. main bearings, the lack of counterweighting, and a lubrication system which can best be described as casual. Model A's initial performance was spectacular by virtue of its light weight, but the car actually became slower as it evolved, even while Chevrolet and Plymouth were closing the performance gap. The big 21-in. wheels of 1929, coupled with a 3.7:1 axle, gave Model A a top speed of about 60 mph, but in 1930 the wheel size dropped to 19 ins. and the 4.11:1 axle began to appear. This development forced a hard-pressed and somewhat breathless engine to rev even faster. Sustained high speeds were never really safe in the Model A after the "newness" had worn off because the flexible crankshaft tended to whip away the babbitt of the center main bearing, resulting in a fracture at that point. A common signal for trouble was the appearance of a vibration range, often at around 45 mph, which prudent owners took as the limit for a useful cruising speed. It was wise thinking.

Fred Thoms acted directly upon Mr. Ford's orders and secured nine V-8 engines. One wonders at the nine engines that Thoms secured, or where he went to get them. The DeDion V-8 introduced in 1910—the first true production engine of its type—lasted until 1923 though it is doubtful if many examples were even available, much less known in the United States. The Cadillac V-8, introduced in October 1914, was the pioneer in this country and had many imitators including Oldsmobile, Cunningham, Apperson, Cole, Daniels, King, Peerless, Chevrolet Standard, Stearns, Wills St. Claire and, of course, Lincoln. These American V-8 engines were big and low-revving. The 1926 Peerless may be taken as typical with bore and stroke of 3.25 ins x 5 ins. for a displacement of 332 cu. ins. At 2700 rpm this behemoth developed only 70 bhp.

The very early V-8 craze died as quickly as it started. Oldsmobile dropped theirs in 1923. Cole's big Northway engine was finished by 1925. Apperson wound up its affairs in a blaze of 8-cyl. glory, when, during a brief

No engine in America could compare to the mighty Duesenberg J straight-8 whose 265 hp gave .65 hp per cubic inch, all the more remarkable because it was a physically large engine. Contemporary European engines of high power/displacement ratio were all small in comparison, usually under 1½ liters. The J was 6 liters.

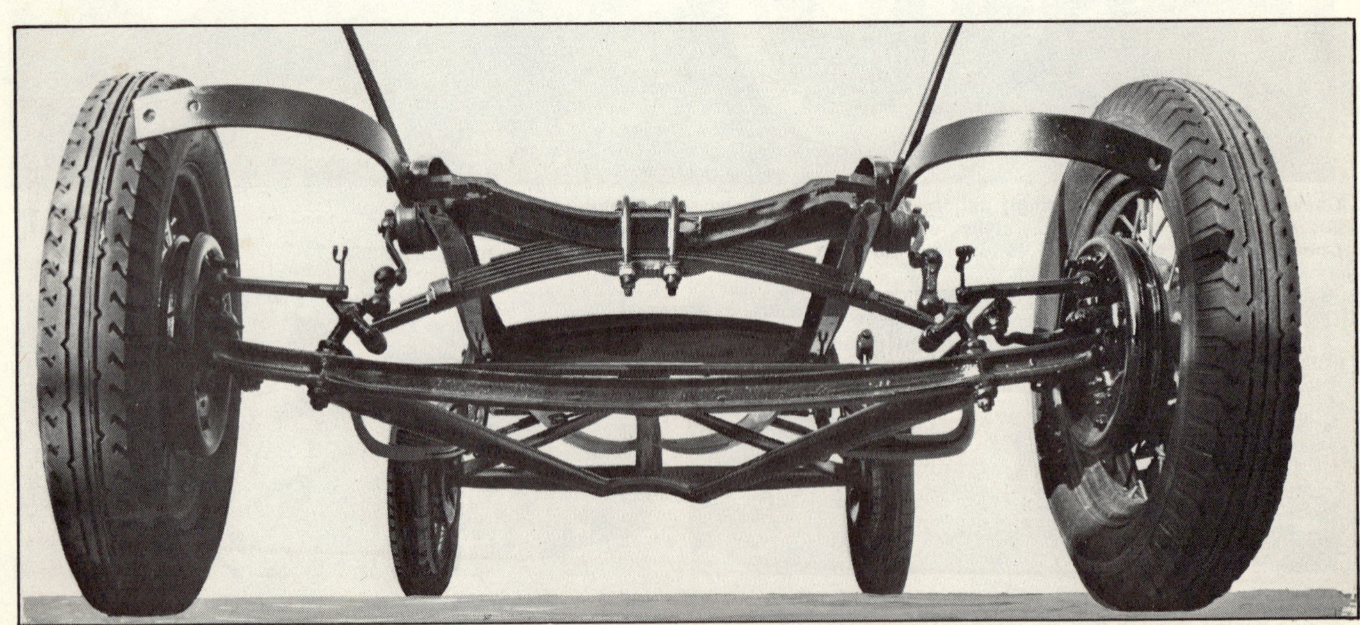

The key to what performance Model A possessed was in its lightweight yet rugged chassis, evident in this example undergoing restoration. The upcoming Fords for 1932 would enjoy the same basic design, but would reflect greater strength to handle the increased engine weight and higher speed.

This engine dominated the luxury class market in 1931, the Packard Straight Eight. It would be the target for V-8 engine development for Packard's Eight was smooth, refined and reliable, but its obvious length precluded its use in the shorter-bodied lower price classes.

Chevrolet had preceded Ford's V-8 concept many years earlier with its 288 cu.-in. version, but Ford could not have cared less, for his Model T at the time was outselling Chevy 12:1 at almost 1/5th the cost.

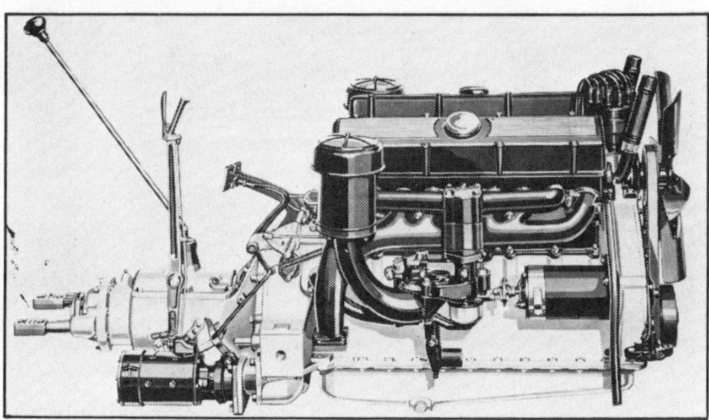

The Vee engine layout found popularity in 12-cylinder configuration, shown here in Cadillac's classic 1931 version. Other luxury cars followed suit shortly; Packard, Franklin, Lincoln, Pierce Arrow, and Auburn in 1932.

period in early 1925, it offered both a V-8 and a Lycoming straight Eight. The Peerless V-8 Model 69 continued through 1928 and was replaced by a Continental straight Eight in 1929. The big Cunningham V-8 was still built in 1929 but would not survive the first wave of the Depression.

Even while the old designs were dying, however, a new generation of V-8's was appearing, fostered primarily by General Motors. The 1927 LaSalle managed 80 bhp from 303 cu. ins. at 3000 rpm, comparable to the 1927 Cadillac's 87 bhp from 314 cu. ins. at the same rpm. In March of 1929, the new Viking from the Oldsmobile Division of GM produced 80 bhp from only 260 cu. ins. and this output, in turn, was bettered in the fall of 1929 when Oakland offered 85 bhp at 3000 rpm from 251 cu. ins. The much-vaunted LaSalle of the same year had reached but 90 bhp from no less than 340 cu. ins. The trend toward smaller displacement engines with equivalent horsepower ratings was evident.

Thus, Fred Thoms could have purchased "off the shelf" in 1929, the Cadillac, LaSalle, Viking, Oakland, Cunningham, the "house" Lincoln and perhaps a leftover Peerless 69. And one could hardly imagine Thoms overlooking the creation of C. Harold Wills, the man so important in the early rise of the Ford Motor Co., who had marketed his own overhead-cam V-8 of advanced design from 1921 to 1926. Could that ninth V-8 have been one of those ohv Mason engines out of a 1918 Model D Chevrolet?

Thoms dismantled and studied the V-8 engines. Their pieced construction and complex manifolding at once made the cost problem clear. The use of aluminum crankcases with cast iron blocks was the mark of quality, but manufacturing and assembly costs were obviously high. Valve location was normally on the inside of the block in order to take advantage of a centrally placed camshaft, but this required that the intake and exhaust manifolding intertwine in carefully and costly produced separate pipings. Mr. Ford saw that a low-cost V-8 engine would require a single casting for its block and crankcase, but in this he faced unanimous doubt from his engineers. "Everybody said it couldn't be done," recalled Thoms, "but Mr. Ford said it could." The costly struggle was thus set into motion.

The development of the V-8 began in the context of previous Ford practice. A 3.625-in. x 3.625-in. engine of 299 cu. ins. was built. Oil was thrown by the flywheel into a tank in the valve chamber, somewhat like Model T. Main bearings were lubricated by gravity flow. According to Eugene Farkas, this engine was built under Chief Engineer Laurence Sheldrick's directions, and it burned out under its first dynamometer test.

THE MECHANICS OF INSPIRATION

One of the eccentricities of Ford Engineering is that several engineers would often be assigned to work independently on a given project, Mr. Ford believing that a competitive spirit would not only uncover the best design but would spur each team to harder work. Thus, when the decision for a 6-cyl. engine was made at the end of the decade, two teams worked independently, and a choice was then made between them. Speaking in relative terms, this practice could and did result in engineering confusion. It was resolved only when Ford management and engineering lines were clarified after Mr. Ford's relinquishing of control.

Meanwhile, at the Fort Myers Laboratory, Schultz and Laird were pursuing a course which would lead to success. In November 1930, they had laid out an engine of

EIGHT-CYLINDER GENIUS

3.375 ins. x 3.5 ins for a displacement of 232.5 cu. ins. The engine was designated as Model 24. In many redrafts this design was developed and the dimensions of the bore were reduced to 3.062 ins. while the stroke was lengthened to 3.75 ins., producing the now familiar 221 cu. ins. The heart of this engine was a sturdy new crankshaft, 1.75-ins. shorter than that of Model A. The three main bearings were 2 ins. in diameter, as the engineers were determined not to repeat the shortcomings of the Model A. The Model B 4-cyl. engine of 1932 also had 2-in. mains, but the V-8 bearings were narrower, with 36.5 sq. ins. of area, compared to the B's 44 sq. ins. This was possible because of the firing overlap of the 8-cyl. engine, the reduced size of the pistons, the new fully counterbalanced crankshaft, and the introduction of full-pressure lubrication. The V-8 crank weighed 65.5 lbs, compared to 38 lbs. for Model B, and was at first forged but later cast.

Model A's 40 hp at 2200 rpm was developed with a 4.2:1 compression ratio. With a heavier crank for Model B, the compression was raised to 4.6:1, which resulted in a peak horsepower reading of 52 at 2800 rpm, yet it was conservatively rated at 50 hp. The first production V-8, with but a 10% increase in displacement, produced 65 bhp at 3400 rpm. and this 60% increase in horsepower over Model A came about with only a modest 5.5:1 compression ratio. It was clear that the new V-8 engine with its higher revving capacity and better breathing was opening up entirely new power potentials. Within three years the V-8 was to develop more than twice the horsepower of Model A, perhaps not so much a tribute to the efficiency of the V-8 as a condemnation of the gross inefficiency of the Model A.

As the V-8 engine developed, Mr. Ford was always seeking the simplest possible solutions to the many new technical problems presented. A typical example was the design of a new distributor. Mr. Ford asked Emil Zoerlein to construct a prototype for Model 24 which would be similar to that of Model A; namely, a fully enclosed Bakelite system in which the plug leads would be brass strips leading from plug to terminals. Zoerlein designed a plastic loom of 1-in. diameter in which the high tension leads were fully enclosed. The

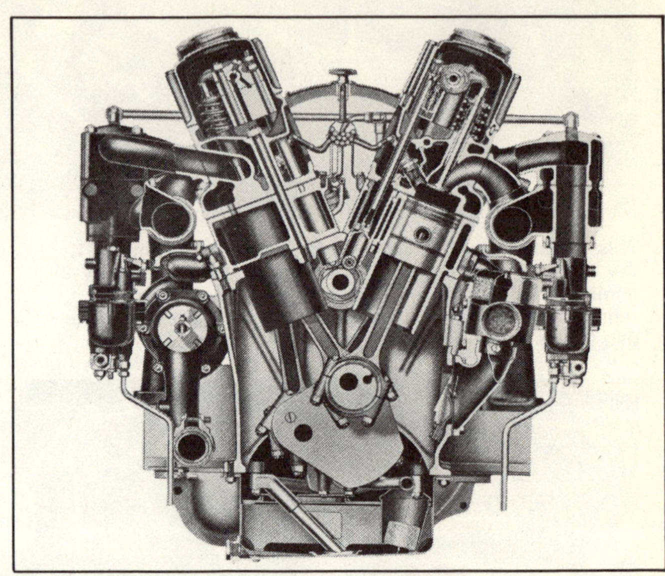

A cross section of the Cadillac V-12 reveals intricate, pieced construction involving pan, crankcase, block and heads. Outside manifolding was possible only by virtue of the overhead valves. Mr. Ford obviously could not follow this concept in his low-cost V-8 design.

A Cadillac classic was its massive V-16, carrying the concept to the logical limit. It helped the motoring public become aware of Vee engine layout, and was followed by the similarly impressive and enormously expensive Marmon V-16. The Vee became the ultimate in engine design, Mr. Ford wanted to capitalize on this fact.

dialectric strength, however, was not sufficient to prevent constant electrical breakdowns. Bakelite tubes were then developed, through which conventional high tension cables were threaded, and this worked satisfactorily. In production, the Bakelite was replaced by simple metal conduits.

The distributor itself was to be mounted directly against the cam gear, an idea of simplicity that was particularly advocated by Mr. Ford, but one which was at variance with engineering thinking of the day. In July 1930, Zoerlein had developed a pilot model and asked Mr. Ford for a suitable electric motor to calibrate it. Mr. Ford noted that only DC current was available in the Fort Myers Laboratory (generated at Greenfield Village by steam power). Mr. Ford then asked Zoerlein to design a small steam engine to provide the motive power to test the distributor! Zoerlein, a man of considerable talent, spent the following month making a superb little engine, 20 ins. long with a 2-in. bore and 2.25-in. stroke, which was able to wind up to 2800 rpm's, which was exceptional for a steam engine. Precise rev accuracy was necessary, and the usual ball-type governor was out of the question. Zoerlein, under Mr. Ford's direction, incorporated a Wright flywheel governor into the engine, and after some intensive steam work was able to proceed with the electrical calibration of the new distributor.

The Marmon V-16 was actually an improvement over the Cadillac design through its unique cross-flow head, but it was too much too late, as even Cadillac's sales had shrunk to near-nothing in the Depression's panic.

It is likely that a 1930 Cadillac V-8 like this one was at the Fort Myers laboratory during Ford's push to finalize his V-8 design. This was a flathead engine, the spark plug covers perhaps fooling some people.

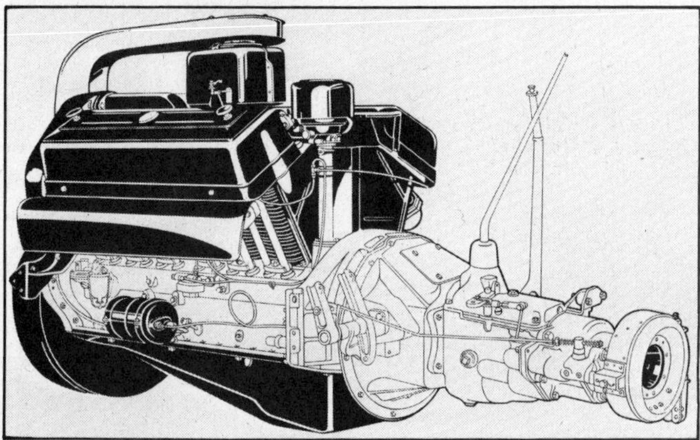

The most remarkable of the V-12's was Franklin's air-cooled concept. But again, it was too complex a configuration to be of any inspiration to Ford who was striving for mass production at low unit cost.

Mr. Ford must have been impressed with Zoerlein's model making, for in October 1930, Zoerlein was removed from development work on the V-8 in order to construct a scale model of Mr. Ford's first car as a Christmas present for Edsel.

As 1931 began the pressure for successful development of the V-8 increased. Though experimental engines were running, the technical difficulties were enormous, and the stakes grew steadily higher as the Depression deepened. It was now obvious that a new car was needed for 1932. The 1931 Chevrolet AE Independence sported a new body on a new 2-in. longer wheelbase of 109 ins. The success of the 6-cyl. engine was clear, since Chevrolet sales were showing more resistance to the declines than those of Ford. Model A sales in 1931 were plummeting to less than half of the 1,055,097 of 1930. Though Chevrolet had sold 618,884 cars in 1930, the 1931 sales were down only 5%, and, in fact, Chevrolet was going to beat Ford for the year—583,429 to 528,581. Quick action was required.

COLOSSAL COMMITMENT

Yet at the beginning of 1931, with normal fall introductions only 10 months away, the new V-8 engine was barely running and, in fact, did not receive serious dynamometer tests until June. The principal problem was in the development of the single casting concept. Combining block and crankcase presented problems enough, but the new design proposed a technical

Beginning with the 1932 model year Ford began a system of coding its vehicles with regard to its model year and body style. It was to remain in effect until the 1938 model year when the system was revised.

Thus a model designation of 68-710 means a 1936 Roadster. The figure "18" indicating a 1932 model stemmed from the first year of the V-8.

MODEL	YEAR
B	1932 (4-cyl)
18	1932 (V-8 from here forward)
40	1933
40	1934
48	1935
68	1936
78	1937

BODY TYPE	NUMBER
Tudor Sedan	700
Roadster	710
3-window Coupe	720
Fordor Sedan	730
Victoria or Convertible Sedan	740
Phaeton	750
Cabriolet	760
5-window Coupe	770
Sedan Delivery	780
Station Wagon	790
Commercial	800

breakthrough in the manifolding which made extraordinary difficulties. Mr. Ford was seeking a way to remove the manifold complications, which often appeared to resemble a spider, astride the central valley of the V-8 block. His answer was to guide the exhaust ports through the block itself so that exhaust manifolds could be attached to the engine on the outside of the Vee. It was a momentous decision, as will be revealed.

The first solution was to have the front and rear cylinder exhaust ports of both banks exit through the ends of the block, with the middle two cylinders siamesed to a single port in the center of the lower outside of each bank. A prototype of this system apparently worked, but the resulting exhaust manifold for each bank was awkwardly shaped like an elongated "W" and added length to the block.

The next development was to bring the front and rear exhaust ports across the block as in the middle cylinders, thus making possible a short exhaust manifold, bolted only on the lower outside of each Vee. The introduction of this porting through the blocks presented huge casting problems. Throughout 1931, Charles Sorensen, production chief at Ford, struggled along with the engineers to solve location problems of the various corings. Failure was endemic. The walls of the various passages were vulnerable to any shifting of the cores, and it seemed impossible to maintain wall dimensions. Even when the design was finalized at the beginning of 1932, there was a 50% rejection of blocks in the first attempts at line production. Not only did the cores shift, but the cupola iron control was faulty, and many of the first production blocks had to be welded and re-annealed. The agonizingly slow start-up production figures for the new engine in 1932 reveal the continuous struggle to solve the problems.

Even the Lincoln V-8 layout was of no help to Ford, for like its contemporaries, it was of difficult design, with pieced construction and complicated manifolding. This was engine very likely dissected at Fort Myers.

A restored 1929 Lincoln V-8 which again shows the complexity of the design and obvious manufacturing expense. Even its unique 60° Vee angle was not duplicated in the Ford search for an affordable V-8. The V-8 Lincoln could hit 70 mph, but from January to November 1930, only 3967 units were sold.

An inherent V-8 shortcoming would soon be revealed which continued to plague the engine throughout the decade. The hot exhaust gasses, passing through the block, acted as a heating system which was responsible for the chronic cooling problems that the engineers attacked again and again. Though the V-8 had only a 10% increase in displacement and a 30% increase in power over the B engine, the radiator capacity for 1932 was increased over the 4-cyl. model A no less than 84%, from 12 to 22 qts., and even this was by no means able to solve the trouble.

Another error in Ford's V-8 design which further compounded the cooling problems was laid down in the first engines. The water pumps were located at the top of the heads to exhaust hot water, rather than at the bottom of the block to pump cold. The pumps thus tended to lower pressure and with it the boiling point of the water. At the first flash of steam, their effectiveness was further reduced.

An early Ford V-8 prototype, in which front and back cylinders exhaust through ends of the block—it created undue engine length and would undoubtably have caused manifold construction problems.

Side view of the above engine shows the Model A coil, the experimental exterior water manifolding on low side of block, and the experimental vacuum clutch. But it was obvious that the design team was on the right track, for there is a lot of similarity between this and the final layout.

Zoerlein called the pumps little more than "agitators," but also noted, "When you make a major change like this on an engine, you're talking millions of dollars. The tooling for the existing pumps was already bought and in operation."

The former research director added: "Mr. Ford tried to get out of this overheating business by adding more radiator capacity, and more water flow through the block in order to get rid of the heat. The problem wasn't solved until after 1937, by putting the water pumps in the cylinder block which *forced* the water through the block, rather than *sucking* it through."

In another knotty problem, the intake manifold at first was little more than an airtight cover which diffused the mixture from the single-throat Detroit Lubricator carburetor to the various ports. But because the manifold lacked the sophisticated intake castings of the expensive V-8's, the system tended to starve the more remote cylinders. This was not corrected until late 1933 production models, which were fitted with the new "over-and-under" manifold, mated to a new dual-throat carburetor. It was first described in a later supplement to the 1933 owner's manual.

It was fairly well agreed that a fuel pump would be necessary for the new engine for two reasons. A rear-mounted gasoline tank was projected for the new 1932 car, in conformity with current practice. The cowl-mounted tank of the Model A had been successful despite criticism that it constituted a fire hazard. But it was obvious that a gasoline tank in the cowl location would pose increasingly severe problems to stylists and engineers, and so a pump was necessary. Secondly, the new carburetor was mounted at the top of the engine and was of down-draft design. The location of a fuel tank for gravity feed was no longer possible.

Mr. Ford hoped to do away with the fuel pump entirely by developing a self-feeding carburetor in which venturi vacuum could be used to draw fuel. Such a carburetor was designed by Mr. Otis Funderburke and when fitted to the V-8 engine actually worked. But the system was acutely sensitive to any changes in atmospheric pressure, and any weather shift disabled the unit. Mr. Ford also ordered an investigation of a pressurized fuel tank, but it was soon discovered that such a tank would not begin to pass numerous safety rules.

The fuel pump finally decided upon was mounted high at the rear of the Vee, an unfortunate location for two reasons. First, the pumps were forced to suck more than push and were prone to vapor lock. Furthermore, water vapor was driven up the fuel pump tower from the crankcase, which served to corrode pump parts. In very cold weather this vapor would freeze after the engine had cooled. Both of these problems were somewhat corrected with subsequent design modifications, but the vapor lock trouble persisted into the postwar period.

DEVELOPMENTAL DIFFICULTIES

These operational problems were not apparent in mid-1931. More important to the engineers were the first results of the dynamometer testing. Power was low, and the engine was rough. Development proceeded through the fall on both valve and ignition timing. The distributor caused considerable problems, because the novelty of its design made it difficult to adjust the points. Eventually, however, it was to become highly reliable.

As Zoerlein explained it, "First of all, Mr. Ford's desire was to have the V-8 distributor mounted in front and driven directly off the camshaft, but through gears.

He wanted to eliminate the gears between the distributor and camshaft, because there are inherent errors and tolerances that stack up. The V-8 distributor, therefore, was a direct drive—camshaft to distributor."

Zoerlein was first given orders to adapt a Model A coil to the V-8's distributor design. Mr. Ford didn't want others in on the project, at that juncture, while Zoerlein was taking an existing Model A coil, with its outside primary and inside secondary, and designing a housing for it. The decision was a prudent one.

"We were able to make a 2-piece Bakelite housing for it. We shoved the tall Model A coil up inside, sealed the base on with oakum, and stuck it on top of the distributor."

But at first, as Zoerlein noted, coil breakdowns were frequent. The Model A's coil wouldn't handle the extra loads. There was more than double the available speed, and nearly twice the rpm with the V-8, and the Model A's Mallory coil, with its outside primary winding, would simply not react fast enough at the vastly improved higher rpm's, finally failing altogether.

Zoerlein next introduced a newer, lower-coil design, which, although a big improvement, still did not offer total satisfaction to Mr. Ford. Dubbed the "hedgehog," the lower-coil design would remain reliable up to 4100 rpm on experimental engines before cutting out. It, too, was shelved. Mr. Ford was a notorious nit-picker for simplicity and reliability in electrical systems, and, as Zoerlein has noted, "was striking out—although he didn't tell me then—to develop an ignition system that would last 50,000 miles."

What Mr. Ford had in mind was to replace a sealed distributor every 50,000 miles with a completely reconditioned unit, and in the process, create a vast revolv-

In the Sugar Mill building at Dearborn's Greenfield Village lie a number of experimental Ford engines, but public access is denied. Here are several V-8's.

Interior of the Fort Myers lab as it appears restored today. In here the developmental work on the Ford V-8 was carried out in deepest secrecy.

A prototype Ford V-8 dating from 1930 and used most likely only for dynamometer testing. It was photographed through a highly reflective window.

Highly experimental, but operationally sound, was Ford's X-8, supposedly destined for a highly refined Model T. It proved too heavy for the lightweight car.

The final configuration okayed for production was this world-famous 90° V-8 nestling neatly here into its first home, a Model 18—and it would shake the world.

ing parts network. National and international rebuilt parts concepts of today can be directly traced to Henry Ford's persistence in this area.

Following the demise of the hedgehog coil, Zoerlein came up with a coil that could boost rpm and higher speeds, by changing from a 4-lobe to an 8-lobe cam and using two breakers. It was this make-and-break design that went into production. Initial distributor and coil combinations used a 4-bolt mounting, yet were almost immediately changed when a vacuum control was added in order to control the road load spark advance, by means of a tube from the intake manifold. In this configuration, one bolt hole was lowered for the fitting, and the fourth eliminated altogether.

In the back of Mr. Ford's mind was the rock-ribbed Model T. As Zoerlein explained, "The Model T had a so-called distributor, in reality not a distributor at all, but a rotary commutator-type, mounted in front of the engine and driven off the camshaft. It was very successful, for that model. Undoubtedly, the success was another reason why Mr. Ford wanted the V-8 distributor mounted in front."

Zoerlein and Ray Laird worked against time and obstacles on the V-8's valve timing, ignition timing, and cam contour changes. Since Mr. Ford's V-8 introduced radical concepts, there were no previously established ignition curve requirements, hence no proper vacuum control figures. Furthermore, there was no equipment to do the job. The test equipment had to be designed in order to analyze the engine, which would in turn rely on the test equipment! Zoerlein's steam engine was a perfect example.

Allan Nevins reports that by the fall of 1931 Mr. Ford was intensly worried about the whole V-8 project. As one of the engineers put it, "He seemed to be getting madder and madder. Of course, we didn't know what he was thinking—but we knew he felt we weren't yet on the right track." Mr. Ford had plenty to worry about. The company was to lose $37 million in 1931. The introduction of slant-windshield styling to the Town Sedan and Cabriolet in mid-year served only to emphasize Chevrolet's styling superiority. William C. Cowling, appointed new sales manager in 1931, raised dealer discounts to 22%, but the discouraged dealers were unable to generate any new enthusiasm. Even in the late fall after Chevrolet had introduced their handsome new BA Confederate Series, Mr. Ford remained silent. For all the dealers knew in that bleak fall, the Model A would go on unchanged into 1932.

According to Laurence Sheldrick, the decision to go into production of the V-8 engine was made in January 1932. Mr. Ford had attended President Hoover's conference on unemployment and had returned with the decision clear in his mind. Ford declared, "We are going into production on the V-8. We are going to stimulate the economy, and stimulate the country, by the production of the V-8." Yet even at this late date, Sheldrick knew that the engine was not ready. Oil consumption was still high, and bearing trouble was continuing. Sorensen had taken the precaution of establishing a pilot production line, which only served to emphasize the foundry problems. In the words of Sheldrick, "The V-8 development was very hurried, and the public was the testing crew,"

It must not be construed that initial production of the new V-8 was in anyway jury-rigged, or that manufacturing quality shortcuts were taken. There was, to state it briefly, much to be done. New manufacturing techniques had to be developed, and new machines devised to perform functions not before required in engine production. An initial goal was to produce 100 V-8 engine block molds per hour in one continuous operation. The sand for the individual molds was fed by gravity through overhead chutes. An automatic vibrator then settled the casting sand firmly in place, where previously this operation had been one of hand labor with workers tamping the sand with mallets.

A raising mechanism was developed which lifted the finished molds onto a conveyor, and which carried them to a juncture with a second conveyor transporting the cores. The automatically assembled mold then rode to a moving molten iron-pouring machine, not unlike a huge furnace in continuous motion. Chemical makeup of the molted iron was carefully controlled to produce uniform iron cooling, as well as consistent material hardness which added to the life of milling machine cutters, drill bits and reamers. Literally hundreds of new machines had to be acquired and installed, and dozens more had to be specially developed. One machine chamfered the eight valve seats in each cylinder bank in a single operation. But despite the complexity of the engine-producing machinery, the new V-8 block was finish-machined at a lower unit lost than was previously possible—an incredible undertaking.

One of the famous photographs of Henry Ford shows him stamping the first serial number, "18-1", onto the first production Ford V-8. Either this engine was later removed from the Victoria and sent to Greenfield Village for display, or a duplicate was later numbered. The date was March 10, 1932.

Chevrolet's 1932 debut came in December 1931, and sales were so strong that Ford's Model B and 18 could not catch it. On a monthly sales comparison, though, beginning with the V-8's first month of March, the new Ford actually outstripped its rival.

LOSING THE LOW-PRICE LEADERSHIP

The world waited long for the arrival of the all-new 1932, but the wait was worth it in terms of engineering, especially the affordable V-8, and styling, exemplified here by the Deluxe Roadster.

While the struggles with the new V-8 were going on at Greenfield Village, the progress of the new 1932 chassis and body was much more satisfactory. The frame was entirely new and had a double drop, though at the front the drop was little more than a bend in the rails at the point of the rear engine mount. It was a much more sophisticated frame than that of the Model A. The wheelbase was lengthened from 103½ to 106 ins., yet it was still 3 ins. shorter than Plymouth and Chevrolet. Spring perches were mounted behind the rear axle, allowing lower bodies and thus lengthening the spring base, the latter of which was to be one of Ford's defenses in the coming criticisms of transverse springing. The brakes were similar to Model A but were enlarged 1 in. to 12-in. diameters and boasted an external rib for cooling and perhaps strength. Area was up—168 sq. ins. to 186 sq. ins.

The wheel diameter was reduced to 18 ins. and the tire section increased to 5.25. Steering gear ratio was increased from 11.5 to 13:1, beginning a dismal trend to ever-reduced controllability. In 1934 the ratio was reduced to 15:1. Then in 1936, plagued by steady complaints of hard steering in 1935, the ratio dropped yet further—17:1. Needle bearings added to the sector shaft in 1936 made for a much lighter steering effort, but the number of turns from lock to lock now meant that precise and rapid directional control was gone. It was about this time that the ubiquitous steering knob began to make headway in accessory shops, a confession of the wretched state of steering found not only in Ford but in most American cars.

A splendid new transmission was incorporated featuring a synchromesh cone on second and high gear. The excessively low-second gear ratio of Model A of 1.85 was improved to 1.6. It was a sound design with little change until the 1939 model. Mr. Ford's conservatism saved him from incorporating freewheeling, a fad which swept the industry in 1931 and would appear on both Chevrolet and the Plymouth PB in 1932. Perhaps in response to the dramatic delivery of the new Plymouth PA, all Fords in 1932 had rubber engine mountings, which went a long way toward giving even the 4-cyl. Model B a competitive smoothness. The rear engine mounts were on the transmission; and driving thrust, which in Model A had been delivered via the torque tube directly to the rear mounts, was now taken by two rods in tension connecting the flywheel housing to the main central frame crossmember.

As noted in the previous chapter, Model B engine development centered on a new crank, 10 lbs. heavier than Model A and blessed with larger crank and rod journals. The new strength of this crank allowed for higher revs, higher compression, and the 25% increase in engine output to an advertised 50 hp.

The improvements were overdue. Since 1930 Plymouth had been offering 48 bhp at 2800 rpm. On Oct. 1, 1930, Durant had introduced a new Four based on the Continental 8W—interesting because the bore and stroke along with hp and peak revs were identical to Model B, and this some 18 months earlier. Even more striking was the new PB Plymouth, the last Four of Walter Chrysler, which premiered in March 1932, the same month as Model B. This engine, still with 196 cu. ins., produced an astonishing 65 bhp at 3000 rpm, equal in power to the new V-8 with 11% less displacement. The V-8, though, had far more potential.

The Model B engine was still without counterweights, and these were supplied on the BB truck engines. The weighting was initially added on to the normal B cranks, but this awkward system eventually gave way to the Model C crank introduced Dec. 5th, 1932, in which

The Model 18 was identified by the bold V-8 emblem on the headlight tiebar, while the 4-cyl. Model B had none. This was the first year that Ford covered the radiator with a grille. The 18 was luxury for a low price.

Prototype V-8's took many forms but this was the version okayed for production that began on March 9, 1932. The first V-8 powered Ford car was assembled the following day. Note low-mounted starter.

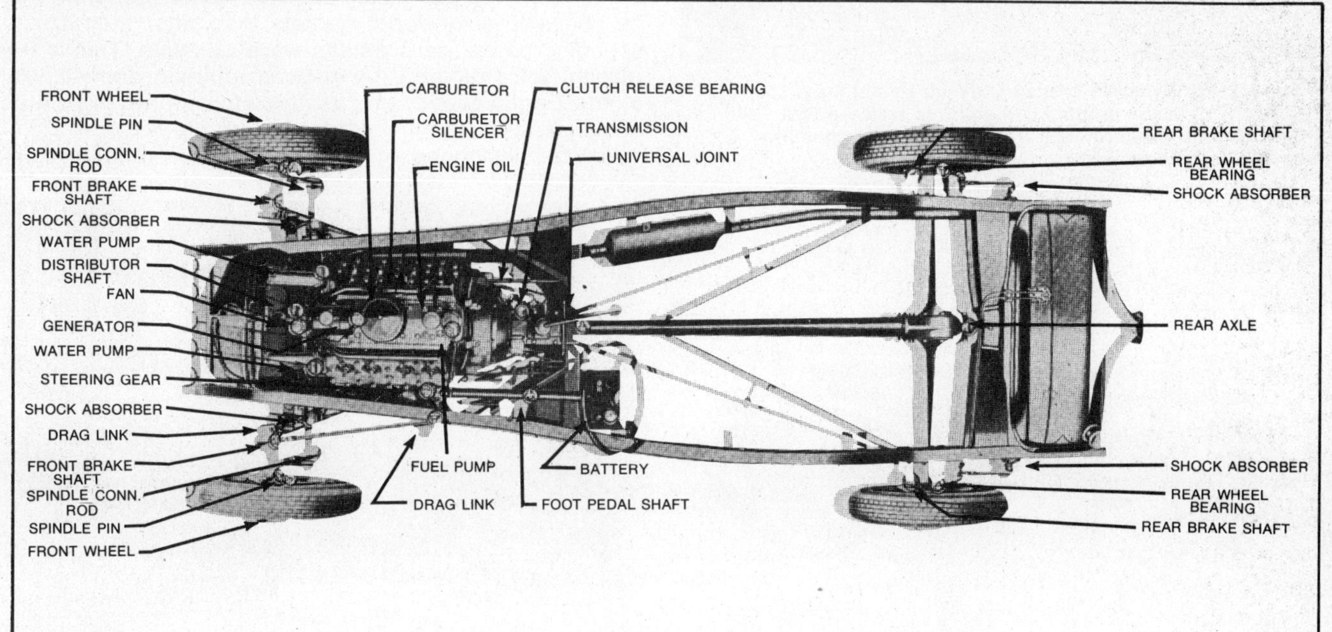

The 1932 Ford frame was much more sophisticated than the Model A, especially in the side rails which were curved as well as double-dropped. The rear spring mounting behind the axle is clearly seen in this Model 18 lubrication chart. The engine was mounted on rubber pads instead of bolts.

the counterweights were cast integrally with the shaft.

Other changes in Model B included an internal oil return with modest pressure to the mains, a 3-bolt water pump, larger venturi size on the Zenith carburetor, and of course a fuel pump to supply the carburetor from the new rear-mounted gas tank. None of these changes was very significant yet the Model B engine, especially with the C crank, was far superior to Model A, its smoothness approaching but not equalling the Plymouth PA. It is a good thing that changes were not troublesome, for in the initial beginning of production in 1932, the Model B took up the slack while V-8 manufacture picked up.

It must be pointed out that Mr. Ford's sense of the dramatic caused him to order the delay of the 1932 models until the V-8 could reach production status. He knew his introduction of the first inexpensive V-8 would stir the world, and to introduce the newly styled car with merely a minor update of the Model A engine would be unthinkable. Thus it was that while the Model B engine was ready for production by late 1931, no cars using this engine were assembled until April 1932.

HERE IT COMES!

The first production-line V-8 engines, 38 in number, were assembled on March 9th, and the first production car was built the following day. For no particular reason, the chassis received a Victoria body. Mr. Ford was on hand as the first car took shape, and he was instructed by Charles Sorenson where to stamp the serial number on the bellhousing. Using single numbering dies, Mr. Ford hammered in 18-1. But even though he put on his glasses to do it, he serialized the engine with the 8 inverted! It is generally believed that the first production engine was later removed from the Victoria and installed in a place of prominence at the Henry Ford Museum, but it is also possible that two No. 18-1's were actually numbered.

Start-up production figures are given in an accompanying chart which reveals, among other things, that no 4-cyl. Model B's were produced in March. As V-8 engine completion grew in April, the Fours were allowed into production at a ratio of approximately 1:3. Production jumped considerably for May, and now the 4-cyl. overwhelmed the V-8, at a ratio approaching 2:1. May's total production of just over 50,000 units was far short of the Rouge Plant's capabilities, but it had to operate at least at this pace for any sort of efficiency. Thus more 4-cyl. cars had to be built than V-8's, a fact that Ford dealers would face with extreme difficulty.

An adjoining chart demonstrates clearly how very tardy Ford was in the general transition from the Model A to the Model 18 and to the Model 40. Production figures for the 4-cyl. Model B engine as it continued into 1933 are also given, and the chart includes production of the Model C engine with the counterbalanced crankshaft after Dec. 5, 1933.

In all, 8743 4-cyl. Model B Ford passenger cars were constructed domestically in 1933. During 1933 and into the following year, 4-cyl. truck production continued steady and remained so until the last Model C 4-cyl. commercial chassis came off the line in September 1934, at Edgewater, New Jersey.

It is not easy to pinpoint the cutoff times of Model A and Model B production. This is especially true of the 1½-ton AA and BB truck chassis, which continued to be competitive in world markets long after their corresponding passenger versions were obsolete. This is the reason for continuing AA truck production domestically at the Edgewater plant, as the accompanying chart demonstrates.

Isolated instances of Model A car production con-

The 1932 PB Plymouth carried Chrysler's final 4-cyl. development of the original design. This was the first Plymouth with synchromesh transmission and "floating power," and produced 65 hp from 196 cu. ins.

This 1930 Model A was built in the last years of Ford's Manchester plant, is right-hand drive and carries the fender lamps required by British law. The big new Dagenham plant was to open for '32 production.

Another 1930 Cabriolet built overseas is this German version, from Cologne, and is virtually indistinguishable from the U.S. counterpart. Some other foreign-built A's were quite different in their styling.

tinued throughout the world amidst truck assemblies. The English plant at Dagenham produced 31,000 Model A's and AA's in 1932, and Canadian production until July 1932, totaled some 3000 units. In the same month Ford Istanbul produced 68 Model A Standard Phaetons. From August through November, Ford Santiago assembled 69 Standard Phaetons. It is likely that Copenhagen continued Standard Phaeton production in small numbers in 1932.

In 1933 world-wide production of Model A's totaled 5796, of which 4254 were AA 131-in. trucks, 938 were 157-in. trucks, and 572 were 112-in. wheelbase commercials. Thirty-two passenger cars remain to be accounted for. In 1933 Santiago assembled 16 more Standard Phaetons.

Model A truck production totaling 4481 continued in 1934, especially the 131-in. truck chassis at Dagenham; and Santiago, still assembling Phaetons, produced 160! In 1935 we hear no more of any Model A passenger cars, but the Dagenham 131-in. chassis continued, with production still in substantial numbers around 3200. In 1936 there were 121 AA's and 60 A's produced, likely the absolute end of Dagenham truck production. It is always possible that a maverick assembly occurred somewhere in the world which escaped even Ford accounting. Sheetmetal shipped here and there may not have found its way into a car or truck for years after assembly had been ostensibly stopped. This practice perhaps accounted not only for the Santiago assemblies but may be illustrated in Dagenham truck production which frequently mixed chassis, fenders, and radiators between A and BB.

Domestic Model B and Model C truck production formally concluded in the fall of 1934. Assembly continued world-wide of both B, BB, and Model 18. In 1935 the total production of all "1932" designs was 5919. In the same year, by a curious overlap, production of the 1933-34 BB design was 7258. In 1936 BB production was still 6286, principally from Cologne and Buenos Aires. In fact, the BB was assembled as late as 1938 in both Cologne and Budapest, and German production undoubtedly went right into the war period. These assemblies were, of course, in Ford-controlled branches.

The Russian Model A Ford, the "Gaz," was in production from 1932 until 1941, according to historian Robert Scoon. Model A engines were cast until 1947 and the AA continued until 1948. Naturally, the Gaz output was wholly independent of Dearborn. It was the Model A engine which powered the Russian Gaz Jeep Model 50 and Model 67 with production beginning in 1943, a year in which Russia sorely needed them.

One last "authentic" Model A was built in Dearborn in 1945 from new parts for Henry Ford II. The body was a "one-off" station wagon convertible designed by Ford stylist E.T. Gregorie and was a harbinger of the immediate postwar Ford Sportsman. It was, however, not constructed using purely Model A components. The steering wheel, for example, was from a 1940 Ford. Bumpers dated from 1941, and so forth.

The Model 40, built domestically in 1933 and 1934, likewise continued along with Model 46, the commercial chassis of those years. Assembly of the Model 40 was active in Cologne and Buenos Aires as late as

FORD ASSEMBLY PLANTS IN 1932

Domestic
1. Atlanta, Georgia
2. Buffalo, New York
3. Charlotte, North Carolina
4. Chester, Pennsylvania
5. Chicago, Illinois
6. Cincinnati, Ohio
7. Cleveland, Ohio
8. Columbus, Ohio
9. Dallas, Texas
10. Dearborn, Michigan.
11. Denver, Colorado
12. Des Moines, Iowa
13. Edgewater, New Jersey
14. Houston, Texas
15. Indianapolis, Indiana
16. Jacksonville, Florida
17. Kansas City, Missouri
18. Long Beach, California
19. Louisville, Kentucky
20. Memphis, Tennessee
21. Milwaukee, Wisconsin
22. New Orleans, Louisiana
23. Norfolk, Virginia
24. Oklahoma City, Oklahoma
25. Omaha, Nebraska
26. Pittsburgh, Pennsylvania
27. Portland, Oregon
28. Richmond, California
29. St. Louis, Missouri
30. Seattle, Washington
31. Somerville, Massachusetts
32. St. Paul, Minnesota

Foreign
33. Amsterdam, Holland
34. Antwerp, Belgium
35. Asnieres, France
36. Barcelona, Spain
37. Buenos Aires, Argentina
38. Cologne, Germany
39. Copenhagen, Denmark
40. Dagenham, England
41. Istanbul, Turkey
42. Mexico City, Mexico
43. Santiago, Chile
44. Sao Paulo, Brazil
45. Yokohama, Japan

A British Model AA with rather crude cab and body by an unknown builder. The worm-drive rear axle mounts cantilever springs, and split rims with spoked wheels help unsprung weight. Rear axle also used radius rods.

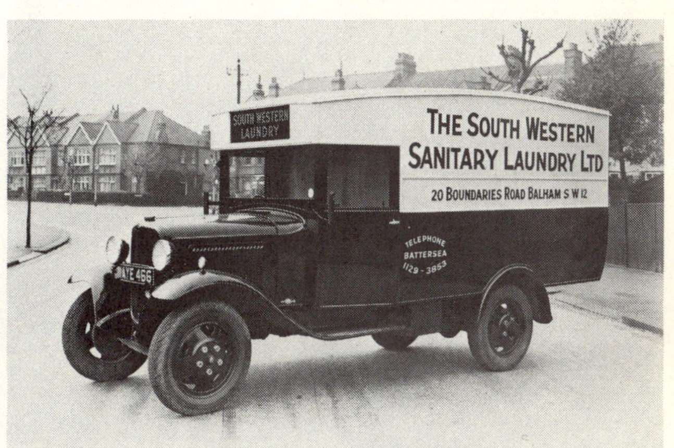

A Model BB Dagenham-built truck that explains something of Ford's assembly methods. Grille shell is 1932, 2-bolt splash aprons and fenders are Model A. Clue to real identity are rear hubs of the 1934 axle.

1936. It should be noted that world continuation of these models, along with even later V-8's such as 1935 Model 48 and 1936 Model 68, is in conformity with European practice where model runs of five or even 10 years is not unusual. Sheetmetal often remained unchanged, which is why each introduction of a new U.S. model was not automatically followed in, say, Cologne or Dagenham. Retooling was felt to be both unnecessary and too expensive for the low-production runs of these assembly plants.

The 1932 Ford was of pleasing outline, and the shape of the car has "worn" well (a tribute to Edsel, Joe Galamb, and others)—better by far than the Plymouth PA whose radiators were moving forward of the axle line, which destroyed any pretense the car might have had to classic styling. The Chevrolet BA Confederate was also a fine design, though Ford's slightly Vee'd radiator was a styling advance over the Chevrolet's flat front.

All of the Model A's body styles were continued for the '32 lineup, with the exception of the 2-door Phaeton. Original plans were to also continue this pleasing configuration, and indeed a number of prototypes were said to have been built (and at least one restored example exists), but it was not listed as an available body type in Model 18's literature. Some of the styles were little changed from '31, as the B400 Convertible Sedan and the Sport Coupe. Yet the Cabriolet, whose landau irons were functional for '31, now was folded entirely with inside ironwork. There was one entirely new configuration; a lovely 3-window Coupe originally offered as a Deluxe model only.

The windshield visors did not harmonize well with slanting windshields of closed cars and had been omitted on the Victoria and the later 1931 Fordor sedans. For 1932, all closed cars had a 10° windshield slant and the visors were dropped entirely.

Refinement was evident in many areas; in particular, the progress in quieting the running gear and body noise transmission. Front carpeting was introduced on

A 1932 Model B open-side Delivery ½-ton truck. Body roof extends over the top of the cab and the truck is minus its windshield visor. Typical in the truck line are the black-painted grille and headlamps.

This ½-ton Model B van was first exhibited in London in October 1932. The peculiar, skirted front fenders are very early for British use and pre-date the American 1933 Model 40 fenders by some five months.

Model B enthusiasts will look long at this "odd" Fordor differing in nearly all details from our own domestic version. It's a 1932 4-cyl., all right, but set on a 112-in. wheelbase which accounts for the "stretched" look overall. Only the most devout Ford purist will credit it as Spanish.

the Deluxe models. The windshield wiper motors were concealed under the header panels. Ash trays appeared, despite Mr. Ford's well-known feelings about the hazards of smoking.

The design of the dashboard and instrument layout was particularly pleasing, the removal of the fuel tank having given new freedom to Joe Galamb and Edsel. The similarity of Lincoln and Ford dash design of the period is evident, and Ford's functional instruments throughout the Thirties were especially attractive when compared to the offerings of some makers who yielded to bizarre styling influences.

V-8 SENSATION VS. DEPRESSION

First public announcement of the new V-8 was carried in the *Detroit News* on Feb. 11, 1932, though the

DATES OF SIGNIFICANCE IN 1932

The following changes were indicated from Instruction and Assembly Change Letters, and Service Letters. The Serial Numbers were taken from the Shop Production Record Book. Unless specifically indicated, the Serial Number is the first unit of the date of the letter involved. In view of Mr. Ford's thrifty ways, it is safe to assume that all existing stocks of phased-out parts would be used up before a change was actually initiated. Therefore, the Serial Numbers listed would be the earliest possible numbers to incorporate such changes. This information was originally published in the March/April 1974, and the January/February 1976 editions of the "V-8 TIMES," a publication of the Early Ford V-8 Club of America, and is used with permission of compiler Pat McFarlane.

(Continuity of dates and Serial Numbers lost after last date).

*This discrepancy cannot be clarified.

DATE	SERIAL NO.	SIGNIFICANCE
3/9	18-1	38 production V-8's built.
3/10	18-1	1st complete car assembled.
4/1	1221	1st unit for April.
4/15	3449	Minor changes including No. 1 and No. 2 floorboard revisions.
4/22	4878	Use automatic control shock absorbers. Use engine-turned instruments panel on all Four and V-8 passenger cars.
4/29	7251	Supply windwings as options on Standard Roadsters and Standard Phaetons. Front frame crossmember engine mount holes changed. Clutch release bearing grease cup moved from side to top. Station Wagon body (B-150) adopted.
5/2	8356	1st unit for May.
5/6	NA	Dash and Dash Insulator re-designed for more toe-room at clutch pedal.
5/6	10572	Use 4-blade fan, in place of 2-blade, and larger fan pulley.
5/13	14962	Brake plate thickness increased. Oil dipstick changed from right to left side starting with serial number 15164 per Service Letter No. 68 dated 6/7/32.*
5/20	20821	Oil dipstick changed from through-block at right rear to through-pan at left.*
5/24	NA	Gear shift lever housing now incorporates a rib extending the full length of the casting opposite the hand brake.
5/24	NA	Larger diameter oil filler pipe released for Models B and BB.
5/26	NA	Frame reinforcement members shipped to dealers for cars already sold.
5/27	28072	Add fuse block to lighting circuit on V-8's. Change to 90 mph speedometer for V-8's, use up 80 mph unit on B's, then 90 mph's for all. Hole added to rear frame covers for anti-squeak rubber. Flat steel with vulcanized rubber for rear brake rod support to replace wires with vulcanized rubber.
6/1	32116	1st unit for June.
6/3	35133	Oil bath air cleaner released for Models B and BB as an accessory.
6/10	43290	Black and white top and side curtain material for Standard Phaetons and Standard Roadsters instead of all black.
6/17	51822	Fuel inlet to carburetor changed from horizontal (with screen) to vertical (without screen). Nut cover added to sidemount spare tire carrier to reduce theft.
6/24	NA	Release fuse block for production on Models B and BB. Starter switch for Models B and BB left-hand drive units changed from the starter to the steering gear with foot control, as on all V-8's.
6/30	78500	The ⅝-in. dia. oil drain hole in the bottom of the flywheel housing is changed to ¼-in. dia. with loose cotter pin.
7/1	80519	Added optional righthand taillight assembly.
7/15	112231	Vibrator horn adopted. Seven notches now put on distributor breaker plate screw washer. Larger radiator released for Model 18.
8/1	139398	1st unit for August.
8/5	NA	V-8 released as option for school or passenger bus chassis.
8/18	NA	Combination temperature and fuel gauge released as option.
9/6	163455	1st unit for September.
9/13	169180	Oil level indicator marks on dipstick changed to 2-in. spacing. "L" mark raised 1 in.
9/16	NA	Sidemount spare wheel locks now available.
9/20	NA	Sedan Delivery production starts, available with either Four or V-8 engine.
9/21	NA	New front brake rod support made of strap steel instead of wire. Battery rock shield released for production.
10/3	NA	1st unit for October.
10/18	NA	Oil bath air cleaner available as a V-8 option. Fuel pump changed from sleeve type to rockerarm type.
10/28	202288	Pressed steel oil pan released. Hood louvers increased from 20 to 25. (Serial number 198035 was first engine assembly with new pan; dated 10/18 in Production Book.)
11/1	203296	1st unit for November.
11/30	NA	Automatic "winter front" available as option.
12/5	B5-175104	First Four (Model C) with counter-balanced crankshaft.

media at large had been speculating on the revelation for some weeks. In fact, *Business Week* in their Dec. 23, 1931 issue correctly predicted a Ford 8-cyl. engine, but made no mention of its Vee configuration. That same issue of *Detroit News* also carried a prediction by Mr. Ford that he would sell 1,500,000 units of the new Model 18 and Model B. This must have caused Sorensen some concern, for production was still some weeks away. As noted, V-8 engines began to flow from the initial line on March 9th, and completed cars started the next day. On March 28th Edsel Ford announced the public showings, which would follow on March 31.

Engine production for the month of March totalled 1220 units, while car production trailed slightly at 1104. The 4-cyl. models began to flow from the line in April, with 1712 completed cars built. V-8 production, meanwhile, was 4967 cars. By the end of April, 17,683 cars of both types meant that dealer distribution of perhaps one car each would not be complete until early May.

It will be noted from the production chart that no Model B's were produced in time for the first showing on March 31. This is especially odd because B engine production had been under way since November 1931, and engines were in hand and waiting for use. Mr. Ford, as has been noted, was apparently anxious for the maximum impact of the new Model 18 and withheld the B until the first wave of enthusiasm had been thoroughly exploited.

What happened was that the B engine was consigned from the very beginning to a second level of use; that is, commercial and utilitarian. On April 29, the company made this quite specific when it informed dealers that the new V-8 engine would be used exclusively in the Deluxe Coupe, Victoria, Cabriolet, and the

This is a Cologne, Germany, B400 Ford Koln, V-8-equipped. It is identical in all respects to the U.S. counterpart. The full range of domestic body types were offered abroad, and produced excellent results.

On the other hand, the German Cabriolet had very distinctive rear-end styling, especially to accommodate the folded top which stores far more neatly than on the U.S. cars. This car is a 4-cyl. B.

The Model B Phaeton was again a duplicate of the domestic version, and was popular in Germany probably because of its superior open-car styling. This is an early model with 20 hood side louvers.

Convertible Sedan, unless a special customer request specified the Model B engine. The shortage of V-8 engines, due to the struggles to get it into full-scale production, made this directive impossible to execute. Had the initial engine design undergone the extensive testing that most all-new automotive components experience, some of its problems would have surfaced and been dealt with before production began. One alteration that probably stopped foundry production for a time was the shifting of the oil dipstick from its right-hand through-block location to the left-hand side where on all subsequent V-8's it entered directly into the pan via a short tube. This occurred after engine serial number 15163 in mid-May, 1932.

In the 1932 model year, the 4-cyl. engine was used in 96.5% of all light commercial units and 98.5% of all heavy trucks.

Another complication in the 1932 model beginnings was the great number of assembly plants, 32 in the United States and 13 abroad. It took more than two months to get production going in all of the domestic branches, and even when this had been achieved, it was quickly apparent that the production capacity was grossly beyond the ability of the market to absorb the cars. Thus for the 1933 model year, only six U.S. plants undertook assembly. Many of the other branches were never to reopen again.

Early Model 18 production revealed some of the weaknesses of the new car, and no model has had more running production line changes than the 1932. Some of the changes were minor; floorboard revision (April 15), front frame crossmember engine mount holes altered (April 29), black and white top and side curtain material for Standard Phaetons and Roadsters, instead of all black, a change made June 10; an optional right taillamp made available July 1. Other revisions were of a more serious nature, and many of these were due to the chronic overheating problems of the V-8 which had not been tested during warm weather. Some of the moves to solve overheating were: a 4-blade fan and larger fan pulley (May 6), a larger capacity radiator released for production (July 15), and 25 hood side-louvers incorporated, instead of 20 (October 28). Buyers welcomed these changes.

Another serious problem that arose as increasingly more cars saw service use, was an inherent frame weakness. This was overcome by the design of a special frame strengthening plate to be mounted at the rear kick-up, and plates were shipped to dealers on May 26 to install on cars already sold.

These changes, as well as some others, are detailed in an accompanying list, arranged chronologically.

Initial consumer demand seemed strong for the new Ford, despite the absolutely disastrous state of the economy in 1932. Five-and-a-half million people reputedly visited Ford showrooms on the opening day of March 30, and attendance was reportedly even greater than this on April 1st and 2nd. But alas, dealers had nothing to sell. The approximately 1000 cars available were being retained by the dealers, in most cases, for display and for order-taking. As we have seen, April production of the V-8 was somewhat better but many small dealers probably didn't receive their first Model 18 until May when just over 50,000 cars were produced. Many people were justifiably sad.

June was even better with 73,858 cars (V-8 and 4-cyl. production combined), but the rate had not been reached to achieve Mr. Ford's goal of 1,500,000 for 1932, though if sales matched output Ford might yet

DOMESTIC 1932 FORD PRODUCTION

Month	Model 18 (V-8)	Model B (4-cyl.)
March 1932	1,104	0
April 1932	4,967	1,712
May 1932	19,499	30,571
June 1932	42,904	30,954
July 1932	35,248	5,982
August 1932	23,062	4,010
September 1932	20,378	4,200
October 1932	16,984	3,872
November 1932	16,872	3,949
December 1932	10,066	2,142
January 1933	2,204	338
February 1933	603	1,306
March 1933	0	0
TOTALS	**193,891**	**89,036**

1932 MODEL A AND MODEL AA DOMESTIC PRODUCTION

Month	Production
January	5,398[1]
February	4,702[1]
March	650[1]
April	27[1]
May	88[2]
June	233
July	327
August	574
September	458
October	239
November	195
December	95

1. These were primarily trucks with perhaps less than 50 passenger cars included.
2. Only 131-in. wheelbase Model AA trucks after this point.

MODEL B ENGINE PRODUCTION FOR 1933

Month	Production
January	0
February	1
March	221
April	1646
May	1852
June	1190
July	1134
August	975
September	717
October	515
November	279
December	213*
TOTAL	**8743**

*Model C engine with counterbalanced crankshaft began production Dec. 5, 1932, with serial number B5-175-104.

LOSING THE LOW-PRICE LEADERSHIP

The 1932 Ford Tudor Sedan shows off the 10° slant of the windshield which was common to all of the body styles. Overall softening of the body surfaces is evident yet the "upright" look inherited from the Model A is clear. This body style was far and away the largest seller with 90,568 units.

Lincoln dashboard reveals the inspiration for the 1932 Ford. Engine-turned inset with round gauges works well with Lincoln. Note the round pedal pads which Ford also adopted this year, as well as the steering/ignition lock, design of brake handle, and the shape of the gearshift knob.

see a 900,000 car model year. Production, however, started to fall back in July and continued at a sharp decline until the last Model 18 was produced in February 1933. The final tally at the end of the model run was 193,891 V-8's and 89,036 Fours, for a grand total of 282,927 units.

Clearly, the Model 18, though sensational in many ways, was not about to lead Ford's recovery in the manner of the 1928 Model A. The Depression was the principal factor in the general decline in production. Chevrolet, which had beaten Ford in 1931 and had benefitted mightily from a full production year, could sell only 322,000 units, down from 583,000.

On this point, one must be exceedingly careful in the use of production statistics. First, shall registrations reported by states, sales reported by sales managers, assemblies, or engine production be used? Second, shall trucks be included? This is a critical factor in 1935 when comparing Ford and Chevrolet. Third, shall world figures be included? Fourth, shall domestic production for export be reported? Fifth, shall the calendar year be used, or the model year? In the case of Plymouth, it must be the calendar year since Chrysler introduced new models sometimes in April, June, and

The 1934 Packard dash is very rich—busier than the Lincoln—and the Packard firm used such highly-styled gauges throughout the Thirties. Lincoln, though, retained dial simplicity during the era, along Ford lines.

The 1932 Ford dash was neatly laid out with a commendable round speedometer. The flanking ammeter and new gas gauge were also clearly legible. Treatment on this Cabriolet was duplicated in all styles.

July. Sixth, shall continuing production of older models be included in calendar year figures, a factor especially important in Ford figures? Alas, in some instances precise answers are not yet possible.

The comparisons cited above and hereafter, unless otherwise noted, generally follow the calendar year with gross domestic production of all vehicles.

Customer demand was plainly not there, and Ford's production figures were a remarkable achievement for what really amounted to no more than a 7- or 8-month full production year. Interesting to note is that while it is generally conceded that Chevrolet had beaten Ford for the 1932 calendar year (320,331 to 256,867 by December 31), Ford actually outstripped its rival during those months when the Models 18 and B were available. Ford led Chevrolet beginning with June, and from that date on Ford delivered 195,988 cars by year's end, but Chevrolet only 138,149.

More threatening, however, was the growth of Plymouth. Despite the state of the economy, Plymouth sales were up again to 121,468, a 14% gain over 1931. The PB introduced in April 1932, was a very good car, indeed, and had served to bring the PA, introduced only the previous June, right up to date. The PB was much better styled than the PA, and along with the mechanical refinement of floating power and the long and reliable use of hydraulic brakes by Chrysler, it was having its effect on sales. Furthermore, Plymouth was ready in November with their new 6-cyl. PC, which would double sales in 1933. Such aggressive change, occurring without the disastrous hiatus of deliveries that seemed to plague Ford's major moves, was a tribute to Chrysler's superb management.

TROUBLE: EXPRESSED AND IMPLIED

Yet another factor undoubtedly hurt Model 18 sales. The V-8 was bold and new. Though few could criticize its performance, rumors abounded about its durability and economy. Eight cylinders suggested high-fuel consumption. People wondered if the new engine would shake the car to pieces. And why did not the cylinders wear more severely on the outside where the weight of the piston would rest in the new Vee configuration? Most of these early rumors were soon proved to be unfounded. The real problems in Model 18 were quickly attended to by an alert engineering group who were entirely conscious of the chances which had been taken in the hasty introduction of the model.

This is not to suggest that Ford's principal competitors were free of engineering problems. Chevrolet's new Six had a bad reputation on axles. The whole rear end was redesigned and strengthened in 1930. In 1932 the axle shafts were again increased in diameter, twice in just one model year. Still another redesign occurred in 1933. (Ford's rear axles, both Model A and the straddle pinion variation introduced in 1933, were without trouble.)

It was not until 1935 that Chevrolet finally solved its inherent valve problem. Chevrolet splash lubrication was a serious weakness—especially against Ford's high-performance full-pressure V-8—even after the "Pressure Stream" oil system (directly aimed at solving bearing troubles) was introduced in 1935.

A more subtle factor in the dismal 1932 sales picture was the disorganized state of Ford dealers. The savage cut of the discount rate to 17% in 1930 had made for bad relations between the company and the dealer network. The effect was cushioned by the fact that 1930 was a splendid year for Model A with registrations exceeding one million, some 400,000 ahead of Chevrolet's AD Universal Six. Ford's penetration of the market exceeded 40%. Few dealers were willing to fight such success as Depression clouds rolled in, but 1931 left the dealers in bad shape with plummeting sales, despite a return to the 20% discount. Mr. Cowling's 22% discount of late 1931 compared favorably with Plymouth's 21% and was not far behind Chevrolet's 24%. Yet even a new high discount could not compensate for the lack of cars which marked the first half of 1932.

DISCOUNT DISCOURSE

It must be made clear that these percentage figures refer only to the price a dealer paid for his car; in Ford's case, 22% below the retail price. Ford's previous volume was high and most of its models were priced low. Chevrolet's model lineup, with its slightly higher-across-the-board price, could offer a higher discount of 24%, while Plymouth was obliged to hold at 21%. While certain automotive practices involved a smaller percentage rebate for successful selling, this figure, in the 5% range, would be applied to gross billing figures that the manufacturer charged the dealer. A rebate or "kickback" is not considered a normal automotive practice, although of normal import among other merchandising lines. A rebate between dealer and consumer is likewise not to be confused with the relations that a dealer has with its manufacturer. In the Thirties, times were sufficiently bleak to force dealers by the scores to close up shop, not withstanding discount rates or any other inducements offered. The important thing, above all else, was simply the fact, that in 1932, critical automotive sales volume was simply not there. Period.

Dealer morale was understandably low. More than this, Ford advertising expenditures in 1932 totaled only $2,700,000, a fraction of the $8,700,000 spent in 1930. At the very moment when Ford engineering advances needed exposure, the company retrenched. It is possible that Mr. Ford expected the same sort of public response and return to his car as had taken place with Model A in 1928 and 1929.

A LOSS IN SPITE OF ITSELF

But times were changing, and Ford had lost his monopoly on the low-priced field, so much so that the public did not automatically presume that the Ford car was the natural leader in the field. The restoration of that mystique would never again come to the Ford Motor Co. (not withstanding some of the die-hard youngsters in the generation). The Thirties witnessed a rather sad change in the sales climate of the company. The aggressiveness and assumption of innate superiority slowly gave way to a defensive attitude on the part of both dealers and advertisers. Apart from the brilliant advances of Model 18, it was possible Mr. Ford was unwilling to innovate in the Ford car on any major scale. The Lincoln-Zephyr would be the only claim to innovation in the decade, and the engineering advances contained in that car were by and large not incorporated into the Ford. In fact, in areas such as brakes and suspension, the Zephyr revealed problems rather than solutions, as will be shown.

The dealers' dismay at the late introduction of Model 18 was compounded by the failure of the new 1933 Model 40 to appear at the end of 1932. Plymouth's new Six was ready in November, and Chevrolet's CA Master, a really new car, was ready in December. Model 40 was not announced until February 1933. Few people were to buy Model 18 Fords in the closing weeks of 1932 in the face of such brilliant competition.

A significant source of income in 1932 was from the parts business, which totaled $46,000,000 or 18% of

Early production Model 18's line up at a San Francisco dealership. The Deluxe Phaeton is fitted with a special see-through hood. Salesman in rear of Phaeton shows off a chassis model of the new Ford in comparison to the "inferior" layout of the typical competition—a sales stunt.

total dollar sales. There were approximately 7 million Fords in service, of which nearly 60% were still Model T's. Spare part demand for Model T was plummeting, yet in 1932 Ford sold 135 brand-new T engines. That any factory parts could be sold against the vast Model T inventories in Ford dealers across the land, plus used parts at give-away prices, is remarkable. The future of spares sales was not promising for another reason; namely, that Model A precision was so improved over Model T that spare parts sales were cut 50%. No longer could Ford or independent manufacturers make a fortune on replacement transmission bands and spark timers.

It is no surprise that Ford lost $74,861,645 in 1932. Though it was a bad year for the country, Mr. Ford's company had performed a good deal worse than his principal competitors. The new V-8, for all of its brilliance, had little opportunity to recapture Ford's position in the low-priced field. Had the V-8 appeared in the fall of 1931 in full production, the story might have been different. By the end of 1932, in that fast-changing styling time, the Model 18 was seen as already outmoded. It was to be the first Ford car in which body dies lasted only one season.

In 1933 the Essex became the Terraplane and this is the 8-cyl. Cabriolet. Hudson stylists were well into the skirted fender theme, but Ford would wait until late 1932 on English trucks and 1933 on the car lines.

1932 FORD PASSENGER, COMMERCIAL AND TRUCK MODELS

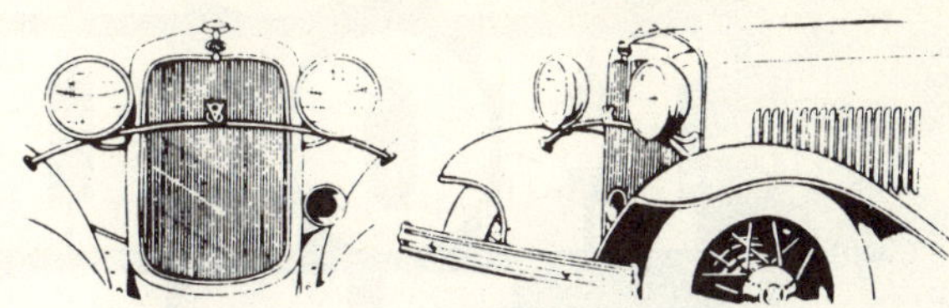

MODEL 18 FORD PASSENGER CAR
8 Cylinder Engine (106″ Wheelbase)

MODEL B FORD PASSENGER CAR
4 Cylinder Engine (106″ Wheelbase)

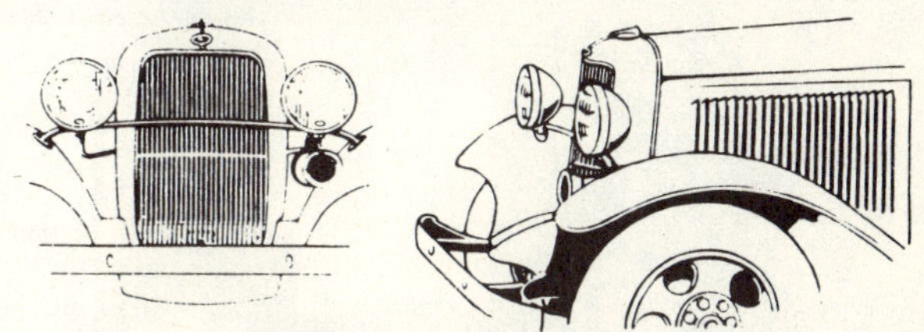

MODEL BB FORD TRUCK
8 Cylinder Engine (131½″ and 157″ Wheelbase)
4 Cylinder Engine (131½″ and 157″ Wheelbase)

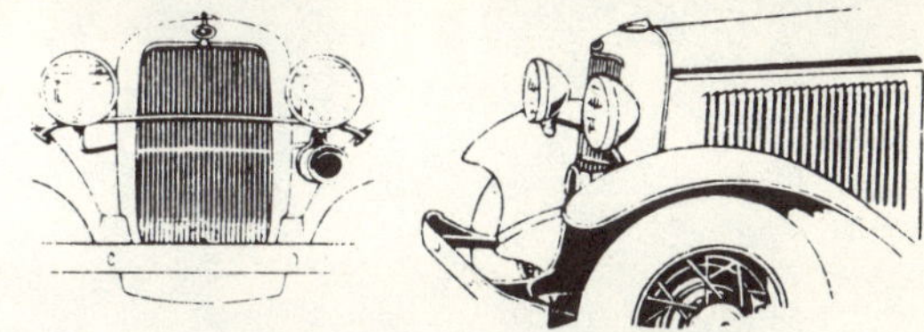

MODEL B FORD COMMERCIAL
8 Cylinder Engine (106″ Wheelbase)
4 Cylinder Engine (106″ Wheelbase)

(Illustration is 4 Cylinder model; 8 Cylinder is the same, with V-8 ornaments)

The 1933 Chevrolet CA Master series was very attractive and was a well-balanced automobile. Introduced in December 1932, it had a three-month sales advantage over Ford and easily beat the Ford in unit sales for the model year. Ford engineering advances were slow, and dealers worried.

FORD AT HOME AND ABROAD

A portion of the gigantic manufacturing complex at Dagenham, England, which opened in March 1931. This view is of the powerhouse as seen from the jetty, where raw materials were unloaded for processing. Construction of the plant was delayed thanks to the hundreds of support pilings that had to be driven into the river banks along the Thames.

Ford's English operations began in 1911 with an assembly plant in Manchester that served the British market well for some 18 years. As the Model T position deteriorated in world markets, Mr. Ford, Edsel, and Sorensen came up with a general reorganization of European marketing which made England the primary production point for Europe and the Middle East. Manchester was ill-suited for the sort of expansion envisioned, and so the construction of the Dagenham plant was begun in 1929 on a swampy site by the Thames. Model A and Model AA would be the standard production units, available either knocked down or assembled and shipped to all other distribution centers in the various European countries.

The Model A was never to have the world-beating uniformity of the Model T because the American and European markets were beginning to diverge. Fuel costs were to be part of the reason, especially as World War II approached. But a more critical factor was the system of taxation as applied in Great Britain. Gasoline there was first taxed in 1928, but much more important was the Motor Taxation Act of 1920 which took effect on Jan. 1, 1921. This Act taxed private cars at the rate of one pound sterling per horsepower, based on the RAC formula of the diameter squared times the number of cylinders divided by 2.5. By this formula Model T was 22.5 hp, and British tax in 1921 would thus be approximately the equivalent of $108 per year, not an inconsiderable amount of money.

The tax formula had several immediate effects upon engine design. In the first place, it tended to spur development of small, high-efficiency engines. In Britain during the Twenties, the most popular engine rating was 11.9 RAC hp implying a displacement of 1½ liters and about 30 bhp. In 1926 in Britain there were some

45 different makes in this category, led by the famous Morris Cowley, the British equivalent of the Model T. The Morris was an altogether first-rate value with a 3-speed gearbox and a wet cork clutch as well as other refinements, which put it in a class well above the T in some respects.

Smaller engines developed during the Twenties, including the very refined Humber 8 and 9, the Rover, and the Talbot 8. The most well-known of them all was the Austin 7 with only 10.5 hp from 747cc's, first introduced in 1922. The Austin turned out to be the smallest car that could stand comparisons with all rivals in terms of quality, reliability, and general utility, and it sold some 150,000 units until its finish in 1937. Yet despite its success, its lower taxable rating of $33.60 equivalent per year and its undeniable excellence, the Austin never seriously challenged the Model T in the Twenties, for one basic reason. In 1926 the Austin 7 Chummy cost 150 pounds; the Model T fourseater cost 120 pounds. In England, as in America, Ford had built a dominance of the low-priced market so total that the erosion of sales by the RAC tax formula had not been sufficient for even Austin to take over leadership.

Thus, Ford successfully resisted the tax formula for at least seven years, and the demise of Model T could not be said to have come simply from taxing, its obsolescence being quite apparent on all sides.

A second development in engine design spurred by the RAC tax was a reduction in bore size and a lengthening of stroke. Since stroke did not affect the taxable rating, designers were free to indulge themselves, and the typical British long-stroke/small-bore engine appeared. The first 3-liter Bentley had dimensions of 80 mm x 149mm for three liters, producing some 65 bhp at 3500 rpm. Piston speeds were high in such engines, in fact reaching speeds of 3500 feet per minute, which is altogether modern.

More typical of utility engines was the Morris Cowley with bore/stroke ratio of 1:1.5. The Delage 11 of 1921 had a ratio of 1:1.7. The lovely little Rolls 20 introduced in 1922 was typical with a ratio of 1:1.5.

HE PREFERRED SHORT STROKES

Mr. Ford had favored short stroke engines from the very beginning. Models N and S had a bore which was actually larger than the stroke, 3.750 ins. x 3.375 ins. In this Mr. Ford was not altogether in bad company, for Henry Royce's Legalimit V-8, not to mention the original Silver Ghost, had bore/stroke ratios of 1:1.

Model T dimensions were 3.375 ins. x 4 ins., almost square. Coupled with a very low top rpm of about 1600, they gave mercifully slow piston speeds. Mr. Ford, along with Mr. Royce, benefited from low cylinder and piston wear by this arrangement, and crank and bearing stresses were light.

Yet the RAC tax spelled the end of such ratios. The new Phantom I Rolls-Royce had dimensions of 4.250 ins. x 5.50 ins. and a ratio of 1:1.3, which allowed salesmen to sell the new model as a tax saver. Model A was fractionally larger than the T on a tax basis, and the bore/stroke ratio remained typically Ford with 1:1.1. One wonders about the equity of this tax when it is remembered that a 3-liter Bentley was taxed at 16 hp while the Model A came in at 24 hp, the brake hp of the Bentley being approximately twice that of the A.

The Model A was thus in a bad position from the very beginning. It was apparent that a smaller engine of some sort would be necessary if Ford were to com-

Thames River site near Dagenham was chosen since the delivery of ore required shipment by water in order to accommodate the vast amounts of the material needed to feed the furnaces, a mammoth task.

Overall view of Dagenham reveals the sprawl of the giant facility. Roof over manufacturing and assembly area totalled 34 acres! Plant served all of Europe.

A portion of the River Rouge plant outside of Detroit, the largest manufacturing complex in the world. There, ore became running Ford cars in a matter of hours.

pete against the British economy car which was challenging Ford directly by growing steadily smaller and yet managing, through engine development, to maintain performance and economy.

It was in response to this situation that Ford announced the AF Model, nothing more than an underbored Model A engine fitted to a regular chassis. With its 3.05-in. bore, the taxable rating was 14.88, but with reciprocating weights much lower and the crankshaft the same, higher revs were possible and brake horsepower was thus down to only 28 at 2000 rpm. Performance was further helped by a 4.56:1 rear-end ratio, though the gearbox was unchanged.

Production for all Model A's and AF's continued at Manchester, for the construction of the Dagenham plant was slowed by the requirement of an incredible number of pilings. The factory did not open until March 19, 1931, and thus played no appreciable part in the early A output.

The AF response to both Morris and Austin was clearly inadequate, and the idea of a truly small Ford gained headway. Percival Perry and A. R. Smith of Dagenham insisted that a Ford for the English market must be truly small; that is, with a wheelbase well under 100 ins. and an engine only slightly larger than the baby Austin. On Oct. 19, 1931, work on project 19 (headed by Laurence Sheldrick) was begun in earnest. The first prototype was ready on Feb. 1, 1932. The engine was 2.23 ins. x 3.64 ins. for 56.93 cu. ins. The first engines had two-bearing cranks, perhaps reflecting the Austin 7 success, though the Austin boasted ball and roller main bearings. After some three or four prototypes, the new engine adopted a three-bearing crank quite like Model A. In fact, the engine was almost a precise scaledown of Model A, including the familiar timing pin Mr. Ford, characteristically, insisted on non-adjustable tappets.

The engine was set in a chassis with a 90-in. wheelbase and 45-in. tread. The body for the new car was designed by Eugene T. Gregorie and was, in simplest terms, a streamlined Model 18. Gregorie's work was imaginative and may be seen in his initial experiments with fender headlight placement reminiscent of Pierce Arrow. The new car was designated Model Y and, like the Rolls 20, would eventually develop to the point where it displaced its bigger brethren as the normative car of the make.

The importance of Gregorie's work on Model Y cannot be underestimated, for it was no one less than Edsel Ford who, upon seeing the prototype Model Y, gave immediate orders for Gregorie to proceed with the development of the design for the 1933 full-sized Ford. In February 1932 Model 18 was not yet in production, and there was no obvious reason to presume that its life would not be extended, at least for two years. But Edsel was undoubtedly in touch with the very rapid changes occurring in body development. Though he may not have known of the plans of Chevrolet and

An early mockup for the English Ford Model Y, which was ready for production in February 1932. Styling for European Fords was largely carried out in Dearborn.

The 1930 Austin 7 (with author Woudenberg) was at mid-point in a 16-year production run, was immensely popular in Britain. The Model Y was developed here.

An English version of the Model T, built at the earlier plant at Manchester for the 1922 model year. The British system of taxation burdened buyers of U.S. Fords.

Plymouth for 1933, he surely suspected that his competitors were not going to stand still.

The Model Y went into production at Dagenham immediately. During the summer of 1932 Gregorie restyled it, the windshield being angled back to 20° and the body and moldings reshaped into a pattern almost identical to a small-scale Model 40. Hood louvers were reduced in number and set to the rear of the hood side panel. The 1932 bumper was retained. The 1933 Y was similar, but skirted fenders were added, and the bumpers now had the characteristic center dip of Model 40.

SHOOK-UP BY STREAMLINING

Gregorie's handling of both the Y and Model 40 must be set amidst the vexing design questions of the moment. Streamlining was clearly on the horizon, but no one was sure how it would be handled. Integrated designs, such as the Cadillac V-16 fastback coupe and the Pierce Silver Arrow, would appear at the 1933 Chicago World's Fair. But in 1932 the stylists were working on Vee radiator shells and their slants, skirted fenders and a general smoothing up of traditional body lines.

The Bentley 3-liter engine was as far removed from the Model T as can be imagined, despite four cylinders and 3-liter displacement. It developed 85 hp at 3500 rpm.

In particular the vertical radiator was about to go, and in 1933 a 10- to 15-degree back-raked Vee radiator was typical. This trend was resisted by Cadillac and Packard, among others. Even the Cadillac World's Fair car, with voluminous convex surfaces which were to become so typical of GM styling, had a near-vertical radiator. The problem in 1933 was that body shapes continued in the old expressions, and the grafting of slanting radiators was never quite right. Perhaps the worst example of mixed styles was the 1933 Oldsmobile, which sported not only a slanting radiator but very full crowned fenders, all grafted onto a most upright sedan body. Oldsmobile adopted an even more radical radiator shell rake in 1934 and still with the conservative body. Buick, using similar body shells, retained concave fenders through 1935 with altogether more successful results, though by 1935 Oldsmobile had come out with the completely new GM round styling, certainly integrated if not handsome.

Packard wisely retained a vertical grille through 1934, and the cars of that year are generally considered to be superbly handsome. The 1935 Packard was an unfortunate effort to enter the new era, though by 1938 Packard should be given credit for developing its frontal appearance into a far more pleasing whole, principally by restoring much of the lost vertical angle of the 1935 radiator. Bentley, Rolls-Royce, Lagonda and a host of other British cars were saved from these problems by simply not altering radiator angles in the Thirties. That Rolls-Royce has yet to do so underscores the vindication of their conservatism.

The Lincoln passed through this styling period with commendable dignity, and though the radiator developed some angle the effect was pleasing. Lincoln's conservatism was such that full crowned fenders did

Short-coupled version of a 1925 3-liter Bentley was the fastest model of the series and could touch 100 mph despite a displacement very near to that of the Model A. Taxation system, though, rated this speedster at 16 bhp and Model A at 24 bhp. It was a displacement formula, which gave a lower taxation rate to long-stroke small-bore engines.

not appear until 1936, while Packard struggled to keep fenders in both worlds by using concave fronts and convex rears on the Senior cars through 1937.

One of the most successful early styling efforts was that of the Graham Blue Streak, introduced in January 1932 and designed by Amos Northup of the Murray Corp. The Blue Streak Graham had numerous features which are remarkably like both the Y and Model 40. It was the first car to have skirted fenders, an idea copied almost universally in 1933. But the Graham had a hood which ran right up to the grille molding, an idea used precisely on Model 40. Furthermore, the general rear slant of the radiator grille with a slight ee and vertical chrome strips was a theme again used very successfully on the Ford. Hood louvers slanted to match the grille angle was yet another idea used by Ford, and similarly copied by others.

One must not suppose that Gregorie simply copied Northup or Ray Dietrich, who also worked on the Graham. Yet one wonders at such styling touches as the Model 40 radiator cap whose upswept center line follows the triple pattern of the Graham, a touch which might even have influenced Model 18's cap, still three months away from production.

In any event, the basic layout of the Y—especially the restyled Y which appeared in summer of 1932—was expanded by Gregorie into the 40. In recent years, upon first seeing the Y and its successors, Americans automatically presumed that it was a shrinking of the contemporary big American Ford models. At the beginning, at least, the precise opposite was true, and the British Ford led the way for American styling.

An entirely new frame was laid down for Model 40 featuring an X-member whose four ends ran along the inside of the frame rails. Wheelbase was extended to 112 ins., and for the first time Ford exceeded both Chevrolet's 110 ins. and the 108 ins. of Plymouth. On the Plymouth PD, introduced in April 1933, wheelbase matched Ford, but the 108-in. chassis was continued in the cheaper lines into 1934. Chevrolet responded with 112 ins. on the Master Series in 1934 but continued to offer short chassis models until 1936.

Wheel size was reduced to 17 ins. Here Ford was about in the middle of contemporary practice. The Chrysler had led the way to smaller wheels, the 1931 Deluxe CD Eight having 17-in. wheels. In 1933 Dodge was the first car to offer 16-in. wheels, DeSoto and the PE Plymouth following in 1934. Chevrolet was the conservative car in wheel size and retained the 17-in. wheel through 1936.

The general layout of other chassis components followed that of Model 18. The rear axle pinion was straddle-mounted, and a 4.44:1 ratio was offered for the first time as an option to the standard 4.11:1, the latter continuing as the standard ratio through 1936.

Springing was unchanged except that the rear load rate was very slightly reduced from 230 to 225 lbs. Ford was not yet worried about the springing of the competition, nor indeed was the ride of the short wheelbase Plymouth and Chevrolet markedly superior to Ford, in any way.

The 22-qt. radiator was of the same capacity as 1932, but core frontal area went up from 374 to 386 ins. There were still no thermostats in the cooling system, the traditional muffling of the radiator being common in the cold winter areas.

MODEL 40's ADVANTAGES

The biggest Model 40 changes, however, were in the engine. Compression was up from 5.5:1 to 6.31:1 while

Prototype Ford Model Y shows design transition between Models 18 and 40 of U.S. Fords. Another prototype, interestingly, tried Pierce Arrow headlights.

Production Model Y is very close to prototype above but with grille and headlight refinements. English auto laws required specific marker lights atop the front fenders.

Gregorie at Dearborn almost immediately restyled the Model Y by slanting the radiator and windshield to a more rakish angle. This was version for 1932.

gross horsepower moved from 70 to about 82. Advertised horsepower went from 65 to 75. The compression increase was possible through the use of aluminum heads with which Ford would flirt until 1939. Peak hp revs were up from 3400 to 3800 where they would remain for the rest of the decade on the 221-cu.-in. engine. Heavy trucks shared the aluminum heads and high compression for just one year, after which Ford backed off to iron and lower compressions. Internally, the engine was much the same except for the installation of high-tungsten chrome alloy steel exhaust valve inserts. Spark plugs of 18 mm were now fitted.

The 1933 V-8 engine was a genuine improvement over Model 18 and further enhanced Ford's already sparkling performance, as Fred Frame would soon convincingly demonstrate in the Elgin Road Races. Happily, Gregorie's new bodies were not only graceful but not much heavier than those of Model 18, perhaps some 60 to 70 lbs. on average. Thus, an increase in car weight of no more than 3% was matched by a 15% increase in horsepower. The cars were much faster than in 1932. A "sustained" 80 mph was now publicized. Truly, the Ford V-8 was creating a glamorous image.

In 1933 numerous features appeared which were to be characteristic of future production. The matched air horns on the Deluxe models may be cited, which received only subtle changes in subsequent years before going "underground" for 1936. Bumpers took on a new center dip. New round taillights continued through 1936 on all production and after that on station wagons and commercials for many years.

The biggest change in the car interior occurred in the appearance of the dashboard. A large and attractive circular speedometer was set directly in front of the driver, flanked by a fuel gauge and ammeter. For the first time a cigar lighter and ash tray were in the center of the deluxe dash, and a large glove compartment was mounted directly in front of the passenger. It was to be the standard layout for Ford through 1936.

Exterior colors were still two-tone, the fenders in black and the body colors in pyroxylin lacquer—the layout since color returned to the Model T's in 1926. The somber mood of the country was reflected in the quiet colors offered. All of the popular body styles of the previous year were continued over for 1933, except the Sport Coupe and the B400 Convertible Sedan configurations which had been derived from Model A origins. The 3-window coupe was no longer exclusively a Deluxe model, nor was the 5-window only a Standard

By 1933 the Model Y had skirted fenders and a grille very much like the 1933 U.S. Ford counterpart. In fact, the overall design looks like a scaled-down Model 40.

There is no resemblance between the 1933 Fords and the 1933 Pierce Arrows—until one studies the grille outline. Headlights like these were tried on Model Y.

In 1933 the Cadillac Division of General Motors exhibited this special V-16 model at the Chicago World's Fair, and it set the styling pattern for GM cars to follow for many years. Not apparent from this angle is a grille markedly similar, then, to the Ford concepts both at home and abroad.

model. All coupes were offered in Standard or Deluxe, and with or without rumbleseats. Only the Cabriolet and Victoria were exclusively Deluxe. There was one standard Roadster without even a rumbleseat, the cheapest car of the lineup at a factory list price of $475. The Deluxe Fordor was the most expensive Ford car at $610. Prices of the Ford convertible body styles were always low in relation to the closed cars, and whereas Plymouth and Chevrolet were charging premiums in the mid-Thirties, the Ford Convertible Coupe was no more expensive than a sedan as late as 1939.

Esthetically, the Model 40 Ford was the final flowering of the classic line. The familiar "D" back was still present in the sedans and Phaeton. The engine was set well back, and the midline of the radiator, though now more concealed, was still directly over the front axle. The concave fender lines were in the best classic tradition, and in earliest model form, were unskirted as were the 1933 Model K Lincolns. It has been taken for granted that very early unskirted-fender '33's—which until recently supposedly existed only in photographic form—were prototype cars not released for production. But by 1975 several derelict examples had been unearthed. With the discovery of a few unused fenders, and the peculiar runningboards to match them, in unsold Ford dealer stock, it is now conceded that the unskirted cars were true production items.

MODELS FOR MILESTONES

With or without the skirted fenders, Ford's fender styling, indeed the entire lineup of body styles, was discreet and successful. The car was a styling success. Gregorie, Galamb and Edsel Ford could be rightly proud of this creation. The long-lived beauty of the

When the domestic Ford Model 40's debuted for 1933 the hood side louvers carried the slightly concave lines of the grille. Note especially the central, plated handle.

The V-8, in its second production year, was the standard domestic engine, but some 4-cyl. C engines with integral crank counterweights have been seen.

Odd angle of the 1933 Pierce Arrow shown on the preceding page looks somehow grotesque, although from standard angles design appears integrated. This show model was termed the "Silver Arrow." Only few were built—at $10,000 a copy. With a souped V-12, the car would do 110 mph-plus.

This was the 1934 Dodge offering while Chrysler and DeSoto were off on their Airflow kick. Grille had the concavity of the 1933 Ford, and a single hood latch.

Ford is all the more apparent when comparing it to Chevrolet and Plymouth of the same period.

The 1933 Model 40 Fords were publically announced on Feb. 9, 1933, clothed in eight basic body styles: Roadster, Phaeton, Tudor, 3-window Coupe, 5-window Coupe, Fordor, Cabriolet, and Victoria. The year also witnessed several major political milestones; Adolph Hitler became the German Chancellor on January 30, Franklin Roosevelt became our 32nd President on March 4, and Prohibition in the U.S. ended on December 5. They were milestones that would have their effects, and the world would not easily forget.

The Chevrolet CA Master was all-new, too. It was marked by a Vee grille which was more vertical and sharper in outline than the Ford's. Hood louvers were found only in the cheaper CC Standard series, the Master having three openable vents on each hood side. New for Chevrolet closed bodies was the no-draft ventilation using vent glass panels in the front doors, an idea that was to sweep the industry and which Ford

Twin 1933 Ford Tudors especially prepared for the Wm. Wrigley, Jr., Co., show the very pleasing lines that Ford's Gregorie had developed for the Model 40's, and which were fairly well retained for 1934's Model 40A. Note that black fenders were still available with alternate body colors.

Studebaker still stayed with older styling idiom in 1933, as this President sedan reveals. Its grille, however, seemed a rather racy departure for the otherwise staid design. Sidemount spares were still popular options on the bigger cars, but Ford did not bother with them after its 1934 year.

resisted until 1940. In the Master series power was up to 65 hp, but those iron pistons and long stroke were no match for the speed and acceleration of the V-8. The Chevrolet was 150 to 200 lbs. heavier than the Ford, another factor contributing to Ford's superior performance. But the Chevrolet was undeniably solid and the quality of the coachwork and trimming was superb. Already Chevrolet was moving toward a reputation of solid construction and finish which would eventually work to Ford's disadvantage.

The Plymouth was less fortunate in its 1933 design. The waterfall grille was peculiar, and the fenders were much tighter around the wheels without benefit of either skirting or the sweep of Ford and Chevrolet. In fact, the whole Chrysler line was conservative, much more so than GM and Ford. Chrysler made up for it, and then some, with the Airflow Series of the following year, but the general evolution of Chrysler styling in these years was particularly erratic.

Yet, Plymouth's sales advances in 1933 were, despite opinions on its styling, spectacular. For the calendar year, production was 255,564 units, and the new 6-cylinder PC and PD models carried Chrysler's fame ever higher. The Plymouth was undeniably the smoothest car of the big three, the combination of 6 cylinders with "floating power" engine mountings being almost unbeatable. The 76 bhp was altogether competitive, though without Ford's sheer speed. And Plymouth was untroubled by Chevrolet's splash lubrication or dropping valves. Its progress rested in fine engineering. Ford sales of 313,225 were still well ahead of Plymouth but behind Chevrolet's, and Ford's gross sales including trucks and Lincolns were 429,638, not quite a 10% increase over 1932. But Ford's percentage of the low-priced field slipped from 37% to 30%. For the first time, Ford sales had fallen below one-third of the market.

By 1935 Pierce Arrow had moved away from the styling of the great Silver Arrow. The declining clientele of the marque apparently preferred the conservative lines.

Comedian Harry Langdon with a 1935 Buick which maintained the conservative line in all respects. Buick would weather the styling revolution with dignity.

The senior Lincolns shared nothing with little brother Ford, and this 1933 tourer showed purely classical lines which have stood the ravages of time. In 1932, the V-8 Lincoln would do 85 mph, but would cost $4600 f.o.b. the factory. In 1933, a 65° V-12 of 150 hp would bring new "awe" to it.

Maurice Olley, GM's brilliant engineer, worked out the splendid independent front suspension on the 1934 Oldsmobile, but the car's body lines were awkward.

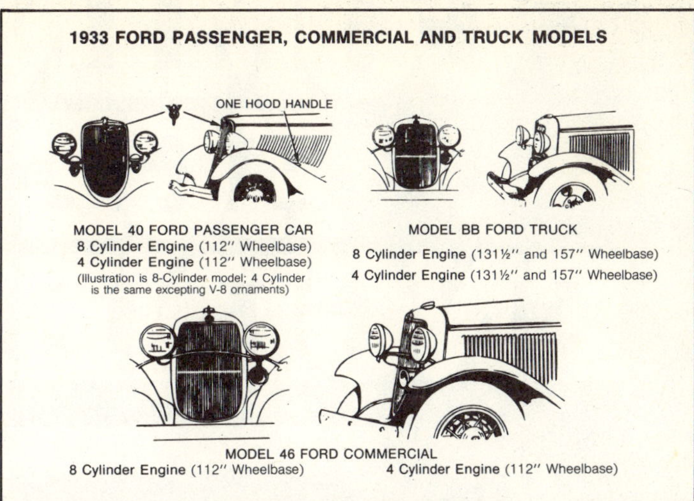

Ford identification drawings for its 1933 models show the disparity between the passenger cars, the commercial line, and the heavier duty Ford trucks.

Packard reached its classic era pinnacle with this 1932 Dietrich Convertible Sedan, a super exercise in styling custom-crafted beauty. Termed the Twin-Six series, this particular example once belonged to singing great Al Jolson. More importantly, it's a near-miracle that such cars sold in the Depression.

In three short years Packard would come up with its 120 Series, carrying the era's "sculptured" styling; and with well-rounded fender lines and an integral trunk. Very little is left from the classic era which Packard had dominated just a few years earlier. The Depression had changed tastes.

COMING OF AGE IN ENGINEERING

The Victoria was the one new 1934 body style, with a decklid that hinged awkwardly at the bottom. It had also lost the concavity which the non-openable version of 1933 had sported. The other body styles were merely face-lifted.

Ford had been unable to make a normal December model introduction after 1929. The late starts for the 1932 and 1933 models had been especially damaging, so it was with some satisfaction that on Dec. 9, 1933, Ford returned to normal patterns with the presentation of the 1934 Model 40. The transition to the new model was made easier by the lack of major changes. When Ford sales literature proudly announced, "There is nothing experimental about this new car," they were more accurate than perhaps should have been admitted.

The most noticeable change was a reshaping of the radiator grille, the Vee now being more pronounced along with a widening of the chrome surround, especially at the top. The Vee was accentuated by making the grille bars straight instead of having the slightly concave shape of 1933. Another subtle and often unnoticed change was the straightening out of the hood louvers to match the grille angle, since the 1933 louvers had followed the earlier concave design. The abandonment of these various curves hardened the frontal appearance of the car with good effect, and the new profile of the grille lengthened the car to the eye.

"HOT" CAR FOR 1934

There were other minor changes. Two painted hood side handles now replaced the single center cast nickle-plated handle of 1933. The V-8 radiator emblem was redesigned, along with the crank hole in the grille. The hubcaps were smoother, the concentric steps in various forms during 1932 and 1933 giving way to a single indentation.

Very little else was changed on the exterior of the car, with the exception of the paint. In 1934 Ford abandoned lacquer and moved to new enamels which did away with the buffing and hand polishing. Black fenders were still optional, at least on the green and gray Standard cars, and sales literature suggests that the Dearborn blue bodies still came with black fenders. The trend, however, was for identical body and fender colors, and this was certainly the normal offering on the Deluxe cars. It was to be the last year of the black intermix of body colors. Black wheels were still used on the Standard cars and this practice was followed through to 1941.

Car interiors were little changed. In mid-1933, the front door handle in closed cars had been moved from the leading edge of the door to near the center so that it could be more easily reached and do double duty as a pull, thus replacing the earlier hand ring. The engine-turned insert instrument panel of the 1933's was jettisoned, and the new panel, of similar general layout, was simply an integral part of the whole dashboard stamping—certainly less expensive, but not unattractive.

Body nomenclatures were unchanged and the styles were merely refinements over the previous year. The Model 40-740 Victoria, however, was all-new; its rear panel was now more nearly flat and was hinged at the bottom to receive luggage. A more awkward loading problem could hardly be imagined. Not only was the opening little more than 15 ins. in width, but luggage had to clear a minimum height of some 3 ft., which meant handles of suitcases needed to be elevated to roof height and held at arm's length while being lowered vertically into the trunk.

GM's system of no-draft ventilation must have given

Ford's V-8 was at last accepted as *the* modern, low-cost powerplant, and for 1934 it had a new intake manifold and dual-throat carburetor that brought it to 85 hp, where the V-8 would stay in the Thirties.

The grille remained little-changed from 1933 when viewed head-on, and still continued to dominate the front end. This nice restoration appears to mount all the available aftermarket accessories of the time.

The new flat lines of the grille are best seen in this angle. Lines duplicated in the hood side louvers have lost their former concavity. This Phaeton body style is easily the most sought-after today. Glamour and speed complemented its styling and led to Ford's domination of the open-car market.

some pause at Dearborn, because in the 1934 Ford the window-winding mechanisms were arranged to give the door and large window glass an initial rearward horizontal motion. The vertical slot thus opened exhausted air from the interior, which was replenished rather curiously through an updraft inside the doors. It may have worked, but in 1936 the rear quarter sedan windows were pivoted, as on the GM system, and in 1940 Ford went over to no-draft front vent windows. Plymouth took no chances in 1934 and with typical Chrysler engineering ingenuity offered the no-draft window which, when locked in the closed position, would also fully wind down.

The V-8 engine was largely unchanged for 1934, the new aluminum heads and the 6.3:1 compression being continued from the 1933 Model 40. One substantial improvement was the new over/under manifold mated to a dual-throat Stromberg carburetor. This single change boosted gross horsepower to 88 and achieved the advertised 85 hp, which was to continue for the rest of the decade. Also new in 1934 were the first thermostats installed in the upper hoses, and a 3.54:1 axle was offered for the first time.

Truck engines reverted to cast iron heads, and compression dropped back to 5.32:1. This compression was even lower than the original 1932 Model 18, but higher revs and the new carburetion held up engine output to 80 hp.

Ford sales started off briskly. In August 1933 the Model 40 had swept to victory in the Elgin Stock Car Races, taking the first seven places. On Feb. 24, 1934, this crushing display of speed was repeated in the Gilmore Cup Race when the first non-Ford finalist placed 11th. There was no longer any doubt about Ford performance. Police departments lined up to order Fords, which were supplied with special generators, radios, and other options.

Ford was unusually progressive in radio development. Though the first Grigsby-Grunow radio in 1932 was a cumbersome motor-generator affair requiring under-floor mounting, by 1933 the glove box could contain the new vibrator superhets complete with a matching dial to the speedometers. Beginning on June 18, 1934, Ford offered a second optional radio with a remote control head mounted in the ash tray space, a sacrifice for smokers which probably caused Mr. Ford no sleepless nights. The radio itself was mounted near the steering column, freeing the glove box. Insulated chicken wire in the closed car roof support provided an excellent built-in aerial. This layout continued through 1936 with steady refinements, one of which was an overhead speaker—quite certainly the best general location for a sound source in closed cars.

Performance was up as well as claimed gasoline mileage—two to three miles per gallon being the advertised increase. Allan Nevins reports that a New Hamp-

The greyhound radiator ornament, grille guard and road lights were available accessories in 1934 but of non-factory origin. Price increases by the competition this year gave Ford a sales advantage.

Rare 1934 Ford Station Wagon shows the awkward spare mounting, a feature that was dropped after this year. The problem can be traced to adoption of the V-8 which necessitated a short hood line. Sidemounts continued in popularity on the larger luxury cars—with their longer hoods.

shire competition was won by a Model 40 delivering some 28 mpg, in the process defeating a Chevrolet.

MOST FOR THE MONEY

More important to sales was the price increases of both Chevrolet and Plymouth for their 1934 models. Mr. Ford refused to follow these increases, and the result was about $60 lower price differential in Ford's favor. In addition, Chevrolet suffered a major strike at the beginning of the year, which further helped Ford.

January production of the Model 40 was 55,000 units. For the first time in the V-8's career, Ford got off to a good annual start, and sales moved forward steadily. Perhaps in response to labor unrest, Ford restored the $5 day in March, producing welcome public relations, a thing very much to the good.

Yet another factor aiding Ford sales was the Ford exhibit planned for the "Century of Progress" World's Fair in Chicago. The exhibit idea had taken root with a Dearborn show on display at the close of 1933 entitled "The Ford Exhibition of Progress." The Ford exhibit became a road show and in June came to rest in Chicago, but on a much enhanced scale. Eleven acres set off a giant rotunda containing a history of transportation, a demonstration of Ford manufacturing methods, and free rides in the new Ford car. Perhaps the most memorable part of the exhibit were three Ford cars, each suspended by a *single wire spoke* from the Rotunda ceiling. It was a startling demonstration of the tensile strength of this component in the Ford wheel. By mid-June Ford was leading Chevrolet in sales.

Ford's success in 1934 was not because Chevrolet was standing still. The Chevrolet 1934 D series, though

The added touch that had been provided by 1933's damascened instrument panel was gone for 1934. This was due largely to Mr. Ford's constant search for ways to reduce costs so that Fords would be affordable by all.

Chevrolet and Pontiac both bowed in 1934 with Dubonnet independent front suspension, but Ford stayed with the transverse springing and solid front axle that had been so successful on the rugged Model T.

A restored knockout is this 1934 Phaeton with rare tonneau windshield, a non-factory accessory. Beautifully restored car by Dave Graham rides on non-stock 16-inch wheels; a definite classic. This would be the last year that Ford would use rear-hinged front doors, perhaps inherently dangerous.

similar to the 1933 lines, had smoothed-up body refinements in the fuller fenders, grille styling, and new horizontal hood louvers. A glove compartment was introduced, one of those all-too-infrequent instances when Ford had led the way. Horsepower was up to 80, but the car was no match for Ford speed, despite a 500-mile run at Indianapolis averaging 75 mph in the hands of Bill Cummings. The most important mechanical advance for Chevrolet (and Pontiac) was the Dubonnet knee-action front suspension. Along with Chevrolet's new 112-in. wheelbase on the Master Series, the knee-action produced a genuinely new ride. The system was not without its faults. After the first Ford test track was built in 1936, Mr. Ford observed the 6-in. bumps in the wobble section and remarked, "You'll never get a car to stand up to that." Emil Zoerlein voiced the opinion that Mr. Ford's car could go through the bumps at 25 mph, for 25 times without trouble—a torture test which it indeed passed. On a comparable Chevrolet put to the same test, the knee action collapsed. In 1937 Pontiac abandoned the Dubonnet system for conventional independent front suspensions, and Chevrolet followed in its 1939 model year.

The 1934 Plymouth was a much improved car, especially the top of the line PE Deluxe series which boasted 114-in. wheelbase and independent suspension. The

Ford bookkeepers announced the firm was once again in the black after the financially dangerous years just past. As 1934 came to a close, however, Ford still had missed the number one spot by more than 4000 units; the Phaeton was the open-car leader, and the millionth V-8 was built.

For 1934 Plymouth featured flow-through ventilation via a windwing which could be opened or closed in the normal manner but which also could be lowered with the side glass by cranking the entire assembly down. Wheelbase of the very popular PE model was now out to 114 ins.

styling was refined, and though the car was still in the old idiom, it had a new solid look. It was solid all right, some 200 lbs. heavier in sedan form than the 2643-lb. 1933 models. The Chevrolet Master sedan weighed 3080 lbs., the first of the low-priced three to break the ton-and-a-half mark. By contrast, Ford Fordor weights were 2684 lbs., unchanged from 1933. This was one of the reasons for Ford's familiar, brisk performance. But that additional weight in Chevrolet and Plymouth was going into body development and chassis refinements, the weight itself perhaps adding as much as the new independent suspensions. It was a trend that Mr. Ford preferred to ignore.

Yet again from a styling standpoint, the Ford must rank as the prettiest car of the three. The Plymouth was a bit upright and had already begun to assume the image of "sensible quality," the car for discerning schoolteachers. The Chevrolet had simply fattened up a bit from 1933 and, despite the new Blue Flame combustion chamber, was a poor third on performance. Ford had it all—performance, style, a splendid new "hot" image, and the refinement of an already superb design which enhanced every good feature. The millionth Ford V-8—a Fordor Sedan—came off the Dearborn assembly line on June 20, attesting to the perfected production techniques of the engine.

Sales figures for the year reflected Ford's comeback. The race between Ford and Chevrolet was neck and neck through the summer, with Chevrolet finally winning by only 4500 cars. Ford's total was 532,589 passenger cars and 128,250 trucks. Plymouth gained again but was well behind with 351,113 units.

The magic 600,000 figure had been exceeded, and Ford moved back into the black. It was about time—losses from 1931 to 1933 had totaled $120,000,000—a figure which would have demolished all but a handful of American companies. The way Mr. Ford's mind worked, it was only a bookkeeping problem.

The owner of this Plymouth Deluxe Sedan boasted that he drove it 200 miles a day, with comfort superior to any other make. Plymouth's comfort came with a 113½-in. wheelbase, but Ford (at right) had a 112-in. wheelbase.

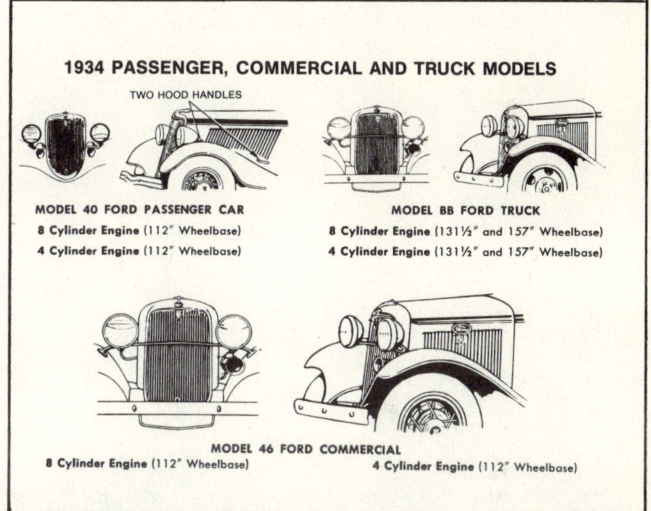

The 1934 Chevrolet was the first of the "big three" low-price cars to go over the ton-and-a-half mark. Chevrolet was the sales leader this year but only by the narrowest of margins. The Standard series, here in 2-door Coach form, had a short 107-in. wheelbase, while the Masters had 112 ins.

GROWING PAINS AND GOOD RESULTS

The 1935 Ford Phaeton, featured a new body this year; one which showed the absolute open-car styling leadership of the company. This would be the last year for exposed horns, as well as the concave fender lines.

If there is a year in the history of the decade in which Ford fortunes reached their zenith, it would certainly have to be 1935. It was a year of great change in the car. It was a year of great commercial success for the company, mainly because it was the one year of V-8 production in the Thirties when Ford beat Chevrolet. And it was a year of research and development which was to have future consequences.

The 1934 Model 40 had not taxed the engineering resources of the company. In fact, those resources were not exactly in first-rate shape. Following the Briggs strike in the low moments of 1933, Mr. Ford had actually sent home the whole engineering department, a short-lived action for the top engineers, of several days at most. Mr. Ford's offhand attitude toward engineers may be illustrated in a remark quoted by Allan Nevins. Said Mr. Ford, "All you have to do is give Sorensen a few sketches on the back of an envelope, and that's all the drawings he needs to make an automobile." The intuitive, experimental, and wholly pragmatic engineering methods of Mr. Ford depended on his innate genius, but automobiles were growing steadily more complex, and their design demanded new theoretical technical knowledge. Ford adamantly refused to consider incorporating into his car ideas that others had pioneered. Thus, he was becoming isolated from trends and innovations essential to the survival of the car. His engineers knew this and were growing restless. They were beginning to come forward with ideas which were rejected time and again by Mr. Ford. The development of an orderly engineering department was sufficiently impeded so that by late 1936 the company was driven to a costly struggle in order to produce the 1937 model. Of course, that car employed far more changes than had been usual.

Some engineers, including Zoerlein and others, re-

Part of the Ford display at the 1935 California-Pacific International Exposition at San Diego, Calif., shows the steps between drawing board and the final car.

The grille for 1935 would have been too overwhelming and massive without the horizontal relief structure. The sealed-beam lamps fit neatly, but are incorrect.

Cadillac for 1935 was barely in the new design idiom and GM designers were still struggling to deal with some of the exterior surfaces. Rear-hinged front doors probably reveal another problem area due to the rearward tilt of the "A" post. It was Cadillac's first year of non-concave fenders.

mained loyal, while still others were anxious to remove themselves from Mr. Ford's mounting interference. Sorensen himself agreed to the necessity of product design apart from Mr. Ford's daily direct supervision, and vowed that there would be no more "agonies" such as had accompanied the development of the 1937 model. It was in this atmosphere that he was able, in March 1937, to move engineering and styling away from Dearborn to the Rouge plant.

All of these later forces were first beginning to be evident as the development of the 1935 car began. It was obvious to everyone that a major redesign was necessary. The GM streamline style had appeared in the 1934 Cadillac and, especially in the LaSalle, the pontoon fenders and convex surfaces were fully developed. The Chrysler Airflow had been ready in January 1934. So confident was Chrysler of this new design that the DeSoto Airflow was marketed without an optional conventional series, a bold misjudgement not repeated in 1935. Edsel had purchased one of the new Chrysler Airflows and had liked the 15-in. seat heights and forward engine mounting.

There were other changes in the industry. GM's policy of filtering down the new body designs from Cadillac to the low-priced cars meant that Chevrolet was in for a major restyling. Though rumor had it that the Airflow line was going to be applied across the board to Dodge and Plymouth, sales resistance and general criticism made it more likely that the Airflow line would be augmented by more conventional, yet new, bodies in the streamline style. The year 1935 was one of great change in styling, punctuated by such standouts as the Packard 120, the very bulbous Oldsmobile, and Pontiac. Holdouts for the old idioms included Buick, Hudson, Nash, and Studebaker, among others. The independents were no doubt reluctant to come up with expensive new tooling, in the light of the precarious economic ordeal that most of them had just been through. Economic lessons carried much weight.

EXPERIMENTING WITH CARE

Ford engineering had been cautiously experimental following the initial settling down of the V-8 engine. In 1933 an experimental V-8 project, number 44, was built with displacement somewhat smaller than the 221 cu. ins. of the Model 18. This engine was peculiar in that it had five main bearings of very large diameter. Sheldrick recalls that the bearings were nearly 5 ins.—about the same diameter as the crank cheeks. Further, these gigantic bearings were splash lubricated. Several engines, and perhaps even some bodies, were constructed for a small V-8, but little more is known of this curious project.

The search for a splash-lubricated bearing, even after the V-8 full pressure pump system had been vindicated, was under the direction of Mr. Ford, as Eugene Farkas recollects. Less likely to be inspired by Mr. Ford was an ohv 6-cylinder engine of some 150 cu. ins. reputedly built in the summer of 1932. This engine also had huge crank diameters, 4 ins. or more. Farkas remembers that the engine was a non-starter when cold, but nothing more was heard of the project.

More promising was a small V-8 engine with 2.6-in. x 3.2-in. bore and stroke of 136 cu. ins., which was begun by Ray Laird in 1934 and known as project 92. The dimensions suggest that this engine was the true prototype of the celebrated V-8 60. Emil Zoerlein remembers that the first 60 had huge bearings of very narrow width which introduced much friction and heat; one suspects splash lubrication was present also. The early engines had the outer walls of the block cut away, perhaps to aid in core control during casting. Stainless steel plates were welded on to complete the wall jacketing. What probably was happening was that in 1933 and 1934 the above-mentioned Model 44 was simply being evolved in stages to a more conventional miniaturized Model 40 engine, whose success and popularity were now becoming very apparent.

Much more interesting than the new prototype 60 engine was the chassis designed to receive it. The layout began with a steel spine with arms extending laterally to support the body, and one wonders if Edsel or one of the engineers had examined Karl Rabe's Austro Daimler ADR introduced in 1928. The design was even more novel for having independent rear suspension combined with the usual Ford transverse springs at the front. There is some question as to whether or not this most radical car was ever developed in 1934, though it would reappear in 1937. It is not all that remarkable that such a unit could have been put on paper by Ford engineering, for experimentation was stronger than popular opinion suggests, but it is a wonder that records of this unusual design survive, for many of the unorthodox experiments were scrapped, often including written and drawn material. A virtual storehouse of "unusual" engines has recently come to public attention on the grounds of Greenfield Village, and one wonders how many odd configurations were destroyed for each one that survives.

Another scheme present in this mid-Thirties moment

The Series 50 LaSalle for 1935 featured a Vee'd windshield but was otherwise little-changed from 1934. The overall design concept, pioneered by Cadillac and LaSalle the previous year, was soon to influence all manufacturers, as did its independent front suspension which was new for 1934.

of bizarre designs was a special frame order by Mr. Ford. In his steady and commendable search for reduction in weight, he came up with the idea that a boxed frame would not only be exceptionally strong but might serve as a conduit for exhaust gases. Such a chassis was actually built and the system worked, but the corrosive elements in the exhaust gases would have quickly eaten the frame away. Also, the box frame presented fresh problems for the attaching of all components; being before the development of the blind rivet. The situation was shelved.

Mr. Ford's insatiable interest in the unusual, taking the form most often in attempts to simplify manufacture, to reduce weight, or both, led him to establish a small workshop at his Fairlane home. Here he sought to develop ideas which may have seemed too unorthodox for even his engineers. One pet project of his own was an inline 5-cyl. engine over which he labored during the early 1930's. The strange configuration surfaced several years later during work on a lightweight experimental car, and at least one of the engines exists in the Greenfield Village storehouse mentioned above.

A more satisfactory engineering achievement was the use of copper-lead bearings which were put into truck engines in the 1934 season.

The development of the 60-hp engine continued through 1934 and into 1935. Production began in July 1935 with 3355 engines manufactured in that year. First announcement for the European market was in October 1935 and the engine was introduced in the French Matford and in the English 1935 Model 48, known thus as Model 60. The Model 60 was built through 1936 until the introduction of all the British Model 62 and the very similar 1937 Matford Model 72, both of which continued with the 60-hp engine.

The V-8 60 engine was also used in the 1936 Model 61 Forward Control truck, shipped to Dagenham on March 6 and in production soon after in the English

The 1934 DeSoto Airflow was a radical and innovative car which influenced Ford development in 1935. Chrysler expected the basic design to sweep the industry and carried through with it until 1937.

The "waterfall" grille is well epitomized on this 1935 Pontiac, one which was singular among the GM offerings; while the balance of the sheetmetal was definitely of the GM "well-rounded" design school.

The 1935 DeSoto Airstream series was luckily added to the marque's model lineup after the previous year's Airflow-only approach. This series helped Chrysler to survive the losses that the Airflows would create.

In 1935 Nash was still trying to mate convex and concave surfaces. Fender roundness is heightened by pressed-in contour lines while the trunk and grille profiles sweep inward. Nash termed its styling "Aeroform" probably to call attention to streamlining concept.

plant. It would remain in the British lineup right up until the war. British truck buyers were not ready to give up the 4-cylinder for the new V-8 and the Model C engine continued to be available on special order in Model 61 and in other heavier truck lines. In 1938 Ford Dagenham bowed to the demand and offered as optional the C engine in all of the truck lines except of course the Y's and E-83W's, which were the little 1172cc commercials. This early use of the 60 in British truck production is the reason why the American 1937 Model 74 60-hp engines begin with the approximate serial number 6602, there having been this number of engines delivered in Europe prior to November 1936.

Laurence Sheldrick claims the credit for the layout of the new 1935 Model 48 chassis. The first problem tackled was the general location of the primary components. As a result, the engine was moved forward by 8.5 ins. The Airflow Chryslers showed what could happen to passenger space with this move, and the industry was to follow the trend. All passenger seats were moved forward, and Ford sales literature now boasted that all passengers had a "front seat ride." There is little doubt that fore and aft balance was greatly improved and, along with a better ride, the Model 48 was a more stable car at high speeds.

"BIRD WINGS ARE TRANSVERSE"

Moving the engine forward produced interference between sump and axle. Independent front suspension was one obvious solution because the engine could be cradled between the suspension elements. Even a conventional beam axle with half-elliptics could accommodate some engine moving through a judicious placement of cross members and the trend of dipping the center of the axle. Transverse springs mounted directly above the axle could not be lowered to make room for an engine because of the thickness of the spring at its center point and the structure of the cross member required to support it. Free travel of the spring was severely restricted already.

Mr. Ford's tenacious belief in his transverse spring led him to utter a famous retort when asked during an interview why he insisted on retaining this archaic system. He explained that he used a transverse spring for the same reason that wheels were round—because they work! He also likened his suspension system to the wings of a bird, in that the tips move the most while the body remains steady.

The transverse front spring situation, however, was giving pause to the engineers on some other counts. First, the length of the front spring (32.6 ins.) was no more than 59% of the tread. Longer springs would have helped to soften the ride. The absolute length of the front spring though, was limited, strangely enough, by the brake rods. If the spring hangers had been spread toward the brake backing plates, the brake rods in turn would have been forced closer to the wheels since they connected to the same hanger forging. This would have reduced the turning arc of the front wheels. On the Model A the wheels virtually touched

Hudson was still firmly in the early Thirties in 1935—with its styling yet to follow the GM school. When Hudson finally did make its move to rounded styling, it was the industry's most extreme.

Hupmobile was bold for 1935, even if in poor taste (with today's hindsight). With a unique 3-pane windshield, it was an early attempt at wrap-around visibility, but it suffered from an ugly roof brow. Overall, it embodied a great disparity of exterior lines with all sorts of curves and angles.

the brake rods on full lock. Even after shortening the brake cross shaft so as to angle the rods toward the center of the car, the clearances were not great. Another related problem was that the shock absorber linkages were mounted in a vertical plane and connected to the axle on the same hanger forging. If the spring length had been increased, the shock linkage would have been offset, since this would have introduced intolerable torque into the shock absorber shaft.

The short front spring, with its restricted travel, had a further undesirable effect; namely, that it had to have a very high load rate, which on the Model 18 and Model 40 was 400 lbs. per deflection inch. In other words, it took 400 lbs. of force to deflect a spring 1 inch. The rate produced a hard ride which was rapidly becoming embarrassing. The situation was even more serious on the 1½-ton trucks. In 1932 the BB started with 550 lbs. per inch of deflection on the front spring, which was raised to 1000 lbs. per inch in 1935, producing a virtually immovable spring. Such was the price paid for transverse springing. Mr. Ford, as has been noted, was firm on the question of transverse springs. Though the BB trucks had been fitted with rear semi-elliptics from the beginning, in 1935 Mr. Ford ordered a Model 51 1½-ton truck fitted with rear transverse springs. The load rate can only be guessed, but it must have ex-

A cutaway 85-hp V-8 on display at Harrah's Automobile Collection in Reno, is very likely a leftover from Ford's great involvement in World's Fairs and Expositions in the Thirties.

Buried deeply in the compartment of a 1940 Ford is the miniscule V-8 60, a well-used and unrestored veteran of uninspired performance but with a stout heart and the will to live on.

The first use of the V-8 60 was in this Type 61 truck announced in Great Britain in October 1935. The grille is basically of '35 U.S. truck inspiration, but without cross bars. Extensive service in British service proved the value there of Ford's new V-8.

ceeded 1500 lbs. per deflection inch! This truck hauled wheat in Michigan for a season and was virtually uncontrollable under load. It was broken up in 1936.

A third factor detrimental to the transverse springs was the necessity of fitting leading radius rods to position the front axle, paralleled in the rear by the torque tube and the trailing radius rods. This extra weight offset the initial advantage of low unsprung weight, especially because as front wheel brakes were fitted, the radius rods had to be heavier to prevent axle wrap-up, when compared to the light structures used on the front brakeless Model T. Likewise, the rear torque structures were all very much heavier than on the Model T, and most advantages in unsprung weight over the Hotchkiss system were lost in the sheer mass of metal required for power transmission and axle location.

Thus, in the minds of not a few observers, a new spring system was needed badly. Sheldrick undoubtedly was aware of the suspension discoveries by Maurice Olley at Cadillac. The research goal there had been to discover the suspension necessary for a truly flat ride so that rear seat passengers would not be thrown about—almost as harmonic balancers for chassis pitching, as Olley humorously put it. The key factor was not the use of an independent suspension, which had long been employed by Lancia, Morgan, and others. Rather, the critical factor was that the front springs needed to be softer with a much lower frequency than the rear. Following this theory, Olley was able to produce a flat ride even with conventional half-elliptics. The Cadillac unequal wishbone system, which fulfilled the requirements of a soft front end, was a brilliant result of fine experimental engineering.

Mercedes was also working on independent suspensions about the same time but missed the lesson that Olley had learned—putting stiffness forward and soft, albeit independent, suspensions in the rear. The resultant ride, at least in the mid-Thirties, could never equal the GM results.

SHELDRICK'S SOLUTION

The Ford situation had parallels to the Mercedes problem, for in 1934 the rear spring stiffness was only 56% of the front. The transverse spring could never permit the kind of soft, free movement which the GM wishbone system soon perfected, but Ford tried steadily for softer ride. By 1940 the ratio of rear-to-front stiffness was 78%, reaching 82% on the Lincoln-Zephyr. Ford could not come much closer to unity without producing a single frequency deflection in equal pitch and bounce, which would have been disastrous. To pass through such unity to the other side of GM's nirvana, with softer front than rear suspensions, was simply out of the question for transverse spring technology.

Sheldrick's solution, then, was made within the limits of Mr. Ford's technical philosophy. The transverse spring was mounted ahead of the front axle, somewhat like the layout used in the rear on Model 18. The front spring was immediately lengthened to 40.3 ins., since it no longer fouled the brake arm or shock linkages. The springbase was now 123.12 ins., more than 11-ins.

A view of the 1936 engine/front suspension layout reveals shock absorber mounting. Overall design shows that by moving the transverse spring ahead of the axle, a longer spring was permitted, which achieved a softer ride through an improved deflection rate. Engine was 8½-ins. forward of 1934's.

longer than the car's 112-in. wheelbase. It was a point useful in advertising. Clearance was immediately opened up over the front axle so that a longer free travel was available. The spring load rate was dropped at once to 245 lbs. with a substantial improvement in the ride. Likewise, the rear spring, with a reduced proportion of the load, had the rate reduced from 225 to 180 lbs. per in. of deflection. The new car was very much softer on the road, and Mr. Ford's transverse springs once again seemed to have caught up with the new IFS technology. This technology, especially in the Chevrolet, was faulty in the beginning and the Dubonnet suspensions were not indestructible, lacking the support and geometry of the wishbone system.

The new Ford springing allowed the engine to be moved forward, as noted previously, and the steering system and other components followed along. The drag link was now so short that the new axle freedom meant adverse steering feedback, so the drag link was placed nearly parallel to the axle, feeding control to the right side.

The Model 40 frame was certainly stronger than Model 18, but as the car lengthened, the tendency for shimmy and frame oscillations increased. The 1935 frame was much stronger, using more box sections and heavier bracing throughout. The car felt more sol-

The 1936 Ford had its hood extended to meet the Vee'd grille, and is the bane of restorers when aligning it to the grille shell and hood sides. Most '36 changing was in the front end, and the horns were hidden at last.

Ford's front suspension layout—altered beginning with the 1935 models—featured the longer transverse spring positioned ahead of the axle. This is the arrangement for '36, with the adjustable-length steering cross shaft.

It is hard to deny the beauty of the 1935 Ford, especially in its Roadster form. Frontal styling was perhaps a little busy with the exposed horns, yet without them the grille area appears bleak. There were less than 3100 open cars built in the Chevrolet lineup in '35, and Ford popularity prevailed.

GROWING PAINS AND GOOD RESULTS

id, and the chassis racking, still noticeable on Model 40 when negotiating sharp road angles, was gone.

The clutch was improved in 1935 by using weights which were forged with the throwout levers that acted centrifugally to increase plate pressure. The system meant lighter pressure at idle by some 20% under that of 1934, yet slipping was reduced, especially as revs increased.

The Ford brake design was refined on Model 48. The primary improvement was self-centering shoes coupled with floating wedges. Shoe dimensions were changed and became shorter but wider, while the 186-sq.-in swept area remained the same. The brakes were good, but two problems were steadily reducing effectiveness. The first was weight. That 186 sq. ins. of brake contact area was standardized in 1932, yet by 1935 sedan weight had increased from 2512 to 2849 pounds. The second problem was speed. The new Model 48 was the fastest Ford yet, and the brakes were likely to have more work to do, especially since highway conditions were improving steadily allowing higher speeds. The cooling ribs were increased by some 40% in an effort to raise efficiency. For one more year Ford could offer mechanical brakes without undue competitive problems because the GM hydraulic changeover in their various makes was not complete.

The 1935 Ford was publically introduced on Dec. 29, 1934, an all-new car from the outside. The proportions were completely different, and the car showed very little of the usual styling evolution. The wheels were still the familiar welded wire spoke design, and the rim diameter had now reached 16 ins., a diameter which remained fixed until 1948. The bumpers were very much like 1934, even if the standard guards had been

Ford's rear fenders for 1935 had concavity, but less pronounced than the fronts. Nevertheless, it was a successful marriage of lines despite the convex shape of the deck and rear body on this Deluxe Coupe.

The inspired styling of Phil Wright who worked at Briggs resulted in the fine 1935 lines, so evident in the fenders—the fronts especially flow nicely into the running boards; a theme to be lost for 1936.

The Phaeton had everything going for it despite the fact that this model and the companion Roadster were beginning to defer to the increased comfort that was offered by the Convertible and Convertible Sedan. The latter styles had roll-up windows.

restyled from the accessory guards offered in 1934.The round taillights were familiar. However, everything else was different. The forward placement of the major components thrust the prow of the radiator well forward of the front axle line—in fact, forward of the fenders—and any classic allusions were destroyed. The Model 48 engine had a few changes; primarily, a new cast alloy crank which once again demonstrated Ford's advanced metallurgy.

The copper-lead truck bearings were now used in all production. Crankcase water vapor had been causing rust on fuel pumps, so a forward facing air scoop replaced the oil filler cap and hopefully collected fan draft which was driven down into the crankcase. The slight pressure forced fumes out another exit below the engine. This system worked providing that blow-by did not become excessive and convert the air scoop into an exhaust port.

STYLING CREDIT

Credit for overall styling of the 1935 Ford must go to Phil Wright who worked under Ralph Roberts at Briggs Manufacturing Co., a major source of Ford bodies. There were two styling sections at the firm; one headed by John Tjaarda being charged with experimental car design exercises, while the Roberts group did speculative designs for Briggs' regular customers, notably Ford and Plymouth. Phil Wright reportedly did the renderings for the 1935 Ford at his home, then showed them to his boss, Ralph Roberts, who in turn showed them to Ford management including Edsel Ford. Ford officials were so pleased, that the order went out to go right to a full-scale mockup of wood, rather than through the customary 1/24th clay scale models. Famed stylist Bob Koto, a compatriot of Wright at Briggs, on the other hand, was later assigned to face-lift the '35's into the following year's 1936 Model 68.

The 1935 Ford has not fared well with modern day enthusiasts who usually judge the 1936 models as superior in almost all respects, especially in styling. This is not fair. The 1935 Ford was a unified design in all of its surfaces while the 1936 Ford shows the mutations resultant from the styling upheaval which was everywhere in the industry in the mid-Thirties. For example, the 1935 fenders, though very deeply crowned, maintained slight but essentially concave flow surfaces which harmonize especially well with the sedan bodies. The Model 48 sedans avoided the extreme bulbousness of the GM idiom and maintained a crispness of line found nowhere else in the industry. The Plymouth married heavy convex fenders to a rather slender body

The Phaeton and Roadster for 1935 shared unique dashboard and separate windshield stanchions. This unrestored example shows the plainness evident at the time in interior design—which was still pleasant.

1935 FORD PASSENGER, COMMERCIAL AND TRUCK MODELS

MODEL 48 FORD PASSENGER CAR
8 Cylinder Engine (112″ Wheelbase)

MODEL 51 FORD TRUCK
8 Cylinder Engine (131½″ and 157″ Wheelbase)

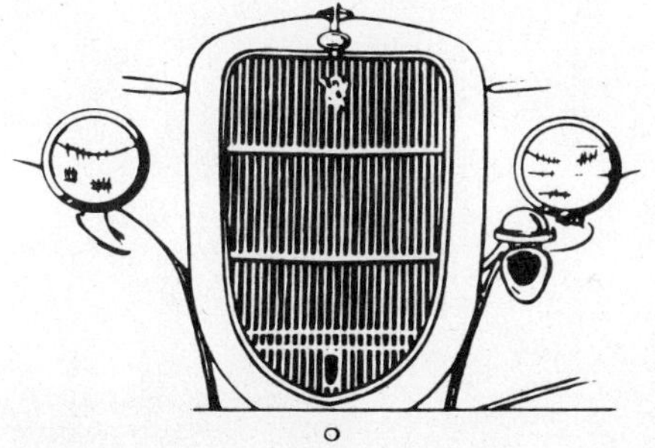

MODEL 50 FORD COMMERCIAL
8 Cylinder Engine (112″ Wheelbase)

Factory identification drawings show the different, yet similar, frontal aspects between the passenger car and commercial lines. Front views are Standards while ¾-views are of the Deluxes. Ford had its best sales year for the decade in 1935.

with only fair result. To many tastes, the independents, such as Studebaker, Hudson, and Nash, were simply downright ugly, challenged only by the incredible roundness of the Master Chevrolet turtled on a 113-in. wheelbase with all pretensions of grace destroyed.

The 1936 Ford line had the convex fender surfaces which were universal in the low-priced lines, except for Willys whose revenge was to come in 1937. These fender surfaces worked best on those bodies which were themselves primarily convex; namely, the coupes, roadsters, cabriolets, and the convertible trunk sedans. The regular sedans in 1936 do not have the unity of 1935 models, a fact often unnoticed since these bodies are not those initially coveted by enthusiasts. The Phaeton, though sharing the rear sheetmetal of the flatbacked sedans, is softened by the door and cowl roll and lacks the hardness in the window reveals which makes the convex fender less damaging.

The 1935 Model 48 had certain virtues. This was the last year in which a hood would properly meet a grille surround. In this regard Ford was distinctly old-fashioned, most other makers having surrendered to vast surfaces of sheetmetal meeting haphazardly. The 1936 Ford grille was particularly vulnerable to bad fitting, as patient restorers know so well.

The 1935 concave front fender lines had a splendid flow into the running boards, not as sweeping as 1934 but still most graceful. The rear fender sweep was inspired, the slight uptilt being just right to lighten the rear profile of the car. The 1936 rear fender could not

Nash held to two series in post-Depression 1936, this Deluxe and an Ambassador with either a Six or an Eight. Concave rear styling seems more pronounced without an opening trunk.

DeSoto Airflow trunk arrangement was bold in a move to improve spare tire location, but its effort to improve styling negated any luggage.

The 1935 Plymouth mated very round fenders with a body that was essentially vertical in feel, beginning with the tall and narrow grille. Porthole motif on the hood sides may be a LaSalle influence. This convertible coupe lacks the grace and unity of the open-top Ford.

compare to it in the sheer subtlety of the shape.

The front doors were hinged from the front, a genuine improvement over the Model 40 rear-hinged "suicide" doors. Strangely enough, Chevrolet went the other way, moving to rear hinged doors on the Master Series in 1935. One wonders if the bulbous shapes and door edges presented hinging problems to Chevrolet, and yet in 1936 Chevrolet went back to the normal pattern. One of the unsightly features of the mid-Thirties was the hinges projecting from curved body surfaces in order to get a hinging center.

The 1935 headlamps were an evolution from 1934—elongated, lens more convex, but using a primary painted surface with a stainless rim. The horns were virtually unchanged from 1934, now perhaps a bit anachronistic but adding a little fussiness to the frontal appearance. Using horizontal break stripes on the vertical grille bars was a technique not repeated by Ford,

Final assembly line at Ford's Long Beach, Calif., facility spews forth 1936's. The West Coast plant had opened in April 1930 and was Ford's 35th U.S. branch plant. It was initially capable of 370 cars per eight-hour shift and was supplanted in August 1931 by a twin in Richmond, Calif.

but they served to break up what would otherwise have been an overpowering massive appearance.

The very sharp change with the past on the exterior was repeated in the interior. The dashboard was fresh, with the big round speedometer now flanked by smaller circular combination gauges. New for 1935 on the Deluxe models was the electric oil pressure gauge. The old hydrostatic fuel gauge survived for another year. The imitation wood grain effect that had been applied to the instrument panel was temporarily gone—a silver gray lacquer now considered to be a Deluxe color, while a mahogany brown served for the Standard models. On the closed cars the windshield would still crank out and would swing out on Roadsters and Phaetons.

The 1935 bodies offered a similar range of choices as in Model 40, with two exceptions. The Victoria was dropped, it being obvious that the new slant-back shape of the sedans, especially the Tudor, made the development of a distinctive Victoria style nearly impossible. The nearest thing to a Victoria would be the Club Coupe, introduced later for 1937 and continued only into the 1938 model. The second change was the introduction of the Convertible Sedan—not patterned on the style of the old 2-door B400, but a genuine 4-door fully collapsible sedan. It was a handsome new design and was the most expensive body in the lineup by nearly $100. Ford was thus put in the interesting position of having both its lowest price and most expensive Deluxe bodies in convertible styles. Apart from the Station Wagon, the Convertible Sedan was the heaviest 1935 body, with all-up weight of 2958 lbs.

Sales got off to a fine start, aided by the momentum developed in 1934. In 1935 Ford had several basic advantages in facing competitors. The car itself, with sub-

The 1936 Fords had lost the fender concavity but to many latter-day buffs it was the ultimate flowering of the styling originally set down for 1935. This would be the last year of the true Roadster and Phaeton.

The 85-hp V-8, now in its 5th year of production, remained the only low-cost Vee and still out-performed the competition. It excelled in acceleration.

Chrysler stylists continued to modify the Airflow grille and the 1936 version was perhaps the most successful of the four attempts. The final try for 1937, the end of the Airflow series, failed to improve on this one. This 4-door Imperial to many observers is the highlight of the series.

stantial changes in styling and chassis, was the best job offered to date. Ford prices were still below those of Chevrolet and Plymouth. And Ford offered a broad selection of body types which were unmatched. For example, the new Chevrolet Master Series with its extreme convex surface development had no convertible in the lineup. The old Standard series retained a Roadster and Phaeton, but these bodies were no match for Ford's four new splendid open styles. Further, Chevrolet once again was crippled by a long strike, which Ford exploited to the full. By the end of the model year, Ford had decisively regained industry leadership in sales with 826,519, compared to Chevrolet's 656,698 and Plymouth's 382,925.

The success of Model 48 in 1935 was perhaps part of the reason for the coming decline of the company in the second half of the decade. Basic criticism of the car was temporarily silenced, and the vindication of Mr. Ford's theories was on the sales charts for all to see. It is probable that in this light there was a mass myopia against the problems which were soon to be apparent as the new 1936 models emerged.

A well-preserved, accessory-bedecked 5-window Coupe receives its daily rub-down from its proud owner. Evident from this angle is the subtle crease that highlights the fully-rounded fenders, and the fine marriage of lines and angles everywhere. Rightside windshield wiper was an option.

Even a low-angle photograph cannot help to reduce the grille angularity and the mismatch of extravagant roundness given this 1935 Chevrolet Master EA 4-door. But GM had mastered one-piece turret top construction—which would not come to Ford until 1937.

WIND OF THE ZEPHYR

The Tjaarda-inspired design of the new Lincoln-Zephyr was the first mass-produced unit construction car in America. Easily as radical as the streamlined Cadillac show car, the Pierce Silver Arrow, or the Chrysler Airflows, the L-Z was the only one to become a commercial success.

The inauguration of the new Lincoln-Zephyr, Nov. 2, 1935, came at a moment of triumph for the Ford Motor Co. Confident now, after back-to-back profitable years plus a resounding sales victory with Model 48, the Zephyr could only augment the expected success seen with the new 1936 Model 68. The introduction of the Zephyr was filling many needs for the company. Production of the great Lincoln K series was no more than a trickle of perhaps 40 cars per week in 1935. The marque was totally subsidized as a prestige item for the company, or perhaps as a whim of Mr. Ford. But that subsidy made possible undiminished quality throughout the Thirties. Commercial value of the K Lincoln was principally in the name, and the new Zephyr was to draw upon that asset.

By 1935 Ford was acutely aware of the marketing gaps between Ford and the K Lincoln; that is, practically the whole market above the lowest priced big three. The problem was extraordinary in that the revolution of the automobile corporate structure and product mix was essentially completed by Alfred P. Sloan of GM and by Walter Chrysler, by the end of the Twenties. The effect on Ford was practically non-existent. There had been no new cars developed, no change in the company structure (whatever that might have been), no attention to consumer research, and precious little attention to dealer attitudes. Major engineering advances, apart from the V-8 engine itself, were not evident. There was no true styling department, and projects emerged as personal assignments to Gregorie, Galamb, Farkas, and others. In 1934 energies of both engineering and styling were focused on Model 48.

It is not surprising, then, that the inspiration for the Zephyr came from the Briggs Co. in the person of John Tjaarda. A car designed by Tjaarda, and shown at the Ford exhibit at the Chicago Century of Progress, embodied the basic body sheetmetal of the Zephyr. This prototype, which seated three in the front seat and two in the rear, was developed by Briggs along with Gregorie and Edsel into a car which was compatible with basic Ford engineering. The essential novelty of the car, apart from the styling, was Tjaarda's unit construction. The V-12 engine configuration was a concession to the Lincoln nameplate, but the execution of the design was Ford inspired. The V-12 had a 2.750-in. x

3.750-in. bore and stroke with a displacement of 267 cu. in. Its 110 bhp made the new Zephyr engine about as efficient as the 221-cu.-in. V-8 on a displacement basis, but peak horsepower appeared at a higher rpm—in the Zephyr's case, 3900 rpm. For 1936 no other engine had a higher rpm for peak horsepower except the blown Lycoming GH, as used in the Auburn, and the blown Graham 110. The torque curve was peculiarly flat, from 1500 to 2500 rpm at about 185 lbs.-ft., again a respectable figure. But the engine seemed anemic, in part because body weight for the 1936 Zephyr sedan was up to 3349 lbs., which quickly escalated to more than 3600 lbs. in 1939, and still with only 110 hp. Since the car offered and advertised 6-passenger carrying capacity, the Zephyr frequently had all-up weights well over half-a-ton above the Ford. Its top speed of about 90 was more a tribute to its efficient streamlining than to engine horsepower, although the strained, high revving capability of the V-12 was certainly a factor.

The engine followed Ford practice at most points,

These 1935 K Lincolns on display at the Chicago Auto Show show the exceptionally conservative line taken throughout the styling revolution of Cadillac and other GM cars. Production was probably 40 per week.

The L-Z's only Lincoln heritage was its 12 cylinders, but through this, Edsel hoped, the senior car's prestige would pass on down. Note flow of runningboard lines.

Typically Ford in construction and appearance, the L-Z V-12 borrowed heavily from Ford's basic design by the relatively simple addition of four more cylinders.

To show that the Long Beach, Calif., Branch Assembly Plant was in production on almost the full line of 1936 Ford body styles, this array of cars was Vee'd for a remarkable photo. Only type not shown was the Station Wagon. By a rare coincidence, barely discernable ship with bowsprit behind lefthand telephone pole was rammed and sunk just prior to WW II by the Japanese!

technically, though the rod bearings were fixed. Pure Ford was the gearbox, including ratios, until 1940. That was the year when the special Zephyr gear ratios appeared—the ones beloved by Ford hot rodders. The clutch was beefed up a bit in diameter, but pedal pressure was up only 15% over 1935 Ford levels.

The cooling problems of the Ford were directly transferred to the Zephyr, since the exhaust passages through the block were similar. The Zephyr put the water pumps in the block, however, a change which the Ford would follow in 1937. The Zephyr coolant capacity was absolutely huge, beginning with 27 quarts and rising to 30 quarts in 1938. The radiator's frontal area of 391 sq. ins., however, was no more than the 1936 Ford's, and even a 17-in. diameter 6-blade fan did not compensate for the basic overheating problem. One must be careful not to fault Ford for any lack of effort in searching for a solution, as Zephyr radiator design moved to ever larger frontal areas, reaching a phenomenal 464 sq. ins. in 1940. No Ford truck radiator ever reached these capacities or surface areas.

Another innovation in the Zephyr was the first use of self-energizing cable brakes. The 12-in. drum diameters were no larger than on the Ford, but the efficiency of these new brakes was so much better that lining area on the Zephyr was only 168 ins., well below the V-8—and exactly equal to the Model A! The cables were used for the obvious reason that the routing of rods was no longer technically feasible with the new unit construction. Bodies were steadily getting lower, and interference problems were increasing.

SPRINGING FOR TROUBLE

Yet another development occurred in the Zephyr which was to have far-reaching consequences. The transverse springs were mounted in a manner similar to those on the Model 48. The 1936 Zephyr front spring was dimensionally about the same as on the 1936 Ford but with two additional leaves and a deflection rate of 300 lbs./in. It was the same at the rear, with a rate of 250 lbs. as compared to the 1935-36 Ford rate of 180 lbs. So far, so good.

Unfortunately, the new Zephyr was to demonstrate dramatically the weakness of the transverse spring for many reasons. The first was that the Zephyr was a much larger car than the Ford. It had a 10-in. longer

To many buffs, the 1936 Roadster is the reigning queen of all the Thirties' Ford open cars. It had a longer hood, a Vee'd grille, and a body unchanged from 1935.

The Roadster and Phaeton shared a dash layout that was unique among all the body styles. While gauge placement was similar, the cowl required a lower dash panel.

1936 was the last year for the "true" Roadster and the Phaeton, for these body types would not boast the separate windshield posts and flowing cowl lines in 1937.

This is perhaps why the Phaeton (and Roadster) fell from buyer's favor; inclement weather necessitated use of inconvenient, snap-on side curtains.

wheelbase and hundreds of pounds more weight. The engineers were seeking a softer ride in order to compete with the new independent front suspensions. In 1937 the Zephyr front spring was lengthened 2½ ins. and the rears 2 ins. But the sheer increase of weight added to the pendulum effect inherent in the shackles or hangers of the transverse spring. The transverse spring cannot be fixed at one end, as is the case with conventional semi-elliptics. The result is that the weight of the car literally hangs and swings on the shackles. This pendulum effect was hardly possible as long as the shackles were mounted above the axle with severely limited movement. But beginning with Model 48, the front springs were both softer and free to move in a new way. The Zephyr suffered from the beginning with sideways movement, especially up front, caused by wind, road camber, cornering, and the weight of the car in relation to springing capabilities.

Now, that sideways movement would be no more than irritating if it were not for another problem. Ford cars always moved sideways a little bit, and up until 1934 it did not make much difference in car handling because the steering linkage was parallel to the frame and lateral motion did not affect the "set." But in 1935 cross-steering was introduced, and the lateral chassis motion converted the steering link into a stabilizing strut. Any lateral motion acted directly on the steering.

The problem was so bad for the Zephyr that in mid-1936 a modification was made to the Zephyr front end. The Ford Service Bulletin said it succinctly: "During 1936 a strut rod was adopted on Lincoln-Zephyr cars to restrict sideways movement which otherwise would be transmitted to the drag link spindle; permitting cross winds to affect the control of the car." That front strut rod continued on the Zephyr even after the torsion bar stabilizers were added.

Again, Ford engineers struggled to make transverse springing work to meet the needs of a soft, controlled ride. The ride-stabilizing torsion bar appeared on the 1940 models of Ford, Mercury, and Lincoln-Zephyr and enabled further reduction of spring deflection rates. However, this was the last refinement possible with transverse springs, and though the improvement was noticeable, it did little good in helping Ford compete against the sophisticated suspensions of its principal competitors. The transverse springs of the Zephyr were one of its weakest points when compared directly to its GM and Chrysler competing lines. Its Houdaille shock absorbers, however, would last longer.

The Zephyr styling was soon to affect Ford design. But in 1936 the new Model 68 was clearly a warmed-over 1935; both Chevrolet and Plymouth were doing the same thing in 1936. The 1936 Master FA Chevrolet basic sheetmetal was unchanged from 1935, though

Here's enough canvas to move a windjammer; a 1936 Roadster is backed by a Convertible Sedan, a Phaeton, a rumbleseat Convertible, another Roadster, and a second Convertible Sedan—all 1936's. (Final two on restorer's row are a 1932 Phaeton, and a 1940 Deluxe Coupe.

the new convex grille harmonized better with the bulbous body shape. The headlights were attached to the radiator shell, which positioned them both higher and closer together, an idea derived perhaps from the 1934 LaSalle. The only important mechanical change was the introduction of hydraulic brakes. Oldsmobile and LaSalle had pioneered hydraulics for GM in 1934, followed by Pontiac in 1935. In 1936 Buick, Chevrolet and Cadillac completed the transition, with only one holdout—the V-16 Cadillac. Now only Ford and Willys retained mechanical brakes.

The Plymouth line for 1936 was unchanged, apart from a grille design which paralleled the new convexity of the Chevrolet. There had been solid sales progress in 1935, and the seemingly endless Plymouth growth of the Thirties was showing no signs of interruption.

Ford styling changes in 1936 were confined to fenders, the hood panels, and grille. The convex fenders paralleled the styling of Chevrolet and Plymouth, but the effect was never as soft in Ford lines because the hardness of the 1935 bodies was unchanged, especially around the windows. Likewise, the new Ford grille had angularity in it, caused by the horizontal cutoff point at the top of the radiator slats which prevented the Ford from slipping into the "Jell-O" effect of Chevrolet. This angularity was further emphasized in the hood side louvers—all straight lines as opposed to the more flowing treatment of Chevrolet and Plymouth. The result was an altogether "tight" car which managed to retain some discipline in the surface development. There is no doubt that the 1936 Ford has become a favorite among latter-day Ford buffs.

BLOSSOMS OF 1936

In 1936, Ford blossomed forth with the greatest array of body types in the V-8 years, no less than 16 including the Station Wagon and Sedan Delivery. The 2- and 4-door sedans could be had with or without trunk, as had been the case since mid-1935. The trunk was awkward and small and hard to load, but it did add length and slight hardness to the body. The 3- and 5-window coupes were available, with or without rumble seats. The beautiful Roadster and Phaeton bodies were still available. And the Convertible Sedan was continued, but in 1936 a new trunk version was made available with a brand new rear line which was to carry through until 1938. It was a very pretty car indeed and the roundness of the trunk offered good parallelism with the new 1936 fenders. The Cabriolet was joined in March by a new body style, a Club Cabriolet, in which all passengers sat under the canvas top, an accurate forecast of things to come. Only half the number of body types available from Ford were offered by Chevrolet and Plymouth, though the latter had a long wheelbase Taxi Special in its regular lineup, which Ford did not. Last Ford taxi production was in the Model A.

One good concession to creature comfort was made for 1936, at least for back-seat passengers in the Fordor and Fordor Touring Sedans. Rear-seat elbow room was increased by 3½ ins., by recessing the rear quarter panel trim beneath the quarter windows. This was made possible by the adoption of pivoting glass, which also served to improve ventilation, in place of the roll-down items used previously for 1935.

A very minor change for 1936, but which nonetheless must have been appreciated by garagemen and service attendants, was made to improve retention of the hood when it was propped open for engine maintenance. For 1935 the rear lower corners of the opened hood side panels engaged a small depression in the cowl, but they could easily jiggle loose allowing the hood to fall. For 1936 the hood was better retained by a raised nub at the same location. This nub, incidentally, plus large X-shaped stiffening ribs pressed into the cowl sides, is an aid to enthusiasts in distinguishing between 1935 and 1936 body shells which are otherwise identical.

The mechanical improvements for Ford in 1936 were useful. Insert main bearings appeared and dome pis-

Fordor Touring Sedan differed from Fordor Sedan by virtue of hump-back trunk design. Trunk was a nice styling touch, but was obviously awkward to load.

Initial Convertible Sedan production was flat-backed with small stowage space behind rear seat. But a mid-year change was to the illustrated configuration.

tons were introduced. The cooling system was reworked because the 1935 car was already earning a bad reputation for overheating, probably because the radiator had less capacity and frontal area than in 1934. This was corrected in Model 68. Cooling capacity returned to 22 quarts and frontal area rose nearly 10 sq. ins. to 391. An extension to the radiator header tank was added and larger louvers were stamped into the inner front fender panels to assist airflow out of the engine compartment. This last feature was especially useful, since the airflow passed by the exhaust manifolds. The largest louvers definitely helped.

The Model 48 steering had been noticeably heavier than in 1934 because of the 600x16 tires and the new weight on the front axle. In 1936, the last year of the worm and sector steering, the ratio reached 17:1, and this combined with a longer spindle arm increased the leverage by 13% but at the expense of more steering wheel winding. Needle bearings were introduced on the sector shaft for this one year only. The net result of these changes meant nearly a 40% reduction in steering wheel effort, one of the most noticeable changes for 1936. Another refinement of the 1936 steering was an adjustable drag link whereas the previous design had a fixed length. The Ford steering gear had a slightly greater tightness at the straight-ahead position, partly to compensate for the great amount of wear experienced at this point and partly to help hold the wheels when traversing varying road conditions. The wheels were supposed to be held dead-ahead at the steering high spot, and the adjustable drag link helped achieve this at the time of manufacture as well as during the car's service life.

The welcome refinement of helical-cut low and reverse transmission gears had been catalogued beginning in mid-1935. It was a design carried over for 1936. The travel of the gear shift lever was reduced by the incorporation of a slightly higher shifter tower, an idea which would be even further developed for 1939.

One last change was the abandonment of wire wheels. The Ford welded spoke system patented in September 1923, had been used steadily since 1926 in five rim sizes. (They were 21″, 19″, 18″, 17″ and 16″.) By the mid-Thirties the vogue for wire wheels had

Popular with salesmen and single people was the Coupe in 3-window configuration. It could be had, like its 5-window counterpart, with or without the handy rumbleseat.

Detail of fender skirt on car at left. The item was a Ford factory accessory, unlatched via exposed lug-type bolt.

High angle photo of a 1936 5-window Deluxe Coupe reveals the fabric top insert shared by all the Ford closed cars. Ford insisted that it lightened car and lessened body drumming, yet it was gone in 1937. Note the relatively recent, narrow whitewall tires.

passed, and they no longer represented the quality choice over wood spokes as in the Twenties. The pressed steel wheel had won the day by virtue of its ease of construction, reliability, and lightness.

Ford was particularly interested in the reduction of unsprung weight, and by reducing wheel weight by 5 lbs., for a total of 20 lbs. —for the four wheels—it was calculated that riding ease was improved by the same amount that adding 200 lbs. to the body would have meant. Much of the reduction of wheel weight came from the respacing of the wheel studs out near the circumference of the drum, thus allowing the center portion of the wheel to be simply omitted. Chevrolet also went over to steel discs in 1936, while Plymouth had made the change the year before. Ford's new wheels were easier to clean and masked any view of brake drum and axles, a feature which added to the substantial appearance of the car.

On paper, the 1936 Ford Model 68 appeared to be a winner, and the company entered the model year with high hopes. An unusually early introduction on Oct. 19, 1935, jumped the gun on Chevrolet, and for the first time Ford got off to a healthy head start. Yet it soon became apparent that 1936 was going to be less than a winning year. The bloom was leaving the rose.

BLOSSOMS CAN WITHER, TOO

The first reason was that in 1936 the Ford car was seen by both dealers and public in terms of its anachronisms. At the head of the list was braking, because the Ford brakes for 1936 were unchanged, and their inadequacies were now accentuated by the final GM switch to hydraulics. Eugene Farkas recalled two problems with Model 68 brakes. The new disc wheels with their wide-spaced stud mountings tended to pull the drums out of shape when carelessly torqued or when the wheel itself was damaged. Thus, the braking quality deteriorated with any abuse of the new wheels. Furthermore, cross-shaft windup continued to be a problem, and the left brakes tended to pull harder than the right brakes. As long as pedal pressure was applied to one end of the shaft, no matter how short, there would be a problem. Consumers complained of groans and seizings. Ford dealers were just about unanimous in condemning mechanical brakes because they were being clobbered by Chevrolet on this one detail, alone.

The Station Wagon was beginning to get over its stigma of being a Commercial vehicle, and was coming into its own as purely a car. Yet, even with wood panels, this 1936 was very spartan in interior appointments.

While Ford's Iron Mountain, Michigan, plant is generally credited with producing Station Wagon bodies, it actually fabricated only the wooden sub-assemblies which were then sent to the Murray Body Co., Detroit, and Baker-Rauling, Cleveland, for final body assembly. Then the 1936 "box" was sent to the Ford Branch Assembly plants where it was married to the chassis and sheetmetal.

Edsel was well aware of the dealers' troubles and had a Model 68 fitted with hydraulics, which were successful, but Mr. Ford stopped the project at once. Mr. Ford was still stubborn in the notion that mechanical brakes were more reliable.

One little-known fact about Ford mechanical brakes of this era was that they were adjustable in the amount of pressure exerted to activate them. This was accomplished by means of two holes in the cross-shaft lever to which the rod from the pedal was attached. When the rod was attached to one hole, required pedal pressure was reduced, but at the expense of available pedal travel. This gave a "softer" pedal for those who desired it. Utmost braking effectiveness came from attaching the pedal rod to the second hole and achieving a higher required pedal pressure with shorter travel.

Overheating problems were hurting Ford by 1936. Chevrolet and Plymouth had little radiator trouble, and the public was now unwilling to put up with a car that simply could not do the job in whatever climate and on whatever kind of mountain grade. Likewise, the high-mounted Ford fuel pump with its tendency to vapor lock from high under-hood temperatures was a noticeable flaw, a problem which was not solved before World War II.

Even more important was the growling public awareness that the Ford car was inferior to both Chevrolet and Plymouth on a comfort and luxury basis. The transverse springs were now a genuine sales liability, and many Ford engineers knew it. Sheldrick remembers that on several occasions attempts were made with no success to introduce half-elliptics on independent suspensions, with coils or transverse springs at both front and rear. The prototype Mercury had longitudinal springs, but when Mr. Ford found out, he immediately cancelled the project.

Having no V-8 to capitalize upon, Plymouth advertising pressed hard on the idea of smoothness. With floating power engine mounts, no-shock steering, rubber-cushioned bodies, and spring advances, Plymouth had succeeded in convincing the public that its car was indeed "smoother" than its competitors. Attention to sound insulation in the low-priced field was another innovation in which Plymouth had particular success. Everything came together for Plymouth in 1936 when the company sold half-a-million cars.

The first Jensen-Ford was built on a 1935 chassis for Edsel's personal use, but limited production began shortly afterwards. This stunning creation was built as a 1936 model of which three were produced.

Many coachbuilders of the Thirties utilized Ford chassis and running gear on which to fabricate custom-crafted bodies, but the only enterprise outside of the Ford empire to be so blessed was Jensen of England.

DeSoto's final fling with a Convertible Sedan was this 1936 Airstream, the hurriedly introduced line of cars to fill the void created by the Airflow. Though Chrysler Corp. managed to chalk up roughly 45,000 new car registrations this year, only some 5000 were Airflows, attesting to the hesitation of buyers to fall for truly advanced automotive concepts. In 4-door sedan form, Airstreams cost $795.

Chevrolet was doing even better. The 1935-36 styling which seems so dated to the eye 40 years later looked altogether different to the average buyer in 1936. The Chevrolet appeared bigger, longer, and heavier, which in fact it was.

The new one-piece turret top without fabric insert proved to be a resounding sales success and tended to emphasize Ford's old-fashioned body construction. Ford countered that while one-piece turrets were easily within their technology, they continued to favor the fabric insert which lessened body weight, reduced body noise, and gave better insulation.

The interior of the Chevrolet was especially effective and showed a level of trim and fit which Ford simply could not duplicate. In 1936 the Chevrolet 2-door sedan offered bench front seats. The no-draft ventilation was now industry wide. In the many details of finish and design, Chevrolet had moved ahead, and the public responded by buying some 930,000 units. Ford sales of 764,126 were substantial, and profit was $17,930,000—well back from the record levels of 1935. Once again, both Chevrolet and Plymouth had gained on Ford, and in the process Ford moved into third place in the total market.

Ford did not stand still during the model year. In an apparently desperate attempt to stave off the growing competition, several interior refinements were announced in mid-July; including a new mahagony-

The 1936 Chevrolet expressed the ultimate roundness of early GM streamlining. The car sold well and out-stripped the Ford, but the styling was quickly outdated, while the Ford aged more gracefully.

Buyers were quick to notice the higher level of fit and finish of the Chevrolet interior against Ford's, perhaps helping move Ford back to third place in the total market. GM had mastered one-piece turret top.

The 2-door version of this 1936 Buick Series 68 was touted by GM as a "Young man's car of exceptional performance." Thus did the marque enter a period of desirableness (which would wind down again in 1942) under the able direction of the legendary Harlow H. Curtice.

grained dashboard finish, new carpeting, redesigned seats and a choice of upholstery between broadcloth or mohair in the closed cars. Two exterior colors were announced simultaneously, a new green and a maroon which became standard finishes for all Deluxe cars.

The recognition that Model 68 had not held off the competition sent serious signals throughout the top leadership of the Ford Motor Co., and was the principal reason for the many changes which were now to occur. The tragedy of this period is that Mr. Ford was no longer the prime mover in change and that, in fact, the new ideas which would soon appear were to find their fruition in spite of, and not because of, the leadership of the company's founder.

Rumble seats were beginning to be considered a nuisance in the GM line for 1936, and only some 11,000 copies were produced by Chevrolet. This car sports the optional spoke wheels, the all-steel, stamped wheels having been made standard equipment in mid-season.

1936 FORD PASSENGER, COMMERCIAL AND TRUCK MODELS

MODEL 68 FORD PASSENGER CAR

8 Cylinder Engine (112″ Wheelbase)

MODEL 51 FORD TRUCK

8 Cylinder Engine (131½″ and 157″ Wheelbase)

MODEL 67 FORD COMMERCIAL

8 Cylinder Engine (112″ Wheelbase)

STYLING DRAWS BATTLE LINES

Taken overall, the 1937 Ford was an almost total break from the styling of its predecessor. Although first-time viewers probably labelled it correctly, the front end bore very little resemblance to the 1936's, especially in the sharply Vee'd grille and inset headlights.

The new sales year opened on Nov. 6, 1936. William C. Cowling, still sales manager at Ford after six turbulent years, pulled out the stops at the Detroit Coliseum to introduce the new 1937 models. The dealers were entertained in a new style, and enthusiasm for the Ford was high. It was an auspicious time to launch a major sales effort because the economy was enjoying a boomlet, the despair of the Depression somewhat erased by general gains in 1936.

The 1937 car was indeed fresh in every way, and visually it showed little influence from Model 68. The new grille was the most striking change. It had a strong resemblance to the Lincoln-Zephyr grille of 1936, a design conceived originally by John Tjaarda of the Briggs Co. Briggs' Bob Gregorie is generally credited with the 1937 Ford design, but he later denied it, perhaps due to the unfortunately small following that the '37's have today among Ford buffs.

The horizontal grille bars were cleanly set in a sharply defined Vee grille, and the hood louvers repeated the motifs. (One observer called it "speedboat" styling.) Headlamp housings were no longer round nor freestanding but were styled into the fender aprons. The front fenders were deeply crowned, with additional roundness which ended abruptly at their bases, and there was no attempt to flare the fender line into the running boards. The new roundness everywhere was emphasized by the roof—finally all metal. The single roof stamping required a slightly increased arch, so that in profile it had additional thickness.

These changes produced an undeniably smooth car, which might have been a genuinely beautiful car but for one problem. On direct orders from Mr. Ford, the car was shortened—from its prototype. All of the roundness and roof heightening, along with the 3 to 4 fewer inches, combined to produce a distinctly stubby appearance. This may be seen most dramatically in pictures of the Fordor Sedan without trunk, which in profile, through some of today's eyes, appears homely.

The new Ford was to be compared immediately to the Chevrolet G series. In 1937 GM corrected the excessive roundness of the 1935-36 streamlined bodies by using hardened surfaces all over the car. The box fender appeared in every GM make except Chevrolet; roof lines were flattened, and windows picked up new angularity. The general result was a control of the surfaces which was missing in the earlier cars. Chevrolet benefited from this styling trend, though it retained more of its 1936 roundness than any other GM car. The stylists introduced angularity in the new grille, along with hood louvers, and a novel crease which tied the front fender into the front door. The Chevrolet was a stylistically busier car. Nevertheless, there was new tautness in surface development.

These differences between Ford and Chevrolet were very important during the rest of the decade. Chevrolet moved steadily in the direction of the developing GM "square" style, which may be found fully expressed in the 1939 Buick. To be sure, the Chevrolet was always more round than its more expensive stablemates and had a softness which was not nearly as successful as Pontiac—for example—in year-by-year comparisons. But the Ford body, at the very moment in the decade when styling trends were undergoing a second revolution, moved resolutely toward the roundness which was to become increasingly dated. Ford's problems were compounded by the fact that from 1938 to 1940—three model years—there was very little change in the basic body dies, apart from grille and hood refinement. In these same three years, Chevrolet had made substantial advances from its 1937 car.

The Plymouth development was somewhat different. In 1937 the sheetmetal development was all toward convex surfaces, and though the car was more massive and more unified, it was still in the "Jell-O" school. The Chrysler products for 1938 had the lightest of facelifts, with unfortunate results. This was especially true for Plymouth, whose grille now looked like the top of a waterfall. But in 1939 the corporation pulled itself together and set a new trend in the "full face" look, in which the fender aprons were involved directly in the grille development. Though bodies were nearly the same, the massiveness of the frontal area brought a

The 1937 Ford debuted in early November 1936 and offered eleven body styles including the all-new Club Coupe. The V-8 60 was new to the American buyer.

The somewhat stubby appearance of the 1937's was evident even in the Fordor Sedan. A 4-in. length reduction from the 1936's made resolution of the rear surfaces awkward at best. The new, one-piece turret top was "thickened" in profile for strength, and this added to the stubby look.

welcome antidote to the roundness. And then in 1940 Plymouth came out with an entirely new car, even more square than the Chevrolet.

SPLENDID ISOLATION

It is difficult to understand why Ford sat relatively still in styling during the latter part of the decade. It was not just a question of inactivity, for the Mercury was produced in the middle of this period. Yet the Mercury was the most rounded convex shape that the Ford Motor Co. had ever produced, and this at a time when GM was going strongly in the opposite direction. A comparison of the 1939 Mercury and 1939 Buick will reveal the utter disparity of styling ideas. Zephyr styling offers few clues. The fenders did become a bit boxy in 1938, but the car was voluptuous right up until 1941. The success of the Continental is due in part to the flat roof and hood line which, in combination with the squarish trunk, successfully overwhelmed the teardrop softness of the sedans.

It must be concluded, then, that Ford styling moved in splendid isolation. This in itself would not be serious if Ford had dominated the market and thus had led styling trends. But the closing years of the Thirties saw Ford in a steadily deteriorating market position where the battle was not for first place but for second, against the Chrysler Corp. To many critics at the time, the normative "look" for a car was no longer the Ford, and by 1940 both Plymouth and Chevrolet had evolved into cars of substantially similar appearance and size, the agreement of which made Ford look out of date.

The dealers gathered at the Detroit Coliseum in November 1936. They would not have analyzed Ford's styling in the above way. They saw a brand-new car, aggressively streamlined with a new Vee windshield, and their hopes for a great sales year were lifted.

The technical innovations on the new 1937 car were numerous. The big news was the new 60-hp engine, now well proven in the European market. The bore/stroke dimensions were 2.6 ins. x 3.2 ins. for 136 cu. ins. Though similar in layout to the 221-cu.-in. engine,

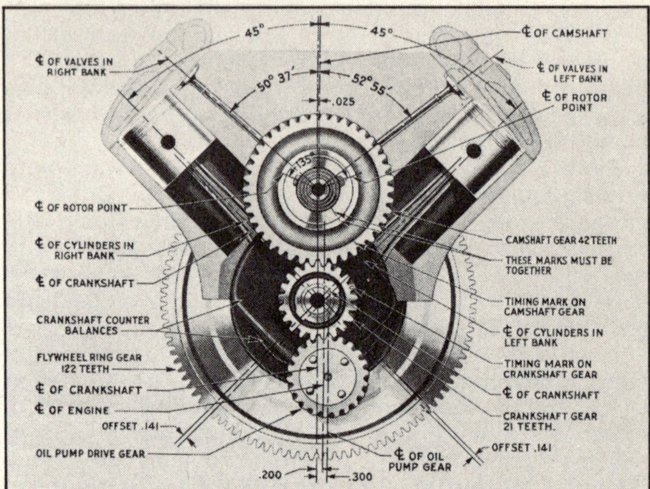

Layout of the V-8 60 engine was very similar to the larger V-8, and it was based on a proven design. It had bowed the previous year in English truck use, but tended to be overworked in passenger car service.

The flat-backed Tudor Sedan suffered most of all from the decrease of overall vehicle length. The wide whitewall tires on this car are almost too large for the overall styling to handle, yet are the center of interest in what many observers term mediocre styling. But Ford plotted its own course.

the 60 was altogether different in performance. Compression was 6.6:1, the highest of all the company's engines. Rated horsepower was reached at 3500 rpm but the horsepower curve was not peaked even at 4000 rpm, the lighter reciprocating masses making the new engine a real "revver." Even more unusual was the flat torque curve, which was constant within 10 lbs. from 1000 to 4000 rpm, though the torque was not much, about 95-lbs.-ft.

The new V-8 engine was offered solely in the Standard passenger cars. There was a general scaling down of auxiliary components to fit the 60. The front spring was light, with a 215-lb./in. deflection rate. The clutch was smaller, the cooling shrank to 15 qts., and the rear-end ratio went up to 4.44:1. The transmission reverted to spur gear for 1937, but with wide ratios of 1.765 and 3.071. Tires were 5.50 x 16-in.

William Cowling was especially pleased with the new car and spoke glowingly—"speeds over 70 with super economy." The claims of the sales manager eclipsed the potentials of the car. At a speed of 70 mph, the little 60 engine would have to be turning somewhere in the neighborhood of 4000 rpm, a feat some 400 revs beyond the advertised maximum horsepower rating point. Even Ford engine quality would not sustain this sort of pounding for long.

The 60 was also offered across the board in the truck lines. The Model 73 pickup had a 4.55:1 rear axle ratio with a 1.9 second gear and a 3.65 low. It provided reasonable, low-cost light hauling. But when the 60 was installed in the 1½-ton chassis, as Model 75, the result must have been nearly hopeless, for the empty weight of the stake-bodied unit was nearly 4400 lbs. With a 6.6:1 axle ratio, the highest offered in 1937, and 7.00 x 20-in. tires, revs were 3950 at 60 mph, surely a speed unreachable with the truck's frontal area and weight. A more typical scene would be a 1½-ton 60-hp grinding along at 15 mph in second gear at 3000 revs on a slight grade. The 60 was mercifully dropped from the heavy truck lineup at the end of its first season. The level torque curve and steadily rising horsepower soon convinced truckers that the only way to drive a 60 was flat out in whatever gear seemed appropriate. Thus the longevity of the 60 in truck use was notoriously low.

Somewhat of the same kind of driving habits were picked up by the passenger car owners, and the poor little engines screamed along without mercy. One can only imagine the treatment that the 60's received at the hands of Wisconsin taxi drivers after a Milwaukee firm ordered up 150 in 1939.

STRUGGLING TO IMPROVE

The now-famed 221 cu.-in., 85-hp V-8 was given changes which were the most extensive to date, with special emphasis on the earlier version's tendency to overheat. Water pump capacity was increased substantially from the 36 gals./minute at 3600 rpm of the previous year, to 45 gpm at 3000 rpm. But more importantly, the pumps were relocated to the upper front of the block where they could push the water through the jacketing instead of sucking it through. The water outlets were shifted to the center of the cylinder heads where a better advantage could be taken of exiting distribution, instead of having them at the front of the heads where the water from the rear of the block had had a greater opportunity to overheat before entering the radiator. The engineers probably felt that at long last overheating was licked, for the frontal area of the radiator core was reduced to 362 sq. ins. And yet, the

The 1937 Ford instrument panel was entirely new and set a general pattern which would remain through 1939. Steering wheel spokes were placed for good driver vision of the gauges. Vee windshield opened outward.

The non-opening Vee windshield of the 1937 Chevrolet necessitated a dashboard shape quite like Fords, but the gauges were contained within a single, glass-covered panel. Steering wheel shown was an option.

Plymouth's dash for 1937 was not as attractive as Ford's or Chevrolet's. Windshield was flat and one-piece. This unrestored veteran has substituted a '39 windshield. Dash depth muddied the '37's design.

STYLING DRAWS BATTLE LINES

coolant capacity of the total system remained the same at 22 qts.

The new cylinder heads, now free of the water pump mounting flanges, were of cast iron and incorporated revised combustion chamber shapes. Domed pistons introduced in '36, and the new combination reduced potential knock through a better quench area. Compression became somewhat less, now down to 6.12:1.

The old "48" carburetor gave way to the Stromberg "97", so-named by virtue of the .97-in. venturis. Main jets were set at .045-in. The forged crankshaft received enlarged mains at 2.4 ins., and insert bearings were incorporated to replace the former poured-babbitt type. Horsepower remained the self-same 85.

A worm and roller steering gear appeared, similar to the unit used on the 1936 Zephyr. Efficiency was sufficiently increased that the needle bearings, used on the sector shaft solely in 1936, were dropped. However, the steering ratio was now increased to its nadir of 18.2:1, beautifully light but making rapid steering impossible. This figure was to remain relatively constant for years, and represented the American norm. The Zephyr moved to an impossible 20.2:1 ratio in 1937 but returned to 18.4:1 in 1938. Apparently, then, the outer limits of steering wheel winding had been explored.

Cable brakes were introduced in 1937, not so much for any inherent superiority, but because the routing of the rods was growing ever more difficult. In the Model A, a long cross-shaft allowed parallelism of the brake rods to the frame in an uncluttered area. Shaft windup, however, made the left brakes always more likely to come on before the right, in all left-hand drive cars; so

While GM had thankfully gotten away from the heavily rounded styling in 1937, the Chrysler lineup stayed with it and this Plymouth coupe is a perfect example.

From the front, the Plymouth still carries the grille of "waterfall" heritage. Effect of height is due to the vertical grille bars. Still, it was a good car.

The Chevrolet for 1937 is the first step of GM's stylists to get away from roundness. The effect of length was heightened by the "speed line" pressed into the cowl and doors. Fender treatment is good, but concept was more pronounced on the heavier GM car lines. Grille has nice angularity.

As car owners began appreciating creature comforts during the decade, the Convertible Sedan and Cabriolet body styles with their roll-up side windows began supplanting the wind-in-the-face Phaetons and Roadsters. The following table reveals the declines in Ford sales of the one type against the increases of the others.

	Roadster	Phaeton	Cabriolet	Convertible Sedan
1932	8,996	2,706	7,063	1,142
1933-34	11,187	8,366	24,299	NA
1935	4,896	6,073	17,000	4,234
1936	3,862	5,555	14,068	5,601
1937	1,250	3,723	18,185	4,378
1938	NA	1,169	10,782	2,843
1939	NA	NA	10,422	3,561

The rock-ribbed Plymouth in-line Six was a slouch in comparison to Ford's peppy V-8's, yet it had earned a reputation for durability and would retain its basic layout for another seventeen years, a fine testimonial.

The Lincoln-Zephyr dash for 1937 inherited nothing at all from Ford, except the round central gauges. It boasts very early use of a center console and had glove boxes convenient to driver and passenger. Shallow depth of dash made for large empty area, especially ahead of the right seat.

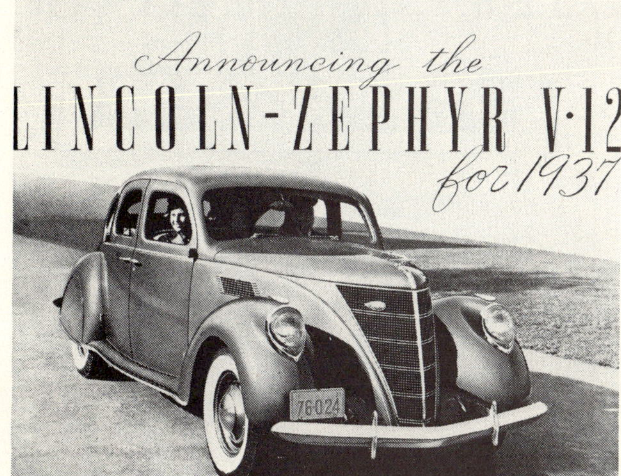

The exterior of the L-Z line was considerably smoother than earlier versions and carried nicely styled bumpers. The bright grille bars relieved the plain-bar treatment of 1936. More than 25,000 Zephyrs were built in '37.

As with its open cars, Ford was style leader with Station Wagons. Standard snap-on window curtains were phased out in 1936, by offering glass windows as an option. For '37, safety glass was the norm.

shaft lengths were progressively shortened, and rods passed diagonally to a more common central point. As frames lowered and became more complex, this arrangement was impossible. The cable brakes allowed a very short cross-shaft with irregular routings.

Self-energizing brakes were also added to the new cable system. These brakes were much more powerful and utilized the drum rotation as a source of energy for one shoe to aid in the application of the other. The new brake was also more erratic in operation and was prone to sudden seizure and shuddering. One peculiar aspect of the new brake was that the Ford braking area remained at 186 ins., which meant that the Zephyr brakes of very similar design were smaller in area by 18 sq. ins. and were required to stop a car some 750-lbs. heavier. The Zephyr brake linings were a shade thicker, perhaps because they wore a good deal faster.

The interior of the 1937 Ford was entirely new. The instrumentation layout began a three-year cycle in which two large dials encompassed all instruments. The dials and gauges lost something of their utilitarian clarity and were "styled." The installation of a radio no longer displaced the ashtray, both items now being located in the center of the dash, but the speaker and works were still tucked away from the remote control head unit. The starter solenoid was mounted on the engine side of the firewall and was actuated by a convenient, dash-mounted starter button. The pistol-grip parking brake lever was mounted under the lower edge of the dash to the driver's left, the move being a part of the trend to "clean up" the front compartment. On the closed cars, the new Vee'd windshield still cranked out as on the new model's predecessors.

Body styles were reduced in number from the complex range of 1936, dropping from 16 to 11. Most lamented by enthusiasts were losses of the special Roadster and Phaeton bodies with their unique cowl roll and slanted dashes. The body designations were still listed—though this would be the final year for the Roadster while the Phaeton lived on into 1938—but were now simply side window-less versions of the Cabriolet and the Convertible Sedan. In fact, while the 1936 versions of these decreasingly less popular configurations used unique doors and cowls, the '37's shared sheetmetal with the roll-up window versions except for a cap welded to the door tops which hid the glass slots. The one new body was the Club Coupe, a popular style which survived through 1938. The pretty 3-window coupes of the early V-8 years had disappeared, and the coupe was now a 5-window. A large, full-opening trunk lid provided easy access to the rear storage area, but the spare tire was moved inside.

A major milestone was reached by the Ford Motor Co., on Jan. 18, 1937 when the 25-millionth car to bear the Ford name rolled from the final assembly line at the Rouge plant, with Edsel Ford at the wheel, and his father alongside him. The cream-colored Fordor Touring Sedan was placed on exhibit along with other Ford production milestone cars.

The 1937 Ford offered major revisions in nearly all of its components, except the basic running gear. The all-new design strained capacities of engineering, styling, and tooling to the utmost, largely because clear and advance directives were late in arriving from the top level. That the car appeared on time was something of a marvel, and a tribute to Sorensen's driving production genius. But "Cast Iron Charlie" vowed that such confusion would not happen again; and in March 1937, product design was moved from Dearborn to Gate 4 of the Rouge. Only experimental engineering remained at Dearborn, under Zoerlein's eye. Mr. Ford's almost daily visits to Dearborn continued, but he did

The 1937 Ford suffered weakness in its single "alligator" hood retaining latch. When locked in the up position, it had to be raised before it was lowered. Careless operation bent left side of hood; evident here.

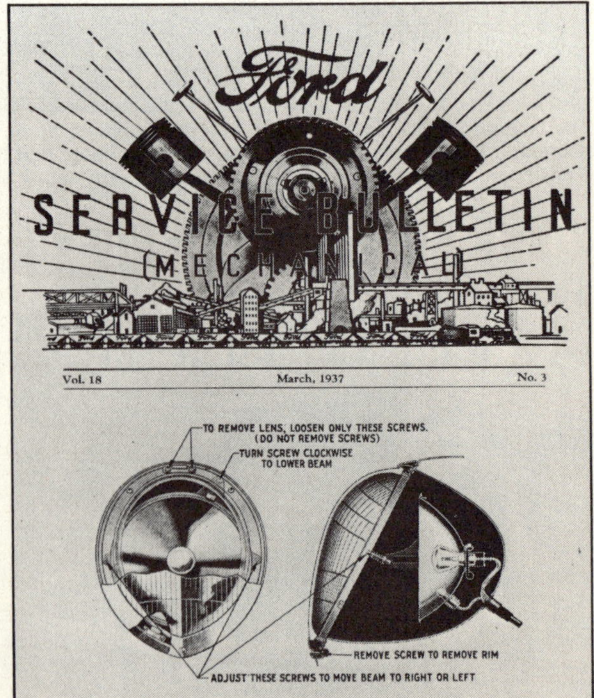

New, inset headlamps required different adjustment techniques, as explained in this 1937 Service Bulletin schematic. Invariably, do-it-yourselfers would foul up adjustment when changing bulbs.

not get over to the new engineering department perhaps more than two or three times a week.

Beginning in mid-1937, therefore, engineering changes began to appear which were in some contrast to previous Ford practice. A conspicuous example would be the first Ford truck with all half-elliptic suspension—the Cab-Over-Engine model laid out by Dale Roeder in 1937 and offered in the 1938 model line. Mr. Ford's interest in trucks was always less than in automobiles—although he certainly had a fondness for them—but the point is that truck engineering being "left alone," frequently pioneered ideas which worked their way into passenger car production. One example would be the copper-lead bearings of 1934.

BUGGED WITH SIMILARITY

In December 1937, the Model 92A experimental car appeared. In the Ford manner of designating its models, the "9" indicates that this would be slated for a 1939 introduction. The experimental car embodied a 60-hp engine, swinging-type rear axles, and tubular side frame rails, which would serve as exhaust outlets. Another design in which Ford was involved, appeared earlier. The rear-engined Tjaarda prototype was a combined effort between the Briggs Co., designer John Tjaarda, who worked for Briggs at the time, and Edsel Ford, who consulted with Tjaarda much of the way. According to several documented reports, Dr. Ferdinand Porsche was a visitor to America on at least two occasions; one, a reported visit with Tjaarda himself; the other, as guest at a party hosted by the Ford Motor Co. at the Dearborn Inn, at which time, he met and talked with Henry and Edsel Ford.

In no case is it being implied that design and developmental similarities existed between the Tjaarda prototype and the Series 3 Volkswagen prototype which reached mock-up stagé following June 1934. But what is suggested is to direct attention to the similarity of front-end appearance between the eventual Type 1 Volkswagen Beetle and the Tjaarda prototype. Tjaarda's car, although built in 1933, did not reach widespread public view until 1934, when it was unveiled at the Chicago World's Fair.

While the Tjaarda prototype had four doors, it was built of unit-body construction, with no separate frame needed because the body structure was solid enough to allow an integral suspension and drivetrain. A Ford V-8 was set in the rear of the car, and connected to a trans-axle, with independent axle halfshafts and two constant velocity U-joints.

In Mr. Ford's case, he liked the Tjaarda prototype, but not the large, four-door, rear-engined concept as an answer to a low priced passenger vehicle concept. Mr.

Proud the Willys-Overland Co. was of their restyled 1937 Four, a radical new body style from the holdover Model 77, which was first introduced in 1933, and saved the company from bankruptcy. With its L-head, 4-cyl. engine that delivered 26 mpg, the 1937 model had four body styles on a 100-in. wheelbase, but sales were a disappointment.

STYLING DRAWS BATTLE LINES

Ford saw the tooling obstacles, in light of his heavy commitment to other designs. While the Tjaarda prototype quickly evolved into the Lincoln-Zephyr, Mr. Ford was adamant in ordering the conventional front engine location. As it moved through several design stages, it gained four more cylinders along the way.

Another project, begun in August 1937, was a V-8 engine layout requested by Ford of Canada, of 2.875-in. bore by 3.50-in. stroke for 182-cu.ins. This engine was given a 7.5:1 compression, but in October work was discontinued because excessive pre-detonation (or ignition knock) could not be controlled.

1937: A QUESTION OF CONVENTION

If there can be any doubt that the move to the Rouge was releasing product design from previous restraints, it should be noted that by October 1937, three of the new Mercurys were on test. Also to be noted is the fact that at no time during the Thirties, did the Ford Motor Co. automotive design staff number more than 36 men. Today, the FoMoCo design staff numbers some 700 men. On a man-to-man basis, that 36-man staff of the Thirties must have been one of the hardest-working groups ever assembled.

The sales race of 1937 was very close. The prosperity early in the year got Ford and its rivals off to good starts, but the economy stumbled late in the season, and sales slowed drastically. This was to be the first year since 1930 that Plymouth sales faltered, dropping to about 500,000 cars. Ford sold 756,933 cars, but Chevrolet was ahead by a scant 2000 units. Truck sales, however, were in Ford's favor, enough to overcome the Chevrolet car lead with the final gross figures of 955,309 to 951,714. The Lincoln-Zephyr had had a fine year, with 25,186 units delivered. And yet even with this success in sales—which was to be the best year that Ford would have until 1950—the company barely made money, showing a net profit of $6,760,967. That

Basic lines of Lincoln-Zephyr were inspired by this Tjaarda-designed prototype which was displayed at Chicago's Century of Progress Exposition—a five-month extravaganza from May 26 to Oct 31 of 1934. The prototype had a Ford V-8 engine mounted in the rear. Gizmo on roof was radio antenna housing.

To many, the 1937 Chrysler Imperial convertible sedan had lost any pretense of beauty or grace and marked a low point in Chrysler Corp. styling. The relationships of the exterior surfaces are simply uncoordinated and wheelwells do not match the fenders. Sidemounts are awkwardly placed.

alone reflects that the 1937 Ford was a costly car to bring into production. Also, the move of product design to the Rouge initiated an orgy of spending as the engineers sought to catch up. It is incredible to realize that a dynamometer room was established for the first time in 1937. An axle-testing machine was bought, a wind tunnel was built in 1936 which was given hot and cold capacities in 1937, and the test track was finally approved in late 1936. At the end of 1937, Ford engineers were in a position to match facilities with both Chrysler and GM for the first time.

Despite Cadillac's exclusive use of Vee'd engines, the marque always sported relatively narrow hood lines, as this 1937 Series 60 displays. Grille is nearly LaSalle-ish, but the distinctive bumper crest is an identity clue.

Until recently—a comment with reservation—it is apparent that time has not dealt kindly with the 1937 Ford. The streamlining which made the dealers cheer at the Detroit Coliseum did not wear well. By the mid-Forties, high school students ignored it in favor of the ever-popular 1936, 1934, and increasingly rare 1932. Perhaps it was the 1937 Ford which cemented the myth of the even-numbered years as the best years for the early V-8's. In truth, there is reason to suspect that product design people knew the faults of the car's styling even as it was being hailed, for the Deluxe sedan body received a major body-design overhaul after only one season of production.

The 1937 Ford marks a break in the development of Ford in the Thirties. The 1935 Ford was a different car by virtue of chassis changes, but it still had the hard performance feel of the Model 40. The 1937 Model 78 was a more civilized car. The brakes were easier to press, though perhaps not altogether foolproof. The steering was light to the touch, though controllability was down. The battery was recessed into the firewall. The engine sounds were better insulated from the passenger compartment. Interior dimensions were improved. Paradoxically the Model 78 was a step toward conventionality, in Ford's unconventional way.

The Chrysler Airflow was—in its last year—still very much in evidence in 1937. Yet only a slightly different grille treatment was tried in comparison to the design of this 1935 4-door Imperial. Buyers shied from its styling in droves, and relegated the great Airflow dream to the sidestreets of America.

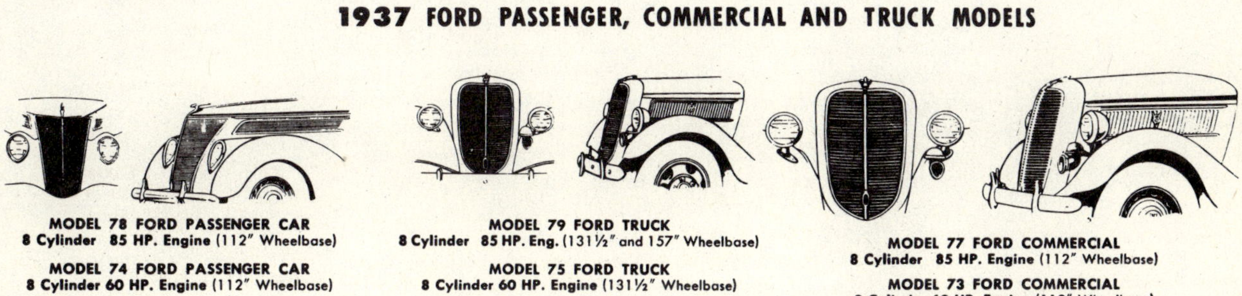

THE RECOVERY OF PROPORTIONS

If any Ford of the Thirties can fairly be described today as the least-loved, it is the 1938 model with the curious heart-shaped grille. Yet the car embodied the fresh thinking of the design group.

The 1938 Ford passenger car, 81A, with the regular 221-cu.-in. V-8 engine, was the first car to reflect the new thinking of the design team at the Rouge. Lead time on this car was incredibly short. Sorensen recalled that in March 1937 it was realized that there was no dashboard designed for the 81A. Sorensen and Sheldrick planned and patterned the dash in one day.

There were few mechanical changes for 1938. However, in mid-year the engine was fitted with a 24-stud head, but the performance figures were unchanged. The brakes were unchanged and, alas, unimproved. The heavy trucks went over to self-energizing cable systems on big 15-in. drums with 368 sq. ins. of lining. And, cooling improvements were negligible, though a flat-tube radiator replaced the round-tube type.

A curious malady was attacked in 1938. The driveshaft would occasionally whip and would tend to tear out the rear splines at the pinion gear. One solution would have been to weld the pinion gear to the shaft. Another would have been to put an extension on the transmission to shorten the shaft. Mr. Ford refused both ideas, and as a consequence the shaft diameter was enlarged to the absolute maximum permitted by interior dimensions of the torque tube.

It was in 1938 that the first experiments were made with generator regulators. Tests were begun with an R.B.&M. regulator made by a subsidiary of the Essex Wire Co. There were failures experienced on the rapidly vibrating contact points. Emil Zoerlein wanted 10% production of this regulator, for test and servicing purposes, with Detroit area distribution only, but by summer the unit was in 100% production, with much trouble. Eventually an American Bosch regulator was standardized.

UP AND DOWN ADVANCES

The absence of substantial engineering advances on Model 81A should not be interpreted as an indication of the idleness of the new Rouge Engineering Center. Sheldrick remembered that by 1938 the new team had come forward with independent suspension, vertical ignition, conventional connecting rod bearings, split valve guides, valves with a large foot at bottom, barrel-type lifters, and Hotchkiss drive—all of which Mr. Ford vetoed, and all of which were eventually to make their way into production after Mr. Ford departed. The frustrations of the engineering team could hardly have been imagined. However, Mr. Ford was to suffer a stroke, about this time—which must have been a factor.

They did push forward one project in 1938 which bore great fruit. The Mercury car had been under way since July 20, 1937, using the 221-cu.-in. engine bored out .125-in. for a displacement of 239 cu. ins. Originally a 122-in. wheelbase car was planned, with nearly identical dimensions to the Pontiac 8. In those days the GM cars used many varied wheelbase lengths, the Sixes and Eights of both Olds and Pontiac always being different. In 1937 each of the four Buick models were offered on a different wheelbase. This curious extravagance continued until 1949 in Pontiacs and even later in the Oldsmobile, though it must be admitted that the "88" and the Six shared the same chassis in 1949.

An extended wheelbase to accommodate a Straight

The Phaeton is as fine a looking car as ever rolled from Dearborn, yet it is the last year to be deemed collectable by restoration buffs. The unfortunately stubby appearance of the 1937's was gone, thanks to new rear body styling and the overall improvement of lines.

Ford tried a new ploy beginning in 1938 by offering a new line of Standard models that made use of the previous year's frontal sheetmetal tooling, in answer to Mr. Ford's continual search for ways to lower costs and retail prices. It was a practice that would last through 1940.

Eight engine was not necessary for the Mercury, and it was shrunk instead to 116 ins., 1-in. shorter than the Pontiac Six for 1937. The four extra inches beyond the Ford car were put into the hood. Body dimensions between the pillars were the same as Ford, but the steering wheel and the front seat were moved 4 ins. forward, much closer to the instrument panel, which added passenger room. The more powerful engine was able to pull a taller 3.54 axle ratio, giving equal or better economy than the Ford. Already in 1938, thought was given to standardizing the new 239-cu.-in. engine in all cars and trucks, but the idea was discarded.

Dec. 9, 1937, the 239-cu.-in. engine was rated at 95 bhp at 3600 rpm. Torque was 170 lbs.-ft., a 13% increase over the 81A engine. Cars were under heavy testing throughout the winter. The Mercury chassis had given opportunity for the Rouge engineering team to try all sorts of suspensions, as noted in Chapter 7, but all were vetoed by Mr. Ford.

Other engine ideas of 1938 were not as successful as the new 239-in. Mercury. During the year Mr. Ford ordered a 180° crank to be built into the 221-in. V-8 engine. It was impossible to balance and may be cited as one of the last instances where Mr. Ford pursued an independent course, with little regard to known engineering practices.

Another interesting engine appeared in 1938. The 6-cyl. idea had not perished among the Rouge engineers because their principal competition was from Chevrolet and Plymouth. This must be the only explanation for a 150-cu.-in. overhead-camshaft Six of 80 bhp laid out in the middle of the year. Mr. Ford did not know about this project and insisted after a brief look that the originally designed conventional distributor be removed and the traditional Ford front distributor be fitted. A low cam gear in the usual Ford manner was provided with

Chevrolet really only offered four body types for 1938; a 2-door sedan without or with a trunk (illustrated), the same variation in 4-doors, a coupe and a convertible.

Chrysler's big gun for 1938 was its Plymouth, with little change from the previous year. New was the vertical grille, here dented.

A Plymouth look-alike was the Dodge, and reveals how family-oriented the Chrysler Corp. designers were. Dodge offered a total of 10 models for 1938, in two wheelbase lengths; 115 ins. and 132 ins. Dodge was always considered a senior car to the DeSoto.

appropriate drive for the distributor, and a new chain carried the power up to the overhead cam. Incredible as it must seem, the cam rotation was now reversed and thus the engine ran left-handed. The project was abandoned, perhaps out of embarrassment, but more likely because oil seeped down the valve guides on idle to the point of fouling the plugs. Also, the chains were quite unreliable, requiring tightening every 5000 miles.

This engine had been programmed for a 105-in. wheelbase car. Mr. Ford and the engineering division had never given up the notion of producing a smaller car, and the 60-hp unit of 1937 was a step in that direction. However, the 60 was a very uneconomical proposition, for the chassis and coachwork were identical in cost to the standard 85. In 1937 the 60-hp engine cost $93 to build, while the 85-engine cost $96. Thus the profit margin on the 60 was much reduced because it was priced $41 lower than the comparable 85. It was clear to engineering that any smaller car would require a new engine, chassis, and body, which may be the reason why experiments tended to the more radical proposals.

WINNERS FROM DAGENHAM

Ford's European operations gave ample scope for genuine progress in the truly small car field. The British

---

Ford announced a **new system of coding** its very diversified lines of cars and trucks beginning with the 1938 model year. The nearly infinite variety of its engines, body types, year models, countries of manufacture, and vehicle wheelbase where applicable, could thus be designated in as few as 4 figures and by a maximum of 5 figures. For example, **19AM** indicates a **1941 Mercury** with the **95 hp V-8 engine;** or, **A817W** indicates a **1938, 85-hp V-8, 157-in. wheelbase, 1½-ton Cab-Over-Engine truck** assembled in **Australia.** The full system explanation follows:

The **first digit** indicates the **year.** Thus **"8"** means 1938.

The **second digit** indicates the **type of engine** fitted:

1.–30 taxable hp	221 cu. ins.	V-8	85 bhp
2.–22 taxable hp	136 cu. ins.	V-8	60 bhp
3.–10 taxable hp	1172cc	4-cyl.	32.5 bhp (British Model C.)
4.–8 taxable hp	933cc	4-cyl.	22 bhp (Model Y)
5.–none			
6.–36.4 taxable hp	267 cu. ins.	V-12	110 bhp (Lincoln-Zephyr)
7.–27.4 taxable hp		6-cyl.	
8.–24 taxable hp	200.5 cu. ins.	4-cyl.	40 or 50 bhp (Model A, B)
9.–32.5 taxable hp	239 cu. ins.	V-8	95 bhp (Mercury)
N.–16.28 taxable hp	119.5 cu. ins.	4-cyl.	30/40 bhp (tractor, truck)
G.–26.1 taxable hp	226 cu. ins.	6-cyl.	90 bhp

The **third digit,** if any, indicates **wheelbase:**

1.–101" Cab-Over-Engine (COE) truck
1.–191" bus chassis
2.–112" commercial
4.–194" bus chassis
7.–157" truck chassis
8.–158" truck chassis
9.–138" Lincoln Custom
none–134" truck chassis

The **type of vehicle** is indicated by the **last letter:**

A.–Passenger car or Sedan Delivery
B.–Rear engine bus
C.–½-ton commercial
D.–¾-ton commercial
H.–Lincoln-Zephyr
L.–Continental
M.–Mercury
N.–Tractor and engine indicator for 1941 4-cylinder trucks
T.–1 ½-ton truck
TH.–2-ton truck
W.–1 ½-ton Cab-Over-Engine
WH.–2-ton Cab-Over-Engine
Y.–1-ton truck
Z.–COE dump truck

The **country of orgin** is indicated by an **initial letter** before the first digit:

A.–Australia
C.–Canada
E.–England
Q.–South Africa
none–USA.

Some examples will show the system:

817W –1938, 85 hp, 157" COE 1 ½-ton truck
29Y –1942, 95 hp, 1-ton truck
1ND –1941, 4-cyl., ¾-ton truck
6G4T –1946, 6-cyl., 194" chassis used for bus work
19A –1941, 95 hp, car (Mercury)
69M –1946, 95 hp, Mercury
7GA –1947, 6-cyl., car (Ford)
E83W –1938, 10 hp, English Forward Control (COE) light truck
268H –1942, V-12, 138" Lincoln Custom

The **letter F,** meaning **foreign,** attached to the end of any number indicates a variation from normal production, usually implying a difference in left-hand or right-hand drive. An **English chassis** with an **F** will mean **left-hand drive,** while an **American chassis** with an **F** means **right-hand drive.**

Battle-scarred, unrestored 1938 Plymouth shows the direction Chrysler took in dashboard design. Novel were the two gloveboxes, shown with doors removed.

Dashboard of the Ford Deluxe seems well thought out yet was basically designed in a single day when it was found at the last moment that it had been overlooked.

8-hp Model Y had saved Dagenham (which had actually been forced to borrow money from its Belgian subsidiary at the end of Model A production). In 1933 at the very bottom of the Depression, Dagenham returned a profit of $7 million—one of the bright spots in the Ford empire. The Y was joined in 1935 by the Deluxe Model C, built on the same wheelbase and to the same scale. The Y engine of 933cc was bored out to 1172cc (63.5mm x 92.5mm), and output went up from 22 to 32.5 bhp. The styling of the Model C was something like the 1935 American Ford, except that the radiator grille lacked the horizontal bars. It was to be a very popular car in England; and in October 1935, the price there of the Model Y was reduced to 100 pounds—some $480—which spurred sales again.

Meanwhile, the big Fords were produced in Dagenham, model for model. The 60-hp engine, however, was fitted into sedan production as soon as the engine appeared as noted in Chapter 6.

An entirely new car appeared in 1936—Model 62—which was the 60-hp engine in an American chassis, but with distinctive coachwork which was wholly British-made. The lines are a strange mix of 1936 and 1937 styles, the grille and fenders being similar to 1937 American styles, but with 1936 headlamps and body configurations. A Fordor Club Sedan was the first and only big production body. Model 62 was produced in France by Mathis-Ford in almost identical shape and specification.

Hudson, and its counterpart Terraplane, was commited to the heavily-rounded idiom even as the industry majors were taking a different tack.

Dagenham had real winners in Models Y and C. In 1937 both were restyled as the 7Y and 7W. The 7Y emerged after World War II as the Anglia, and later the Popular, still being built in 1959 with the bigger 1172cc engine and chassis layout of 25 years earlier. The 1939 10 was restyled again as the 4-door Ford Prefect, another car which was produced well into the postwar period.

The French Ford operation, working in combination with the Mathis Co. (as Matford), produced Model 62 and the big Ford in the prewar period. By mid-1938 Ford had absorbed Mathis, but little further development occurred before the war.

The German assembly plant at Cologne produced the Model B (Rheinland) and the British Y (Koln and Eifel) throughout the Thirties. Later V-8 American models were gradually introduced at Cologne, and some attractive coachwork by German firms was fitted on Models 40 through 78.

Ford operations in both France and Germany were heavily burdened with political problems, and independent engineering development was virtually unknown. In October 1937, Dr. Heinrich F. Albert of Cologne asked Dearborn for a small 10-hp engine, even while the German plant was tooling up for production of the 221-in. V-8 for the first time. The British 1172cc engine seemed to be the answer, but nothing more came of this until after the war. Design studies on the small car suggest that it may well have been initially laid out in 1938, for the first postwar Taunus has a striking resemblance to the original Mercury.

Ford did very well in Barcelona with Model 18 until 1936 when the civil war engulfed Spain. From an engineering and styling standpoint, the other Ford subsidiaries across Europe were simply assembly points for engines and sheetmetal from Dagenham and produced nothing of novelty.

Apart from the 60, no European development had any effect upon the American car. Dagenham was the only part of the Ford empire which had any pretension at independence, and yet even there the major decisions came from Dearborn, both in styling and engineering. The success of the 8- and 10-hp engines could hardly have been of any significance in the American

Ford, the open-car styling leader, no longer numbered a true roadster among its 1938 car line. Buyers had come to appreciate the comforts of Cabriolets.

A Fordor Deluxe in motion with bug-catcher grille guard and another of the era's popular accessories, the bumper-hung water bag.

market where the American Austin had been a conspicuous failure.

The preparation for the 1938 car was already under way when Sorensen moved product design to the Rouge. The immediate problem was to correct the stubby appearance of the 1937 car. Chevrolet had gone to hypoid axles with the 1937 G series, and as a result of the lower driveshaft the cars were dropped and appeared longer. Even the 1937 Plymouth, not the best-looking car from Chrysler during the decade, had a decided lengthened appearance.

DESIGNING THE '37'S.

Steps to improve the appearance of the Model 78 took two paths. First, a new grille was laid out, with a curious heart-shaped pattern that had no precedent in the Ford design history. Only two American cars had flirted with this idea—the Hudson Terraplane, and the Willys 77. Both the Terraplane and the Willys 77 were in a period of exceptional convexity in 1937, necessary for such a rounded grille pattern. The Terraplane hood shape was not unlike that of the Triumph Dolomite, the only British car that attempted to mate traditional coachwork with the radical streamlined American grille design. The Ford grille was saved from the excesses of the Willys by a return to a more vertical profile with a sharper prow and peak to the grille. The hood was thus extended, and the front of the car recovered some of the aggressive line of the 1936 model.

The second path to correct the 1937 stubbiness was

The Lincoln-Zephyr dash layout for 1938 in no way reflected general Ford thinking, perhaps a tribute to Edsel who had sired the L-Z marque.

Edsel had insisted on a 12-cyl. engine, long a mark of the senior Lincolns, but here Ford thinking was closely paralleled in the L-Z rendition.

Although Ford loudly proclaimed that the L-Z's possessed unit construction, the low-production Convertible Sedan had an "almost-frame"; a series of strength-adding members to make up for the lack of body rigidity.

THE RECOVERY OF PROPORTIONS

the complete reworking of the body sheetmetal aft of the rear door on the Fordor Sedan. A long, uninterrupted flowing curve took the roof line right to the rear bumper, which extended the body by no less than 10 ins. With this move, the proportions of the 1936 car were recovered, and once again the car seemed more "like a Ford." The sedan shape was now heavier at the rear, but it was not unsuccessful. This can be perhaps proven by the fact that the basic dies were left unchanged through the 1940 model, a record unmatched by any other Ford design since Model T days. The confidence the Ford design team had in this line at the very time of major revolution in both Chevrolet and Plymouth is remarkable.

A reason for partial neglect of the Ford body development could be that the energies of Gregorie and his group were absorbed with the Mercury and the Lincoln Continental projects. Certainly Edsel was engrossed with the Continental. Thus lacking specific orders from Mr. Ford or Edsel, the 81A body was simply continued. Lead times were also lengthening radically in the late Thirties as cars grew in complexity. A new 1940 Ford would have required running prototypes by late 1938, and this was simply not possible in the situation that then existed. It was "built-in."

The front and rear fenders were also changed. The rear fender was reshaped to parallel the new sedan body, and the result was good. Additional, and maybe unforeseen, benefits occurred when this new fender was mated to the coupe, for it extended beyond the coupe deck, reducing the convexity of the coupe rear. The coupes were not only a bit longer in profile but were "harder" in appearance. The front fender was substantially increased in size, the crown even fuller

This photo is dated July 1, 1938 and is of the E-93A, the 1939 Ford Prefect. Unlike most Ford products, it bore no resemblance to the domestic car lines.

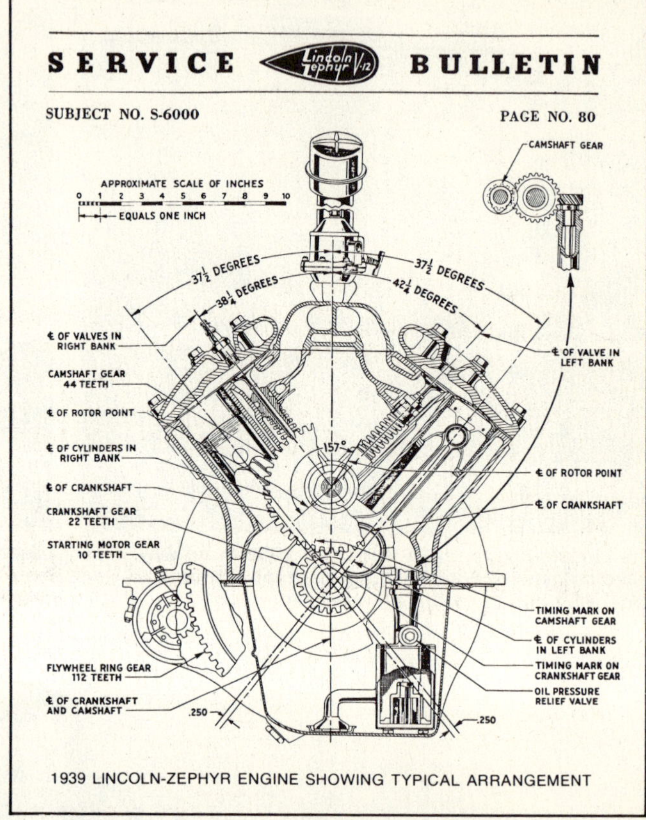

1939 LINCOLN-ZEPHYR ENGINE SHOWING TYPICAL ARRANGEMENT

Superb coachwork by Willoughby has transformed this K Lincoln into a Brougham. Edsel insisted such heritage be carried down to the Lincoln-Zephyr; but what resulted, while indeed a near-classic, inherited only the Vee engine configuration and was closely patterned after the Ford V-8.

than in 1937 but saved by the introduction of some of the GM boxiness. Again, the effect was good because it served to break up the roundness of the body. Apart from detailing at the running board edges and headlight placement, these fenders were substantially unchanged through 1940.

An entirely new idea for 1938 was the introduction of the Standard model series in the sheetmetal of the previous year. In 1938 this meant a considerable difference, though in 1939 and 1940 the changes were principally in grille design and trim.

The 1938 Standards were easily identified as 1937's worked over. The body shape was identical. The front fenders were unchanged, though the rears were similar of those of the new 81A body. But the best feature of the standard was the grille, in general outline quite like the 1937 but simplified and strengthened. The horizontal grille bars were extended back as louvers, and the vertical trim brightwork of 1937 was omitted, which helped to overcome the stubby feel. The Standard grille was so simple and devoid of almost all trim that it sold very badly at first, outdistanced 20 to 1 by the Deluxe. Additional horizontal chrome strips were hastily added, especially on the grille. The absolutely straight belt line of the Standard series helped once more to harden the general roundness of the body, and from this standpoint was actually superior to the Deluxe 81A grille. That straight belt line suffered in the hood because in 1937 a support with a locking catch was fitted to the left side of the hood. Anxious service station attendants would attempt to force the hood down without first lifting it to release, and the hoods invariably became buckled on the left side. This was corrected in 1939 when the hood side panels were incorporated into a one-piece, spring-loaded hood structure.

Sheldrick's hastily laid out dashboard followed 1937 ideas, except for one bold difference. Space was provided for the radio speaker in the center of the dash, a logical final resting place. It was only a matter of time until a truly integrated radio would be designed, in the style of the '34 glove box unit. The 1938 radio came close, but the controls and speaker were still not fully combined with the unit itself.

A SUDDEN RECESSION

The dashboard dials in 1938 were even more fussy than in 1937. A peculiar gold motif was used in the dial background, which admittedly blended nicely with the red fluid of the heat gauge in a sort of final, regal display. The dashboard layout was neater, however. The

GM was strongly design-conscious by 1938, and this Buick Special shows the designer's attention to detail. This particular car has the Hydramatic.

This was the 1935 Deluxe Model C Ford from Dagenham that pioneered the 1172cc engine size. The same engine powered postwar Anglias and Prefects.

Cadillac introduced this lovely 60 Special for 1938, again showing GM's design consciousness. Body shell would be carried forward through 1941, but would be frequently disguised through clever arrangement of front sheetmetal and fenders. The 60 Special would always be a showcase.

protrusions of knobs and controls in 1937 was muted. Ford persisted with the opening windshield thru 1939, perhaps a compensation for the lack of windwings.

The year 1938 was not one of great variety in body types. The sharp and sudden recession seemed to turn the clock back to 1933. It was not a time for frivolous coachwork.

Chevrolet in 1938 really offered only four body types. The coupe was available with a rumble seat option, the 2-door and 4-door sedans could be had with or without a trunk, and the fourth body was a Cabriolet. Chevrolet never came to grips with convertibles in the Thirties. Production was always low and ceased entirely for one year in 1939. The 1938 Cabriolet (this term for convertible being used until 1939) was mounted, strangely, only on the plain Master series without knee-action, a situation begun in 1936. Chevrolet had not offered a Cabriolet in 1935, but the roadster and phaeton had appeared on the old-style standard EC series. The 1938 Chevrolet was unchanged in almost all respects, the grille receiving a minor but pleasing facelift.

Plymouth for 1938 was almost unchanged also, though the grille bars were now vertical with a waterfall top, altogether ugly. Body styles, plus the 132-in. wheelbase commercial sedans, paralleled Chevrolet.

Ford was somewhat reduced in the number of body styles but still managed to blossom forth with four convertibles. The Convertible Coupe and Club Coupe continued the 1937 styles, as did the Convertible Sedan, the latter virtually unchanged from 1936. The Phaeton was built for the last time in 1938, with the window slots of the Convertible Sedan being capped and snap-on side curtains fitted. The old Phaetons of 1936 and before had been relatively inexpensive cars, priced with the coupes. In 1938 the Phaeton was the third most expensive body in the lineup, costing $820, just $5 less than the Station Wagon. If offered no virtues not found in the cheaper Club Coupe which had roll-up windows.

By 1938 the Station Wagon had become a standard car in the passenger car lineup and had shed most of its earlier commercial overtones. Ford had pioneered the Station Wagon (if one overlooks the short-lived 1923 Star), and had produced a steady stream of handsome units since the 1929 Model A. In 1938 the Station Wagon was offered only as a Deluxe model, the Standard sheetmetal never being used for wagon purposes. From 1939 through 1941 the wagon was offered both in Deluxe and Standard forms, when sheetmetal usage was again the same for both trim levels, the Deluxe model including not only the additional trim but genuine leather upholstery. By 1940 it was the most expensive body available, as it had been in 1934 before the Convertible Sedan displaced it.

The sales problem in the recession year of 1938 was

This 1936 Ford Koln was the German equivalent of the English Model C from Dagenham. The grille reflects the thinking that would come to the domestic Ford in 1937.

The German Kolns had a way with convertibles which varied greatly from our domestic models, but this 1938 variant did not follow Dagenham's Model Y grille.

1938 FORD PASSENGER CAR MODELS

MODEL 81A FORD DELUXE
85 HP. 8-Cylinder Engine
(112" Wheelbase)

MODEL 81A FORD STANDARD
85 HP. 8-Cylinder Engine
MODEL 82A FORD 60 HP. 8-Cylinder Engine
(112" Wheelbase)

compounded by the presence of large numbers of used cars which dealers had received in the high-volume 1937 season. John R. Davis, the new sales manager, worked hard to dispose of used car stocks with various programs which were well received by the dealer network. But it was tough going in 1938, despite the early model announcement date of November 30, 1937, and sales fell drastically. Ford prices were still fractionally under both Chevrolet and Plymouth but offered little sales advantage. Chevrolet sales fell to 464,337, but Ford reached only 363,688. Plymouth fell below 300,000, and for the first time in the decade it was unable to grow against any economic or competitive trends.

The 1938 Ford deserved a better reception than it received in that gloomy recession year. It was a more handsome car than its predecessors and should have sold well against the unchanged Chevrolet and Plymouth. However, the cable brakes were still fitted, complete with juddering, groans, seizures, and scorings—which no amount of salesmanship could overcome. The general fit and finish of the Chevrolet and Plymouth continued to emphasize Ford's tardiness in improving coachwork assembly. The transverse springs remained, with all of their inadequacies. The 1938 Ford has always lived in the shadow of its successors, for though it had the outward appearance of the new, underneath it was still the old. The real results of the engineering efforts in the new laboratories at the Rouge plant were about to be revealed.

An unusual variant indeed, the 1937 German Ford Koln body mounted on what appears to be the English Model C chassis. This rather handsome convertible was referred to as the Eifel, and is a curious admixture of various-year components. In the background are more Kolns for shipment.

Another variation of the Koln Eifel. Fenders and runningboards are U.S.-type Model 48 (1935), the hood and grille are 1937, the bumpers resemble 1935's, but are smooth, while the metal spare cover is similar to 1935 but the wheels are 1936. What is visible of the dash resembles 1935-36.

MR. FORD, EDSEL, AND MERCURY

Edsel deserved the apparently "I told you so" attitude when he faced his father during the Oct. 24th press preview showing of the 1939 Mercury, for he had literally moved heaven and earth to bring "his" car to fruition over the objections of his father.

During 1938 Mr. Ford's health declined considerably following his stroke, and he exercised less leadership than ever before. The story of the engineering development of the Ford automobile now moved independently of Mr. Ford's guidance. There were, however, rare exceptions. In 1938 Mr. Ford ordered serious development on the hydraulic brake. Since he refused to follow designs produced by others, the work on hydraulics took an independent and eccentric course. The first effort, under direct orders of Mr. Ford, was the development of an all-metal hydraulic brake system, and to him, the fact that Chrysler had used Wagner designs since 1924, incorporating rubber seals, made no difference.

Initially, this perspective led to results that were not satisfactory. Metal-to-metal pumps might be used in Rolls-Royce Phantom II's for vacuum production, but an all-metal, oil-tight brake cylinder for a mass produced car was out of the question.

Brake development then proceeded along conventional lines, resulting in a very nice system which appeared on all Ford products for 1939 except the K Lincoln. The Lincoln-Zephyr retained the self-energizing brakes with hydraulic application. Ford and Mercury used non-energizing brakes. Since, in this design, the leading shoe does the greater amount of work, the wheel cylinders were proportioned for proper loading. Area ratios of the leading to the trailing cylinder were 56% greater on the front wheels and 26.5% greater on the rears.

In truck use these proportions were balanced in anticipation of loads. The ¾-ton truck used passenger car dimensions in the front cylinder with a 56% cylinder area weighting on the leading shoe. The rear basic cylinder was the same size as the car, but the leading forward cylinder had the same 56% increased area. On the 1-ton truck, the front cylinders were identical to the passenger car, but the rear cylinder had 89% more area on both cylinders. On the big trucks, the front cylinders both had 89% more area than the passenger car, while the rears had 125% more area on both cylinders. Master cylinder dimensions were the same for all trucks so that braking proportions could be finely adjusted. The improvement over the best mechanical brake was obvious, since adjustment was all too often the product of the experience and intelligence of the mechanic. The hydraulic design not only was inherently equalized but it allowed the engineers to design the braking proportions for the life of the vehicle, regardless of adjustment abuse.

The effectiveness of the new brakes may be seen in the immediate reduction of lining area. The Ford car lining area dropped from 186 to 163 sq. ins., a 12% decrease. The 1-ton truck lining area fell from 277 to 187 sq. ins., a 32% decrease. The big truck dropped

An early production Mercury: One of four body styles, and boasting of 95 hp, more than in any previous Ford Motor Co. car. The styling is one of bulk with grace.

"Ford-Mercury" read the hood emblems and hubcaps on the fully trimmed version of the Mercury prototype, but Edsel himself picked the final Mercury appelation.

First working prototype of the then-unlabeled Mercury carried no identifying emblems or side trim, but sported unique hubcaps and taillights to appear later on Fords.

from 368 to 303 sq. ins., an 18% decrease in area. Lincoln-Zephyr area remained the same, possibly because the brakes were too small to begin with and, of course, because the self-energizing feature was retained. Actually, Zephyr brakes *were* competitive.

The new brakes were everything the dealers had been clamoring for, and in one jump Ford had only caught up with the Chrysler engineering philosophy that had begun in 1924.

Suspension and steering were unchanged for 1939, but the cooling system received another major overhaul. The sheetmetal of the Standard models retained the 1938 grille, which meant that the 1938 radiator had to be used, but a new low radiator was introduced on the 1939 Deluxe models. Though of the same 22-qt. capacity, the new radiator increased frontal area to 384 sq. ins. A 6-blade fan was fastened to the end of the crankshaft, very low in the chassis. The direct mounting of the fan created two new problems. A torsional damper was required since the fan belt no longer acted as a flexible coupling. And secondly, a most unusual problem occurred in rough usage, especially in wilderness areas. In fording deep streams, the fan would propel itself into the radiator. These were part of the reasons why the fan was relocated in the 1942 model to a mid-position, driven once again by a belt. Farkas designed a successful electric fan in the meantime—which was never used. The new body design of 1939 was the best yet, but it was soon to be burdened with larger engines, needing more efficient cooling system.

The 1939 221-in. 85-hp engine was beefed up with larger diameter bearings of 2.5 ins., the same as the Mercury. The rods were heavier, as was the crank, with stiffer junctions between cheeks and journals. Compression was up slightly to 6.2:1, and torque was raised to 155 lbs.-ft. Gross horsepower without fan or muffler was now 93, up four from 1938, through still advertised as 85. This new engine was to be essentially unchanged through the remainder of the flathead run.

The goal was an eventual integration of Ford and Mercury blocks—achieved in principle in 1939 by uniformity of bearing widths, even though crank pin diameters, for example, remained different. That integration was taken a step further when, on August 26, steel

First-year production Mercurys carried unusual, barrel-shaped taillights, were aesthetically less pleasing than the units shown on the prototype.

Edsel's struggle to bring the Mercury to reality was vindicated when at year's end 65,884 units had been sold, though at the expense of some Ford sales.

The Mercury dash set a style which Ford would follow with the exception of the sweeping speedometer. The wheel, though, was closer to the dash and windshield.

The Ford dash, though similar to Mercury's, stayed with circular instrumentation through 1939, came back to it for 1942. Column shifts would bow on both for 1940.

sleeves were patented. The system did not work because the sleeves got hot at the top and warped, scored, and went out of round. Full integration was achieved in 1946.

New-type transmission blocker synchronizers were introduced in 1939, using initially the spring retainer and then shifting to ball retainers. Shift lever motion was reduced by a heightening of the shift tower.

The engineering department had done well with the revised 85-hp engine. Once the new engine was in production, attention was turned to a 6-cylinder unit. Edsel had met with six of the major Ford dealers, and all had urged the production of a 6-cyl. engine. Edsel then ordered the design of an L-head Six at the Rouge under Sheldrick's direction. Mr. Ford got wind of this and ordered parallel designs by Farkas. Sheldrick's engine was entirely conventional, including the distributor, which Mr. Ford immediately vetoed. It was a good engine, heavy and well-suited to trucks. The Farkas engine had siamesed ports, and he believed it to be superior on all counts to Sheldrick's, but the Sheldrick engine was eventually put into production.

Another 6-cylinder project was begun after Edsel saw the new Studebaker Champion on Jan. 6, 1939. This engine was another attempt at a power plant for a smaller car. The bore of 3.237 ins. x 3.50 ins. produced 72 bhp. The project was apparently stopped in April or May, although not permanently.

A small ohc Six, perhaps even the above engine, was designed for a most unusual chassis, ostensibly for English use. A unit body and frame was the basic beginning, following Zephyr practice. The engine was up front and was mounted on a single lateral pivot to the body. The transmission and torque tube were rigid extensions of the engine. The purpose of this design was to eliminate universal joints entirely at the cost of making the engine oscillate with any motion of the rear axle. It was an oddity, which fortunately, perhaps, was never built.

Throughout 1939, prototype Lincoln Continentals were under construction, the first one being completed for Edsel on March 1, with two others for Henry II and Benson ready in mid-summer. Limited production started in the fall, and some 25 cars had been hand-made

Though the Mercury was a "different" car than the Ford with greater length and width, Ford Deluxe styling in general was similar to Mercury except for vertical grille.

Ford's Standard series, on the other hand, shared front sheetmetal with the former '38's using a trifle fussier grille. Both 1939 lines totalled sales of almost 482,000.

by the end of the year. The running gear was Zephyr in all respects.

MERCURY: THE MESSENGER

Of much commercial value was the new Mercury, which was named by Edsel himself, and formally announced on Oct. 6, 1938. The car was like the Ford mechanically and structurally but had a 4-in. longer wheelbase and the 239-cu.-in. engine. The body style of the car was defiantly rounded, in essence a "fatter" Ford. The front fenders were very deeply crowned and boxed, while the rear fenders encroached over the wheels so as to be semi-skirted.

The unity of the Mercury design was superior. The soft line everywhere was relieved a bit by the horizontal grille set in the general pattern of the 1939 Ford, to which it was most often compared. The extreme windshield slant fitted well and gave the car a fleet appearance. The windshield did not open, and the wipers could thus be mounted at the base.

The rather flat dashboard had a general layout much like the Ford. Instruments were laid out in little chrome-trimmed rectangular panels with a big sweeping arc speedometer over all. The steering wheel was 18 ins. in diameter, 1 in. larger than the Ford, and it was set closer to the dash (and windshield) in the interest of passenger seating space. Owners liked the slightly different placement of the wheel.

The 3.54 gears gave the Mercury a fine high-speed cruising capacity, 60 mph requiring only 2550 rpm. Top speed was around 90. The Mercury Fordor Sedan had an f.o.b. list price of $957. An accompanying scale

The motoring world at last had hydraulic-braked Fords in 1939, and Mr. Ford had caught up with the industry. The 15-millionth Ford was built in Richmond, Calif.

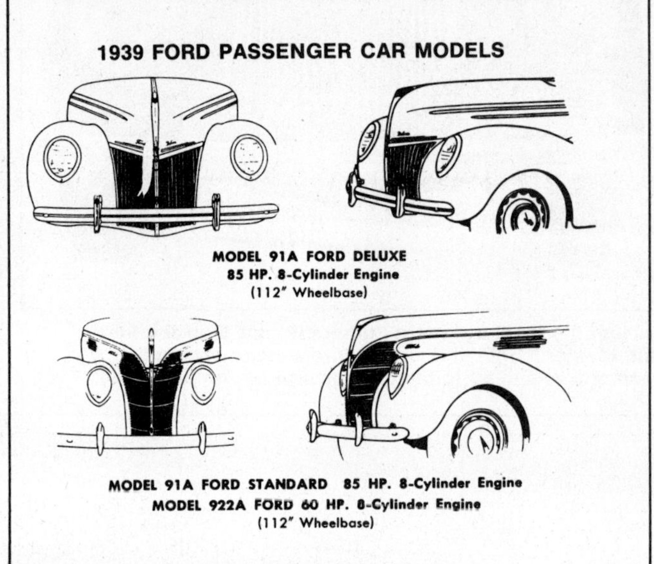

Factory identification drawings of the 1939 Ford Standard and Deluxes. All Deluxes had the 85 hp V-8, while either it or the 60 hp V-8 came in the Standards.

Much-sought after today is the 1939 Convertible Sedan, the final year for the style in the Ford line but which would strangely surface for just one year as a Mercury for 1940. The Club Convertible would supplant this body configuration, to the small but avid following of buyers.

shows exactly where it fell into the sales market target area. The target area was hit perfectly, but the competition was heavy.

Showing evidence of an incredible amount of preplanning, the entire Ford line of vehicles—Ford, Mercury and Lincoln-Zephyr—was announced simultaneously on Nov. 5, 1938. The commercial vehicles and trucks premiered one week earlier on October 29.

The 1939 Ford was unchanged in basic body sheetmetal from the 81A. The new grille of the Deluxe was unusually neat, and the vertical bars were graceful matches to the fender contours. The headlights moved out to the fender crown, which served to simplify the front end. Apart from the headlight rims, all frontal lines were straight. The belt molding had only the slightest dip toward the front.

The Standard series now picked up the 1938 grille with slight modifications. It was satisfactory but busier than even the 81A grille.

PRICE COMPARISONS OF SOME 1939 MODELS

Dodge Luxury Liner	$905
Pontiac Deluxe Six	$922
Oldsmobile Six	$952
Mercury	$957
Studebaker Commander	$965
DeSoto Deluxe	$970
Pontiac Eight	$970
Nash Ambassador Six	$985
Hudson Country Club Six	$995
Packard Six	$995
Buick Special	$996
Chrysler Royal Six	$1010
Lincoln-Zephyr	$1401

The dashboard was an evolution of 1938. Angularity was the theme, and, except for the actual dial faces, there were no curves present in the design. The instrument faces were cleaner, bolder, and much more readable than in 1938.

RUMBLE SEATS ARE OUT IN THE COLD

In the light of the slow economy, even Ford could not maintain its variety of body styles which had been available for 1938. In the Deluxe series the choice was narrowed down from 8 to 5. The Phaeton was, alas, gone. But it must have been hardly missed at the time if the production figure of 1169 units is to be believed. Harder to explain is the phase out of the Club Coupe and Club Convertible, the latter having appeared first in mid-1936. Also, the Club Convertible had reached a 1938 sales level of 6080 copies. This was to be the last year for a Ford rumble seat, which meant that 4702 Convertible buyers preferred putting their backseat passengers out in the wind. Oddly, both the Club Coupe and Club Convertible would reappear in later years, making them conspicuous by their absence from the 1939 lineup.

In 1939, the Convertible Sedan was given the normal sedan trunk section, and the canvas top was much more massive in the rear section than on the model's predecessors. It was to be the final year for this body style in the Ford car line, but the style would surface briefly for 1940 as a Mercury. This, incidentally, is difficult to understand, for the rising costs of engineering and tooling for a unique body configuration dictates that it remain in production until its costs have been amortised. But such was not the case with Mercury unfortunately.

The Coupe was now listed as a 3-passenger car, somewhat optimistic in the light of the fact that the listed Sedan capacity was still five passengers. It would

Chevrolet for 1939 offered competition sufficiently stiff to out-gun Ford by some 100,000 units. The new styling was well-integrated although the headlights had yet to be swallowed by the fenders. The Ford, however, continued to be the peppiest car in this hotly contested marketplace.

be a tight squeeze in the Coupe for three, and that ever-present gearshift was still in the middle of the floor—a bit disconcerting for sliding in and out.

Overall, the 1939 Ford was surely a "neat" car and showed the attention to refinement that Gregorie and his stylists had given. With the hydraulic brakes, it was also now a thoroughly competitive car. But alas, the 1939 Ford faced new developments from both Chevrolet and Plymouth which were very strong.

The 1939 Chevrolet was a very new car and reflected the new integration of GM body shells. The hood and fender crease disappeared, and the belt molding and window reveals were simplified. The GM box fender was sharply drawn. The grille was strongly Vee'd, the grille bars simple, and the prow very smooth. It was a good-looking car, much bigger in appearance and yet slightly lighter in weight. The integral sedan trunk with the notch roof back was the hallmark of GM in 1939 and would never again have such a sharp definition. The commercial importance of the trunk was that it emphasized the dated look of the unchanged Ford.

Mechanically there were surprises. The Dubonnet suspension was finally dropped in favor of the normal, unequal wishbone system, a very sturdy new unit which gave little trouble. New rear shocks further improved the ride. This was the last year in which Chevrolet offered the 4.2 axle ratio on the deluxe cars and the 3.73:1 on the standard series, a concession to weight. The lighter Master series were much better highway cruisers, but the 4.22 ratio made the Master Deluxe series very flexible in high gear.

A genuine advance was the introduction of the optional steering column gearshift. Unfortunately, Chevrolet used a vacuum-assisted unit instead of following the simpler mechanism introduced in 1938 on the Cadillac, LaSalle, and Pontiac. Chevrolet shifting was smooth but sluggish; the vacuum assist persisted through 1948. The column shift was a critically important change because of its direct impact on the driving public. The Chrysler Corp. also switched over to column shifting in 1939. Though Jack Warham at Lincoln had begun work on the column shift early in 1938, right after the introduction of the GM unit, the new transmission was not

Chevrolet's 1939 dashboard showed general industry thinking, though Ford stayed with circular gauges and Mercury mounted its speedometer sweep separately.

Hudson was deep into the well-rounded design idiom, though the smaller series as this 112 Sedan did not have inset headlights, and was priced to compete with various models of the "Big Three" offerings. This version had 112-in. wheelbase, on a par with Ford's.

ready until the 1940 model. As with hydraulic brakes, Ford once again brought up the rear with an important technical improvement.

COMPETITION STIFFENS

Plymouth in 1939 made major changes too. The Chrysler Corp., perhaps bruised from the experiences with the Airflow, had become more conservative by 1938. Chrysler had offered Vee-type windshields in their first Eight by 1931; yet by 1938 Chrysler products had reverted to flat windshields, which looked old-fashioned. Chrysler bodies in the mid-Thirties, apart from the Airflow, had been relatively narrow and were accentuated by long vertical grille designs. In 1937 the senior Chrysler, with high, narrow-set headlamps and a bulbous grille, was downright ugly. Little in the way of improvement was added in 1938.

In 1939 the Chrysler line received a major front-end development, emphasizing massiveness. Of the four Chrysler Corp. products—all following similar motifs—the Plymouth was easily the most successful because of its simplicity. The grille openings were carried in all cases into the fender aprons, but only Plymouth used a harmonious and consistent pattern. The worst looking of the lot was the Chrysler. It was a potent illustration of the chrome styling brigade running amuck.

The Chrysler line was helped by a major restyling of the dashboard in 1939. By the absence of a Vee-windshield in 1938, the dashboard had dropped vertically from the base of the windshield, with a peculiar flat-

Dodge Luxury Liner for 1939 received Chrysler stylists' idea of streamlining, with integrated headlights and pleasant but unexciting overall appearance.

Cream of the Plymouth crop for 1939 was this convertible sedan which had all the engineering amenities of the time including inset headlights.

Obviously proud Hudson workers show off their 30th anniversary car, boldly emblazoned with milestone number; a Model 92 6-cyl. which would carry an f.o.b. price of $898. But even with a rated 96 hp at 3900 rpm, it could hardly get out of a Ford's way, although faster than many.

ness. The gauges and dial designs were questionable, especially after 1935. The new design was much more conventional, and again it was the Plymouth which had a very nice layout with a woodgrain finish. The speedometer featured a glow dot which changed color with speed, and all was clear and readable.

The Plymouth column gearshift was good, a bit notchy and awkward, but far better than 1938. And a fine new independent front suspension was the equal of Chevrolet's.

Thus Chevrolet and Plymouth offered formidable new competition for Ford in 1939, a Ford which did indeed finally have hydraulic brakes, but little else, to sell as new to the consumer.

Ford sales were up for 1939 to 481,496, but Chevrolet was still way out in front with 598,341. Mercury had

Designer Amos Northup receives the credit for the advance-concept styling of the shark-nose Graham which shows the independent course he was following. Thrusting prow of the integrated hood/grille is duplicated by thrusting fenders. "Speed lines" were pressed into rear fenders.

Studebaker Champion for 1939 was the firm's mainstay. Its L-head 6-cyl. engine inspired Edsel to push for Ford Motor Co.'s development of an equivalent powerplant, which would not materialize until 1941. This was a brand-new concept of a compact car, and debuted in three body styles.

a good beginning year with a total of 65,884 cars sold, when the results were tallied, and one suspects that many of these sales were Ford prospects who had moved up. Lincoln sold 19,940 units, only a handful of which were K's. Plymouth sold just over 350,000 a recovery of some 50,000 cars from 1938. But the Ford Motor Co. totals were still behind the Chrysler totals.

This was somewhat disappointing because 1939 spring sales had been strong, and it looked as if it it would be comeback year. A summer sales push had shown good results, and John Davis, the sales manager, was planning for a 900,000 production year in 1940, sufficient to recapture second place from Chrysler and perhaps even overtake Chevrolet.

A tragedy occurred in September, which, according to Allan Nevins, "checked the momentum of the Ford organization." In the locker room of the Dearborn Country Club, a childish fight took place between two Ford executives. Though quickly ended, the fight soon drew Sales Manager Davis into open conflict with Harry Bennett. The end result was that, though Davis' position was vindicated, he was removed as general sales manager. He had been well-liked by the dealers, and his demotion was an ominous sign of the coming breakup of the whole management team, a deterioration which would conclude with the resignation of Sorensen on March 4, 1944. Sheldrick quit in September 1943, followed by Gregorie, Crawford, Wibel and Liebold. Davis' successor was the capable Henry C. Doss, who, somewhat prophetically, would resign in 1944. The dealers rightly sensed that the fight at the 1939 sales meeting and its outcome was a subtle signal of a change in the company's future.

The 1939 Lincoln-Zephyr grille had some design similarities to the Ford including head lamp styling, and a general outline of the grille but with vertical bars.

The '39 Zephyr's Convertible Sedan was a limited number popular offering, highlighted that year by the marque's hydraulic brakes and other refinements.

LIST OF PROPOSED NAMES FOR THE MERCURY

HERMES	OXFORD
CITADEL	CREST
CORONADO	WASHINGTON
COURTIER	CONSUL
CHARTER	VISTA
SOVEREIGN	ARCHER
KENT	FALCON
VERNON	FLEETFORD
FORD-FLEETWING	OLYMPUS
OLYMPIA	SPARTAN
TROJAN	DIANA
MINERVA	EAGLE
SWALLOW	THE TRAIL-BLAZER
STYLETER	FORD-ZEPHYR
PHAROAH 8	EUROPA
TRAFFORD	DRAKE
GULFORD	VICTORINE
ZEPHORD	VANITIE 8
LUXURY 8	THE CONSTELLATION
THE GROUNDFLIGHT	COURAGEOUS
COURSER	FORLIN
FORZELLI	FORD-XL
DART	COURIER
ATHENIAN	STYLEMASTER
STYLIST	MERCURY
THE GAZELLE	KEY
EXPLORER	FORD ARROW
OLYMPIC	CASTLE
WARWICK	ZEST
MANOR	NASSAU
TRITON	LUXOR
HUNTER	NORMANDY
HORIZON	TOWER
FORD-FALCON	FORDUKE
THE DEARBORN	FLEETWING
HERCULES	FORD-OLYMPIC
LEOPARD	MARATHON
REGENT	EROS
THE COMET	PANTHER
EXFORD	CYCLOPS
TRANSFORD	PHOENIX 8
CRUSADER	MERCAR
PATROIT	EDISON
THE WINGED VICTORY	ELFORD
	PLAZA
CORSAIR	FORDOCART
ZEON	FORERUNNER
REXFORD	VALIANT
AUTOCRAT	LEO
THE PATHFINDER	CORINTHAIN
RANGER	BEAU MONDE
RAMBLER	THE QUICKSILVER

Edsel Ford personally selected Mercury.

NEW AGE STIRRING— OLD AGE DYING

The Ford Station Wagon for 1940 continued to be the finest of the wood-bodied passenger vehicles on the market. The year marked Ford's final statement of the Thirties with bodies little-changed from 1939—but the decade's best.

The 1940 Model 01A Ford, announced simultaneously on Oct. 15, 1939, with the 1940 Mercury and Lincoln-Zephyr cars, properly begins a new decade and should therefore stand outside of this study. But the car itself was really a culmination and the final statement of Model 40 introduced in 1933. Though body weight had risen some 290 lbs., over the eight intervening years, the wheelbase was still the same 112 ins. The 1940 60-hp Model 02A was, in fact, but 15 lbs. heavier than the 1933 car. The car was 15 ins. longer than in 1933, two-thirds of which increase was made in the 1938 model. The tread base was unchanged from 1932 and was even ¼-in. narrower than on the Model A. When the public viewed the new 1940 Ford, they had little trouble recognizing the same compact, high-speed automobile which had been in fact familiar since 1933.

In particular, for 1940 the basic sheet metal was unchanged, the sedans carrying along with the 1938 body, and the coupes a continuation of the 1939 style. The Convertible and Convertible Sedan of 1939 were both discontinued in favor of a new club convertible style which combined the virtues of both bodies. A vacuum-operated power top made the 1940 Convertible seem a more modern automobile than its predecessors, but the innovation was hardly novel since Plymouth had pioneered it in 1938, and Chevrolet had followed suit in 1939.

In styling and mechanical details there was much improvement for 1940. The grille and hood layout was

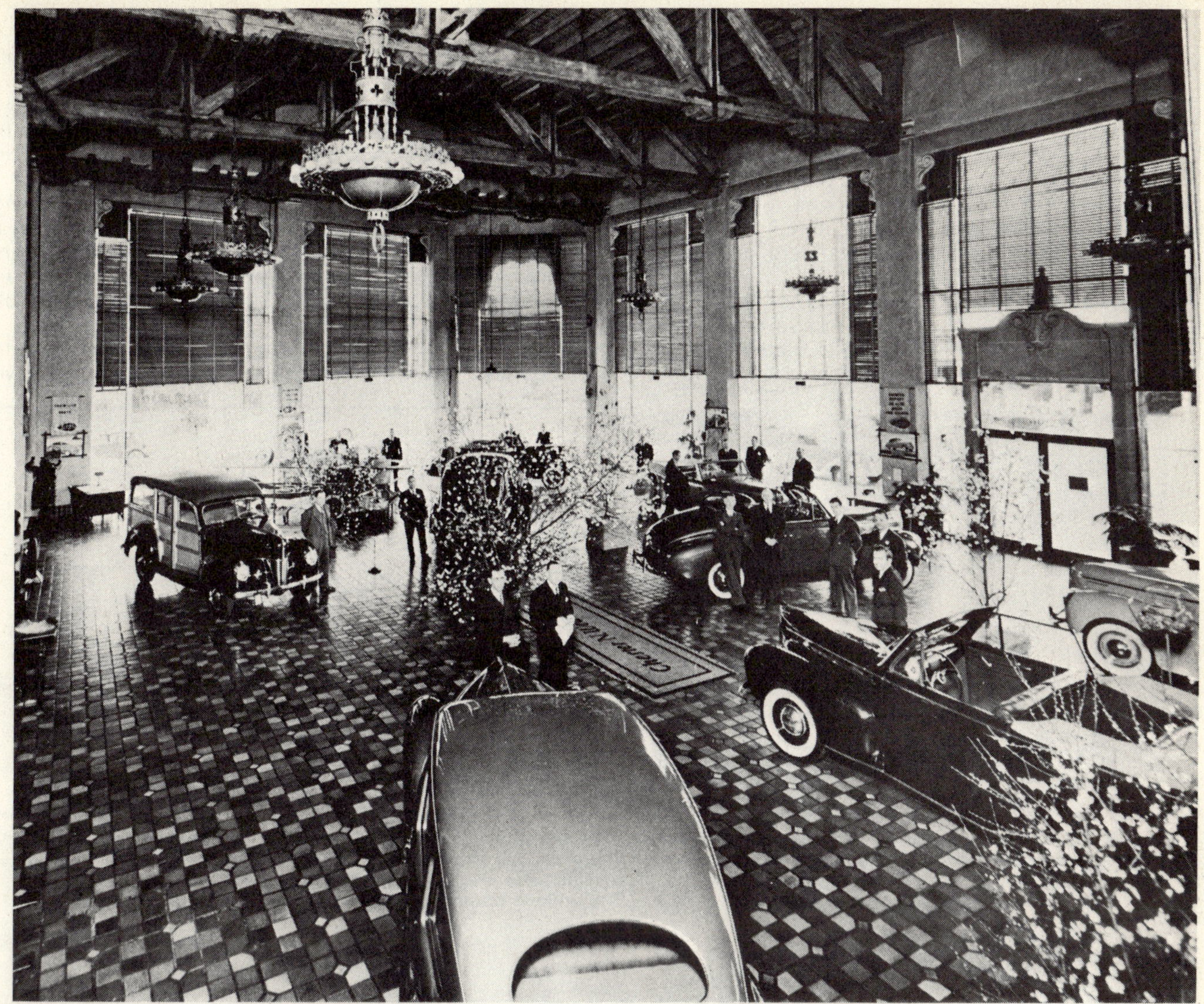

Dealerships often decorated their showrooms with bouquets as an enticement to the ladies, for their influence on family car-buying was beginning to be appreciated. At this introduction of Ford's 1940 models, Ford, Mercury and Lincoln-Zephyr vie for attention. This was typical of a dealer's showings.

entirely new and was cleverly dimensioned to be virtually interchangeable with the 1939 model, requiring no changes in front fenders. The grille was strengthened by a vertical profile utilizing fine horizontal bars, though it was nicely fussier than in 1939. The Standard grille was a mild reworking of the 1939 Deluxe style. Ford stylists had yet to come up with a distinguishing grille motif that could be gradually developed in each succeeding model. This was a problem for almost all designers in the late Thirties, once the traditional radiator shape had been abandoned. The Lincoln-Zephyr had a relatively stable grille design from 1938 through 1941. The Mercury managed an evolutionary grille in their four pre-war models. Buick's frontal appearance in 1939 set long-term patterns. Chevrolet settled down in 1940, and Cadillac hit upon a theme in 1941 which has lasted until our own time. But few cars could achieve the product identification enjoyed by LaSalle from 1934 through 1940 with their long, narrow, graceful grille. It is not suggested that grille styling had to follow a pre-set pattern in which each successive year saw merely a refinement of the preceding model's theme. This would come, of course, but Ford stylists at the time were simply redesigning the grille treatment each year to give the new car a fresh look and to distinguish it from its predecessors. In this they were quite successful, for, with the Standard car series aside, there is no mistaking the year of a Ford.

The teardrop taillights used for 1938 and 1939 gave way to a chevron design. Sealed beam headlights were fitted, in concert with the other major manufacturers. The new lights had been demonstrated in February 1938, and were the result of efforts by the Automobile Manufacturers Association to produce a light that would meet varying state requirements.

A concession to the times was the introduction of front door vent windows, the Ford design having the sealing vertical bar attached to as well as rising and falling with the main door glass, except on the Convertible. But as soon as the window support channels deteriorated and became sloppy, the seal was gone between the window vent and the car. On such details, Chevrolet and Plymouth scored a point against Ford with somewhat superior designs.

A brand-new instrument panel broke sharply with previous practice. The dash, no longer vertical, was full and rounded, the instruments set in a raised panel in front of the driver. On the Deluxe cars the instruments were deep-set beneath a tan plastic facia, while on the Standard cars a single sheet of glass covered all.

NEW AGE STIRRING—OLD AGE DYING

In 1940, and again in 1941, Ford abandoned circular speedometers, which had been one of the best features of the instrument layout since 1932. This mistake, if it could be termed such, was corrected in 1942. The 1940 Standard car instrument panel did retain a fully displayed speedometer pointer, much easier to read than the Deluxe models. The standard panel was continued in the truck lines through 1947.

A welcome change was the abandonment of highly styled panel knobs mounted here and there in favor of uniform round knobs positioned at the base of the panel, a pattern retained for some years.

SMOKERS AND STABILIZERS

Smokers received attention in 1940, for it was the first year when two front ashtrays were fitted to the Ford, one at each end of the instrument panel.

The most immediately noticeable mechanical change was the application of Warham's steering column gearshift to the successful blocker-type synchronized transmission of 1939. The new shift was crisp in action and compared favorably to the designs of both Chevrolet and Plymouth.

New for 1940 were redesigned wheels in which the lugs were returned to the same spacing as on the wire

The 1940 Standard's grille is an obvious rework of the 1939 Deluxes, and is every bit as successful with some finer detailing. It must have been a stylist's dream, to so closely yet precisely update an existing front end.

GM's box styling reached its peak in Buick for 1939. The great curves of 1936 are gone and numerous straight lines and surfaces tighten the whole design. The grille is prophetic and sets a lasting pattern.

The one car that Edsel Ford brought clearly from drawing board to production was the Lincoln-Zephyr Continental, of which this one-off was his personal car. Minor modifications were made before production began. European styling influence is very evident in this handsome machine.

wheels—which were abandoned after 1935—but slight hub differences prevented interchangeability. The new wheels ended the complaints about drum distortion and also reduced the transmission of road noise.

Another important change in 1940 was the introduction of an anti-roll bar or ride stabilizer on the front spring of the Deluxe 85 hp models, the Mercury, and the Lincoln-Zephyr. The front stabilizing strut installed during 1936 on the Zephyrs had been continued with minor changes. A similar rod had been tried in 1937 on the rear of the Zephyrs but was abandoned. These stabilizers on the Lincoln-Zephyrs were used for axle location only and did not affect roll.

There was increasing concern about roll by all of the chassis engineers. The weakness of the transverse spring in fighting roll rooted in several causes:

1. The spring contact with the frame cross member was limited to the small central patch. Any attempts to increase roll resistance by broadening that patch drastically increased the deflection rate.
2. The trend was toward ever-lower deflection rates to produce a soft ride. As the springs grew more flexible, roll increased.
3. Car weight was rising, which intensified both of the above problems. In truck use the transverse spring had reached the end of its usefulness because weight and spring flexibility could no longer be balanced. In 1940 transverse springs were completely phased out of truck production, except in the light ½-ton commercials. That this radical shift away from Ford design axioms could occur at all reveals how withdrawn Mr. Ford had become from truck engineering.
4. The transverse spring was especially weak in combating roll on high center of gravity chassis.

Buick for 1940 evolved from the previous year with somewhat less formal-looking lines, and pleasing front end with integrated headlights but with the bold statement of the grille design that the marque had pioneered.

Only LaSalle maintained a grille identity throughout the Thirties, and the long and thin design of 1934 was consistent until the end. This 1938 grille is a bit fat, but order was restored the following year.

Total refinement of the LaSalle front end for 1939 was a decided improvement over 1938, but the stylists were boxing themselves in, for the trend to lower cars with horizontal grille motifs was on the horizon.

The 1940 LaSalle was the last and perhaps best looking of all its post-1934 models. The massive frontal design was a problem area which was not properly handled on the 1941 LaSalle design proposals.

The Series 62 sedan from Cadillac in 1940 was a clean design, which included a grille shape that could evolve into a horizontal theme without spoiling the Division's front end identity.

NEW AGE STIRRING–OLD AGE DYING

By 1939 the rolling characteristics of the Ford products were painfully obvious, especially on the Lincoln-Zephyr and the new Mercury. The Mercury had a strut rod appear during 1939, but it, like that used on the Zephyr, served only for axle location and did not resist roll. The problem was made more acute by the perfection of the independent front suspensions in GM and Chrysler products which had produced the "flat ride" along with excellent roll resistance. Though Chevrolet still offered the beam front axle in 1940 on the Master 85 series, it was clearly finished on passenger cars.

Ford's answer was the anti-roll bar, a straightforward method of tying down the front axle at its outer ends to limit roll. It also limited free motion of either end of the axle and in one stroke destroyed the old Ford argument that the transverse spring prevented frame wracking. In this sense, the anti-roll bar was a step away from independent front suspension.

The front spring was now relieved of the necessity of providing roll resistance, and the deflection rate was dropped from 245 to 185 lbs./in. The new rate was perilously close to the rear spring rate, which would

The dash layout of the 1940 Ford Deluxe strayed from the circular instrumentation used for so long, but it would return again beginning in 1942. Plastic facia covers gauges, but Standards used a glass pane.

The "competition's dash," here in the form of the 1940 Chevrolet, was perhaps a bit stiffer than Ford's, and the horizontal steering wheel spokes placed above center did not help the driver's readability of the dials.

The 1940 Ford Deluxe Tudor Sedan remains as much of a favorite today as it was when announced. A concession to the times was the addition of the door window vent panes, overdue from Ford. It was a milestone year; the 28-millionth Ford was built on April 8, the 7-millionth V-8 on June 4.

have set up a balanced pitch frequency, and therefore the rears were dropped to 165 lbs./in. The ride was much improved, and the rolling was certainly checked.

Mercury's spring rate went down only 20 lbs. in front for a total of 225 lbs. The strut was abandoned when the roll bar was installed because the new bar was flanged to control sideways movement in both the Ford and the Mercury. Curiously, the Zephyr roll bar did not have this feature, and the strut was continued.

One other approach toward roll resistance might have occurred in 1940. A Hypoid axle appeared in 1938 on the Zephyr, which, if applied to at least the Mercury, could have allowed a somewhat lower body design. The reason for this is easily understood if one stops a moment to ponder the Hypoid design. Ford's conventional straddle-mounted pinion gear meshed with the rear axle ring gear along its center line. This meant that the torque tube joined the differential centersection at its mid-point. In the Hypoid design, the pinion gear meshed with the ring gear below the center line, thus the body floor could be lowered in relation to the rear axle assembly without sacrificing necessary clearance. However, the Hypoid axle never filtered down to the Mercury or Ford until after the torque tube transverse spring era had ended.

AHEAD YET BEHIND

The 1940 Ford was a fine car, tough and strong as Fords had always been, and capable of sustained high speeds. The brakes were good now, and the new gearshift was excellent. Sales were up to 542,755, about a 10% gain over 1939, good in the face of the company's disastrous labor troubles in 1940. The prospects might have seemed bright were it not for the progress made by both Plymouth and Chevrolet.

In retrospect, the Plymouth and Chevrolet were truly cars of the Forties, the first of new breeds. The 1948 Plymouth is entirely recognizable in terms of its 1940 predecessor. The 1940 Ford, however, is entirely recognizable in terms of its 1938 predecessor. The styling revolution for Ford would be in the 1941 model. In that fateful year of 1940 though, the two major competitors of Ford were able to market products which were sufficiently advanced in order to take heavy advantage of Ford's stand-pat styling.

In 1940 the prices of the big three were very close,

Chevrolet for 1940 was all-new and reflected the best of GM's thinking at the time; larger than its predecessors, roomier on the inside, and with quality in terms of assembly and general finish. Chevrolet fell in with the evolutionary grille treatment and would refine this in the next decade.

NEW AGE STIRRING–OLD AGE DYING

with a spread of only $7 between the 4-door sedans and $5 between the Deluxe coupes. Only the Ford Convertible had a price advantage, on the order of $50 under Chevrolet, and $100 under Plymouth. Ford no longer could compete with low prices alone.

The 1940 Plymouth was all-new, easily the best Plymouth to appear in the short history of the marque. The Chrysler Corp. had finally come up with a new style which was handsome, albeit boxy, and in keeping with the latest trends. The Plymouth wheelbase was increased 3 ins. to 117 ins., which allowed the rear sedan doors to have no fender cutouts at all. The car was very roomy, broad on the inside with excellent leg room, and with 15-in. high seat cushions. The car was exceptionally comfortable, and its ride was the best among the low-priced cars.

The 1940 Plymouth dashboard was refined from the 1939 ideas, and was very handsome, the trim in tasteful chrome moldings and stripings without plastic.

The instrument panel, and indeed the whole car, had the feeling that everything was tightly screwed together with not a press fit or snap fastener anywhere. Upholstery fabrics and interior detailing were excellent and spoke volumes about Chrysler's grasp of the importance of quality control.

Technically, the Plymouth offered some nice

Plymouth, like Chevrolet, debuted all-new models for 1940 and this was easily the best yet from Chrysler. It, too, had grown in roominess and its ride was excellent when critically judged against all low-price contenders.

Dodge also made substantial styling and engineering gains for 1940, and was only a step away from an automatic transmission which would bow the next year. Ford's "Ford-O-Matic" would not follow suit until 1951.

The 1940 Mercury grille had the same tendency toward fineness as so well detailed in the Ford. But the horizontal-bar motif was a concession to help broaden the car, since it was a trifle wider than its smaller brother. Ford's stylists continued to lead the way in open-car design.

Edsel Ford's 1939 Lincoln-Zephyr Continental was an instant success and led to limited build of two more before full-scale production began. The base price on the elegant Cabriolet would be in the $3500 range. From the outset, the marque enjoyed a clamorous following.

Very limited production was given the handsome 1940 Lincoln-Zephyr Continental Coupe. Refinements are evident between this example and Edsel's one-off; the hood lines dip downward at the front, rear fenders carry protective shields; the exposed spare tire has a metal covering.

consumer-oriented touches. New rotary door latches allowed one-finger push-shuts in remarkable silence. The gearshift pattern was strongly spring-loaded to the plane of second and third, and once low gear was engaged, the lever returned to the second/third plane. Thus, a shift pattern in the Plymouth was straight up for second and straight down for third with no notch in the movement at all. The second gear was unusually low, virtually useless as a highway passing gear. The idea apparently was to encourage second-gear starts, certainly possible with Plymouth's extra long piston stroke of 4.375 ins., which made for fine flexibility and torque. Perhaps Chrysler engineers were conscious of the new Fluid Drive transmission on the 8-cyl. Chrysler series, which was directing their further attention toward simpler shifting patterns. In any event, the Plymouth was a very easy car to shift and had a soft and smooth clutch. The steering was unusually light and responsive, and the car handled with great ease.

The 1940 Plymouth was a balanced and finely made car, representative of the best in Chrysler engineering, and it properly led a sales recovery up to the half-million mark, a substantial 40% increase over 1939.

The 1940 Chevrolet was an equally advanced car.

By 1941 the marque officially became Lincoln Continental but changes were minimal and limited to the addition of fender-mounted parking lights and bolder edging around the grille halves. Split bumper treatment may have been dictated by engineers to help cool its hot-blooded V-12.

A European influence was the exposed spare, but it helped immeasurably in breaking up rear-end sheetmetal expanse. Tire went undercover for 1940.

Resemblance of the 1940 Pontiac to the Lincoln-Zephyr probably went unnoticed at the time, but in retrospect there is indeed some similarity except for the Zephyr's vertical grille bars, and split front bumper.

Frontal view of Edsel's personal one-off shows a weakness in the disparity of the hood line, yet which was rounded down for production models. The big unusual-for-Ford car must have turned Dearborn heads.

The body was new, larger, and more spacious. Though the wheelbase was 113 ins., a fractional increase over 1939, the car seemed much bigger because the body was positioned farther forward, giving a more solid and coherent look. The new grille abandoned the Vee motif, as had Plymouth, in favor of the massive broad frontal appearance, which emphasized the anachronism of Ford's design.

Mechanical changes were few, but it was in the interior and trim that Chevrolet excelled. The quality of finish everywhere, the neat execution of panels and seats, a rich and handsome dashboard, all combined to give the Chevrolet an expensive feel. The hardware was especially attractive, and, like Plymouth, the car seemed to have a carefully engineered feel.

It was a great sales year for Chevrolet, a total of 894,178 units being delivered. Against these impressive gains, Ford's growth in 1940 is modest and in fact represents a slight decline in market share. The Ford Motor Company was now firmly in third place on gross sales of all products, and Plymouth was threatening more seriously than ever before to displace Ford on an actual sales basis for second place.

It is hard to accept the fact that the 1940 Ford was really a last gasp of the old way and a commercial pause in the success of the company. Its preservation and following among Ford enthusiasts today is a tribute to the tough and sturdy qualities which all Fords have, but easily forgotten is the fact that in its day the 1940 Ford was having a very hard time against the best competition ever. In comfort, room, ride, handling, trim, and to some extent finish, it had surrendered leadership. And what remained was still a wonderful fast pony of a car, able to generate a driver enthusiasm and loyalty—the kind born of speed and acceleration, in which the mechanical forces are readily apparent.

These qualities however were not desired by the American public at that time. But we now have come full circle, and have new appreciation for the excitement which was in the Ford car, especially through 1940. Its virtues remain the stubborn extension of one man's intense vision, whom the world was passing by, but who would yet build what he thought was right.

1940 FORD PASSENGER CAR MODELS

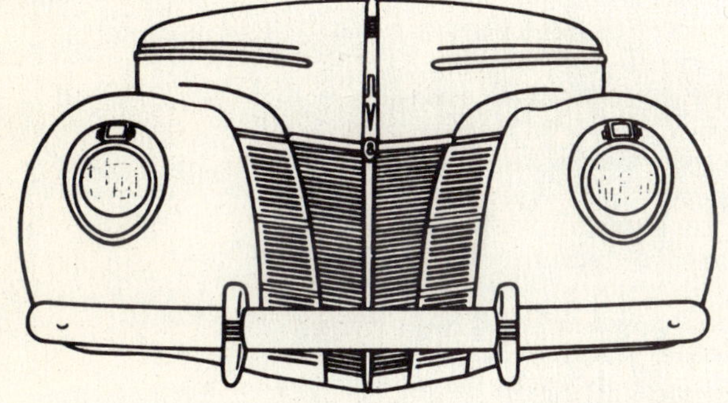

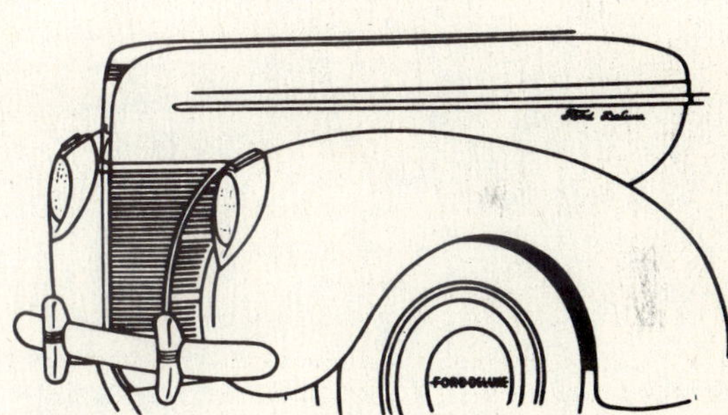

MODEL 01A FORD DELUXE
* **85 HP.** 8-Cylinder Engine
(112" Wheelbase)

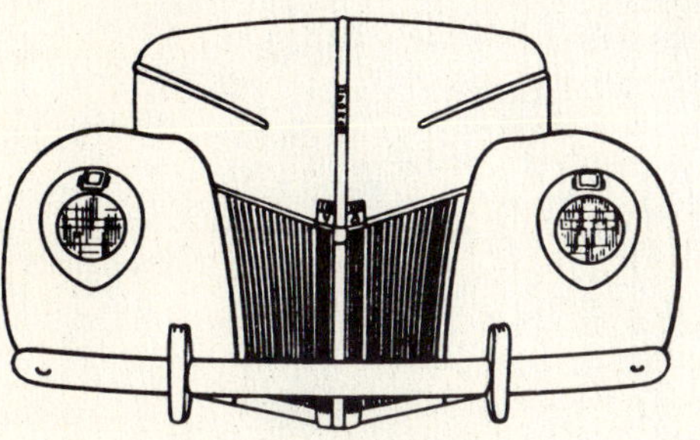

MODEL 01A FORD-STANDARD* 85 HP. 8-Cylinder Engine
MODEL 022A FORD-60 HP. 8-Cylinder Engine
(112" Wheelbase)

Ford Service Bulletin identity drawings of the 1940 Deluxes and Standards show frontal dissimilarity between what were otherwise identical cars. It was a treatment tried by no other U.S. manufacturer. Both were on the same 112-in. wheelbase, and both had the famous V-8.

TRUCKS AND FORD

If a workaday truck can be called glamorous, this 1935 light pickup has to be the queen of the Thirties' crop. Central mounting of medallion on hood side is clue to the year. One wonders how long the metal spare cover remained unscarred in commercial use.

Ford trucks in 1930 bore more than a passing resemblance to their automotive counterparts. The Model A engine was installed in all truck chassis without modification. Maximum torque of 122 lbs. was reached at 1000 rpm, which gave the A and AA 1½-ton trucks a certain slogging power despite only 40 bhp. In the fall of 1929 a 4-speed transmission was standardized, which, with the standard 6.6:1 rear axle ratio, gave a compound low gear of 42:1. With the engine flat out at 2200 revs, this meant a speed of 5 mph, or, at the 1000-rev torque peak, about 2.2 mph (using single 32 x 6 tires on the rear). The introduction of dual rear wheels on 20 x 6.00 tires increased the speed very slightly. In March 1930 Ford introduced an alternate 5.14 ratio, which was claimed to increase speeds at a given rpm by 28%. This 5.14 ratio was to remain standard in the heavy trucks through 1936, with the 6.6 as an optional extra low speed gear ratio.

Truck springing on the heavy AA chassis was cantilever style, in various lengths and thicknesses for specific purposes. Because the rear axle was located by a torque tube, compensation had to be provided at the end of the spring for change in length during flexing. This was accomplished by allowing the rear spring seat to rotate on the rear axle, forming a sort of giant shackle. On the very long 48-in. springs used in lighter loadings, this rotation was so great that special bolts were fitted to the radius rods to act as stops. The front springs were transverse and had up to eight more leaves than the passenger springs.

A further concession to truck duty was the offering in the spring of 1930 of a four-row, flat-tube radiator in the place of the usual three-row passenger type. At first the thicker radiator was uncompensated in the design of the external sheetmetal, with the result that these heavy-duty radiators could be identified by an increased gap between shell and hood.

The very pleasant wire wheels used in early AA production gave way to pressed-steel wheels, particularly necessary when dual rears became standard in 1½-ton production after 1930.

In 1932 the new BB truck had numerous changes. Externally, Ford trucks entered a new, three-year sheetmetal design cycle, new cabs appearing in 1932, 1935, and 1938. The cantilever springs in the rear were abandoned in favor of semi-elliptics, a sign of things to come, though transverse springs were retained in front almost to the end of the decade.

As noted in Chapter 2, the Model BB engine had numerous improvements, the most important of which for truck purposes was the use of add-on counterweights. They greatly improved the smoothness and longevity of the engine. In 1933 the 4-cyl. crank was given integral counterweighting, and this "C" shaft became normative thereafter in world production.

The 4-cyl. engine was in abundant supply in 1932, in contrast to the first V-8's. Trucks, both heavy and light, received the 4-cyl. B or BB engine as normal. In BB production as few as 549 out of 35,506 1½-ton chassis were V-8 powered. This production reflected Mr. Ford's own feeling that his new V-8 had relegated the 4-cyl. engine to commercial and utility purposes. In Britain the public agreed with him, and the Model C engine was retained until World War II despite efforts of Dagenham to kill it in favor of the V-8 60.

When the V-8 was finally used in truck production (first use on Aug. 5, 1932 was in a School-and-Passenger bus chassis), its flat torque curve in combination with Model A gearing quickly earned the reputation for the engine as a "revver," and speeds went up dramatically. At 3600 rpm, the approximate power peaking point of the V-8, torque was still a respectable 100-lbs.-ft., and truckers were thus tempted to run the engine right out to its limits, a fact that tended to cause the early V-8's to suffer from reduced life when compared to the much lower rev limits of contemporary Sixes.

Truck engines followed general V-8 development. In 1933 aluminum heads were used when compression was raised to 6.3 and hp to 75 at 3800 rpm, but cast iron returned in 1934 with compression falling back to 5.32:1. Truck compression remained below passenger use until 1937, when the iron head began to be phased back into passenger production.

Truck grille design for 1932 was similar to the Model 18 passenger car. In 1933 the grille was slightly tilted backward some 5°, with accompanying shell changes. Model 46 replaced "B" as the light commercial designation, and this number was also used for the rare 4-cyl. passenger car, suggesting the commercial intent of that production. The new 112-in. chassis changed the pickup proportions, for the bed remained the same but the wheels and fenders were moved to the rear 6 ins., reducing the overhang at the back.

In 1934 the most conspicuous mechanical change was the introduction of full-floating axles on the BB, which may be recognized by the bolt-on caps visible at the end of the shafts. Shaft diameter was reduced from 1.94 ins. to 1.56 ins., since the shaft now only had to handle torque. In 1934 the 20-in. wheel, which had become standardized for general truck use, was joined

The 4-cyl. Model B engine was originally intended to be reduced to commercial use only, but the slow build-up of V-8 production in 1932 forced the engines into the passenger cars. This is the roadster-pickup ¼-ton truck.

The Australian Branch Assembly Plant tended to uniqueness on some models, particularly in this utility pickup, termed a Ute. It started a trend of integral cab/bed design which would last throughout most of the Thirties. Dimensions of the Ute's loading space included nearly a 5-ft. bed.

by numerous options in tire sizes and corresponding rim width changes, along with some special larger diameters to fit the growing uses of the new truck. A V-8 medallion appeared on the top center of the hood louvers, along with stainless ribbon trim.

BANNER YEARS

For 1935 the truck line was redesigned in the Model 50 ½-ton commercial and the Model 51 1½-ton series. External changes featured a new grille, which reflected 1935 Model 48 passenger styling, and attractive new streamlined cabs. Engines were virtually unchanged, but radiator capacity in Model 51 was upped from 22 to 25 qts., and a six-blade fan was fitted. Core frontal area rose to 444 sq. ins., up from 386. All of these changes brought the truck cooling system to a new

What appears to have started life as a 1932 Phaeton has been transformed into a Swiss Army patrol car. Front seat soldier holds a carbine while the men in the rear hold a tripod and a machine gun. Builder of this special military adaptation is unknown.

The 1935 Ford Panel Delivery, again identified by the centrally mounted hood side emblem, was truck-based, while the Sedan Delivery was car-based. Intended strictly for utilitarian use, Ford trucks during the Thirties exhibited some classic lines, while the competition was mundane.

divergence from passenger car practice, the earlier trucks running virtually identical cooling systems. Ford overheating troubles were now considerable in both car and truck service and were especially bad in the 1935 Model 50 light commercials, which shared the smaller 20-qt. system unfortunately introduced in the 1935 Model 48. Also, the instrument panel was redesigned and followed Model 48 layout.

The new truck was well received. Ford had the satisfaction of beating Chevrolet in the production race.

For 1936, the heavy trucks were continued with virtually no change. A very large 19-in. fan blade was used on the Model 51. The Model 67 ½-ton commercials received the improved 22 qt. capacity cooling system used on passenger also. The iron truck head now was fitted to Model 67 with a slight drop in horsepower. Hood louvers were slightly altered, and the medallion was moved to a forward position. Disc wheels on the light trucks followed Model 68.

Dagenham truck production deviated from the American models quite early. In March 1932, a 1-ton truck was offered, basically using 1931 Model AA sheetmetal and with eight-hole pressed steel wheels. This middle-duty truck continued until October 1935, when the new Model 61 replaced it, powered by the 60-hp V-8 engine. The 60 never was liked in truck service in England, and the Model C 4-cyl. engine was always available on special order. By 1938 Dagenham bowed to demand and recatalogued the C engine as optional in Model 61, which was then called Model E88W. Three-speed transmissions were fitted.

The "W" in Model E88W indicates that this was a Cab-Over-Engine model. Dagenham pioneered this style in the Ford world organization back in October

The 1935 Model 50 ½-ton commercials, and the Model 51 1½-ton series, were totally redesigned for the year. The handsome grille reflected the passenger car counterpart.

Restored 1938 ½-ton pickup is correct except for front bumper which is the 1939 edition. Few changes were made to update the 1938's, except for the bumper and the central grille bar, which was heavier in '38.

The Models 50 and 51 for 1939 shared cabs and some external sheetmetal, but the larger 51's, as the 1½-ton stakebed shown, had their own deep fenders to accommodate larger tires and wheels. Because the V-8 trucks shared car cooling problems, the 51's had larger capacity radiators.

1938 FORD COMMERCIAL AND TRUCK MODELS

MODEL 81C FORD COMMERCIAL
85 HP. 8-Cylinder Engine

MODEL 82C FORD COMMERCIAL
60 HP. 8-Cylinder Engine

(112″ Wheelbase)

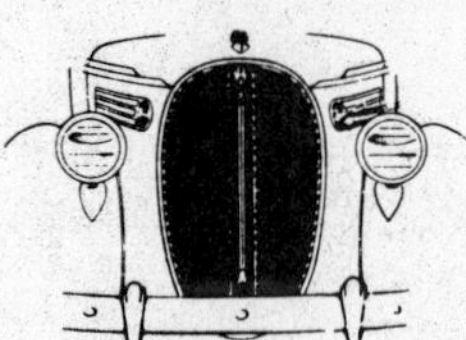

FORD REGULAR TRUCK
85 HP. 8-Cylinder Engine

MODEL	WHEELBASE
81T	134″
817T	157″
• 81U	134″
•• 811T	191″

• Dump Chassis ••School Bus Chassis

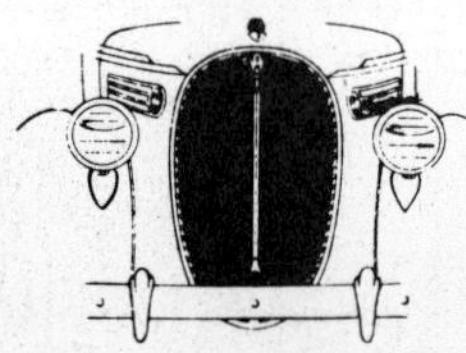

MODEL 81Y FORD 1 TON TRUCK
85 HP. 8-Cylinder Engine

MODEL 82Y FORD 1 TON TRUCK
60 HP. 8-Cylinder Engine

(122″ Wheelbase)

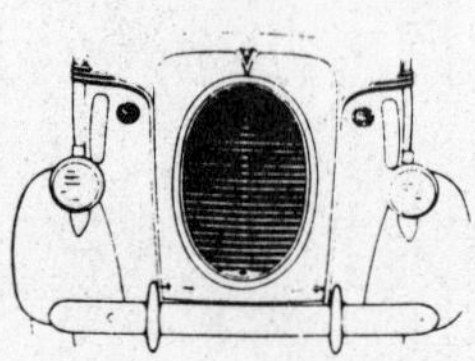

FORD CAB-OVER-ENGINE TRUCK
85 HP. 8-Cylinder Engine

MODEL	WHEELBASE
811W	101″
81W	134″
817W	157″
• 811Z	101″

• Dump Chassis

1939 FORD COMMERCIAL AND TRUCK MODELS

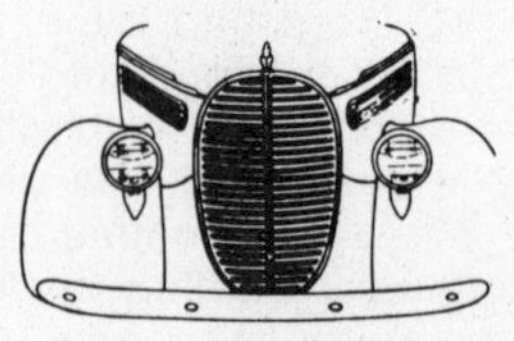

FORD COMMERCIAL

MODEL 60 HP.	85 HP.	95 HP.	WHEELBASE
922C	91C	99C	112″

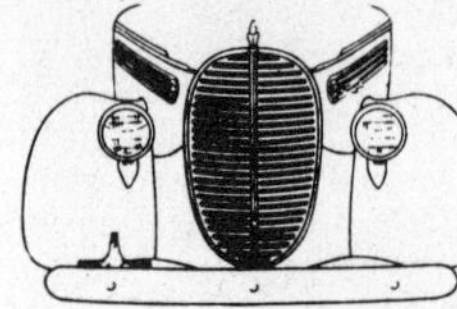

FORD REGULAR TRUCK

MODEL 85 HP.	95 HP.	WHEELBASE
91T	99T	134″
917T	997T	157″
•911T	• 991T	191″
••91U	••99U	134″

•School Bus Chassis •• Dump Chassis

FORD CAB-OVER-ENGINE

MODEL 85 HP.	95 HP.	WHEELBASE
991W	991W	101″
91W	99W	134″
917W	997W	157″
•911Z	•991Z	101″

•Dump Chassis

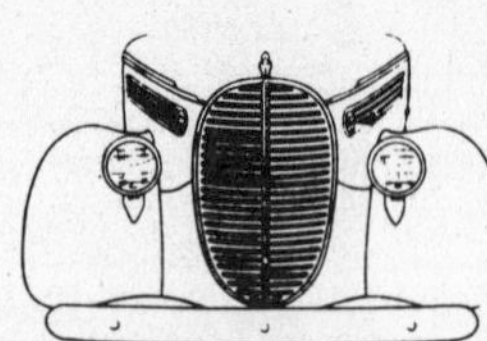

FORD 1 TON TRUCK

MODEL 60 HP.	85 HP.	95 HP.	WHEELBASE
92Y	91Y	99Y	122″

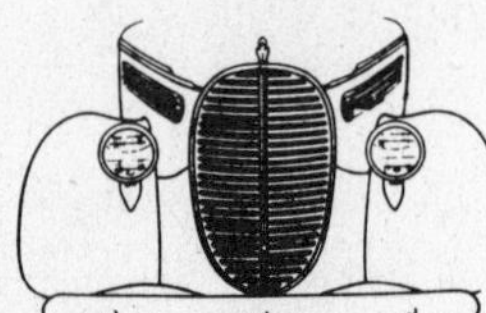

FORD ¾ TON TRUCK

MODEL 60 HP.	85 HP.	95 HP.	WHEELBASE
92D	91D	99D	122″

1940 FORD COMMERCIAL AND TRUCK MODELS

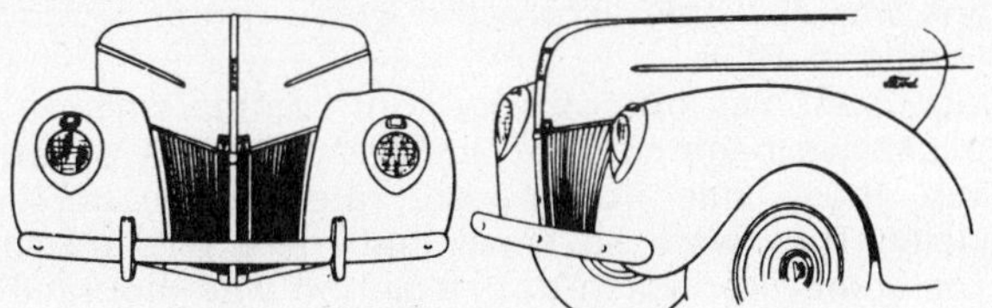

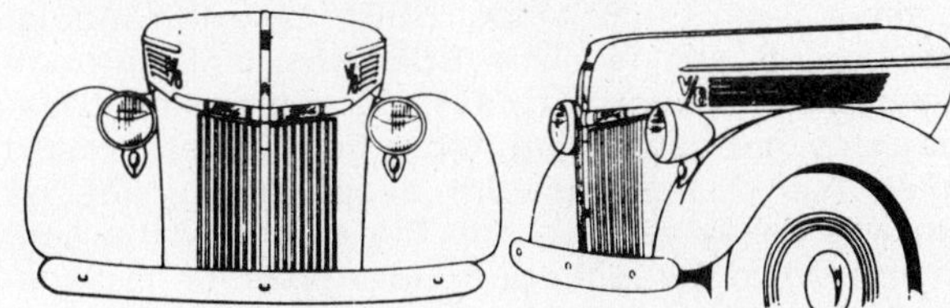

FORD COMMERCIAL				FORD ¾ TON TRUCK			
	MODEL				MODEL		
60 HP.	85 HP.	95 HP.	WHEELBASE	60 HP.	85 HP.	95 HP.	WHEELBASE
02C	01C	09C	112"	02D	01D	09D	122"

The English edition of the 1929 Model AA truck had the typical, square-cut cab of the domestic versions. Earlier wire wheels have given way here to discs which allows rear dual mounting. The curious trailer with a fifth wheel attachment is a low loader, probably for hauling machinery.

One of five styles of dump bodies fitted to the 1930-31 AA 1½-ton chassis. The types were a heavy duty hydraulic unit, light duty hydraulic, mechanical rotating power hoist, gravity dump, and hand hoist. The coal body pictured appears to be the latter with crank just behind cab.

1934, with a 2-ton truck, Model BBE, using the regular 221 cu.-in. V-8 engine. This BBE was built through 1938 and is noteworthy for having a sunroof built into the rather square cab styling. More than driver comfort prompted this pleasant feature because the steering column was nearly vertical, and the only way the light switch rod could be withdrawn for repair or replacement was through the opening in the roof.

Another distinctive British truck was the 7V, a heavy 3-ton model introduced in October 1937. The Model C engine was optional and sold surprisingly well against the big V-8. In 1938 the 2-ton BBE was facelifted to use the same sheetmetal of the 7V, and the trucks were quite similar. Five-lug wheels with 20 x 6.00 tires were used on the 2-ton model, while six lugs were used on the 3-ton truck with 32 x 6.00 tires.

All of the regular American Ford trucks were available in England and were quite similar in specification to the U.S. models, except that the ubiquitous Model C engine was available across the whole range of models beginning in 1938.

Dagenham also offered very light commercials on the 8-hp chassis beginning in October 1932. As a van or pickup, these little trucks were rated at about ¼-ton capacity. They were so small that there was no room for the spare tire, which at one period was mounted on the passenger door, posing some strain for the tiny hinges. In November 1937, the new passenger sheet metal and chassis of the Model Y were incorporated into the revised truck Model 7Y, a design which continued into the postwar period. The little 8-hp car was joined in April 1938, by a semi-forward control truck, built on the 10-hp 1172cc chassis with a load rating of about ½-ton, and called Model E83W. The radiator grille was like the big Dagenham trucks of the period, which in turn was patterned on the 1937 American truck grille.

The 1937 American trucks all began with the number

This 1-ton truck was introduced by Dagenham early in March 1932. An American counterpart was not offered in the Ford line until 1938. The basic truck remained available through 1935, the only year with the V-8 60.

A 1931 AAF 1½-ton truck, the F indicating the smallbore Model A block of 14.9 hp. Heavier tonnage versions were fitted with dual rear wheels. The body is typical of British coach-built units.

A Model AA 6-wheeler would be a rare sight in the U.S. Rear axle arrangement was not a Dagenham product but was built by County Commercial Cars, Ltd. in Fleet, Hampshire.

7, the first step toward a new identification system and one which was finally adopted for the 1938 model year. The light commercials naturally evolved from Model 67 to 77, while the 1½-ton Model 51 became Model 79. The basic sheet metal of the cabs was the same as in 1936, except for a Vee windshield. The grille featured horizontal louvers, and the hood side louvers were again restyled.

Mechanical changes were few; and the light truck utilized and followed passenger chassis development. Cast iron head compression ratios were now back up to 6.12, matching the earlier aluminum head ratios.

The new V-8 60 engine, already in production and used in Dagenham for over a year, was now offered as Model 73 in the ½-ton and Model 75 in the 1½-ton trucks. The torque curve was the flattest yet, with only a 10-lb. variation from 800 right out to 4000 rpm's. Alas, the 90 or so pounds of torque was somewhat inadequate for 1½-ton usage, and after one season the engine was restricted to light commercial duty.

It was a good year for Ford trucks. Again, Chevrolet was beaten in gross commercial sales.

The third and last major body change of the decade appeared in 1938 and in basic form survived for some ten years thereafter. Grille designs were modified, of course, and the initial layout was in the form of a bold oval with horizontal bars. The fenders were heavily rounded, and cab lines were generally softened. Very strong multiple moldings were used under the doors. Interior instrument layout was somewhat like the 1938 passenger car.

CAB-OVER-ENGINE

The Cab-Over-Engine truck appeared in 1938, with semi-elliptics all around, the first breakthrough on Ford suspension, engineered by Dale Roeder. In 1940 the ¾-, 1-ton, and 1½-ton trucks all went over to semi-elliptics at the front. Shortly after this the open-drive Hotchkiss system appeared, reputedly on the urging of, among others, the Armour Co. in Chicago which cited the expensive procedure of clutch replacement with

A Model B with the usual British variation of the raised molding surrounding the hood side louvers, a holdover from Model A design. It is most likely this version was fitted with the BF 14.9 hp, 4-cyl. engine.

The diminutive Model Y "5-hundredweight" light chassis was announced at the White City exhibit in 1932. It had the new 7.96 hp engine.

The 1934 Model BB 1½-ton truck with full-floating rear axle built to U.S. specs. However, the hood design and early-type 1932 grille, and the headlamps distinctly mark this as a Dagenham truck.

torque tube drive in its fleet vehicles.

The 1939 trucks were little changed on the outside but used hydraulic brakes. Also, the 95-hp Mercury engine became optionally available. The 239-cu.-in. engine offered 10% greater torque at 400 fewer revs. It was all to the good for truck purposes.

The 1-ton truck had been introduced in 1938. It was joined in 1939 by a ¾-ton truck, which had much of the passenger car in it (such as the brakes), though a full-floating axle was fitted. Oversize 16-in. tires were used on the ¾-ton truck, and 17-in. wheels with six- and eight-ply tires were offered on the 1-ton truck.

The middle-range trucks were fast, especially when a 4.11 ratio was made optional to the standard 4.857:1. The large wheels and tires used on the ¾- and 1-ton models gave cruising speeds at engine revs little higher than with passenger cars. Clutches were as in the big trucks. Three-speed transmissions were used with a spur low gear and helical second.

For 1940 there were virtually no mechanical changes, apart from the springs. The ½-ton chassis received its first modifications for specific truck use from normal passenger practice, beginning with slightly heavier frame steel. Radiators were beefed up with 450 sq. ins. of frontal area, but capacity fell two quarts to 22 qts. Grilles were changed and picked up styling motifs of the 1939 Deluxe car.

The 1940 Ford trucks had entered into a very stable engineering and styling period, to be revolutionized only in the introduction of a new series in March 1948. The ¾-ton truck would not survive the war, it being too close in specification to the 1-ton model. Commercially, the Ford truck had not displaced Chevrolet, except for the two banner years of 1935 and 1937.

Truck design was more progressive than in the passenger car divisions and frequently led the way in technical innovation. Ford trucks were always strong and tough and lasted well. Their weakness, if it can be called such, was one inherent characteristic of the V-8 engine—it did not seem to possess the pulling capabilities of the 6-cyl. competition. The V-8 seemed to "die" at low revs, and really pushing it suggested rapid wear. Ford trucks always seemed to be working twice as hard as the competition, especially in heavy service. It was in light duty, high-speed service that the V-8 was still the leader, attested by the high survival of the ½-ton pickups to our day.

A variation of the sizeable Model 7V, introduced October 1937 and was rated from 3 to 5 tons with the 85-hp V-8. 7V's were also offered with the 4-cyl. Model C engine, and one wonders how it performed in usage.

This Ford bus photo is dated July 1937 and this particular unit was worked around Dearborn for many years. Ford later produced a handsome city bus which incorporated some of the same ideas.

A Surrey Model AA (the Surreys had one driving rear axle; both were driven on the Sussex). Custom-built on basic Ford chassis with adoption of a second rear axle, this sizable unit was probably the largest body to ever be powered by a 4-cyl. Ford engine.

This is the first Ford Forward Control, or C-O-E, truck. It was announced by Dagenham in October 1934 and was current through 1938. It was normally fitted with the 85 hp V-8. Van-type body was custom-built.

A 1935 1½-ton Model 51 truck, typical of Detroit. The Dagenham plant did not duplicate such a version until 1936 model introduction. The British would rate this truck with dual wheels as a 2-tonner.

The body of this basically Panel Delivery is from a 1937 Model 77 with the Vee'd windshield. The grille and hood side panels are from a 1936 Model 67. Mixed sheetmetal was common in British truck production.

A big 7V Utility Fire Tender from Dagenham, with a body by A.C. Cars of Thames, Ditton. Believe it or not, this whopper was fitted with the 4-cyl. Model C engine. Identity is doors; round corner for V-8's, square for 4's.

Did Ford ever build a 3-wheeler? The answer lies with the Tug, built on the Model Y chassis from October 1935 until the end of 1937. The Ford chassis was ideally suited for 3-wheel adaptation, since the engine load was focused to a single crossmember point. In '37, Tug became a Fordson.

FORD JOINS THE RANKS

Unsuspected at the time of the 1941 Ford's design was that the primary tooling dies would enjoy the longest production run in company history, thanks to World War II. For the first time, the Fords were available in three series of trim.

If the decade of the Thirties was summarized by the 1940 Ford, the 1941 models decisively finished it and set new trends for the Forties. Ford engineers made a mighty effort to produce a new car, at least within Ford's hard-bound parameters of what really constitutes a new car, and which once again would offer Chevrolet a severe challenge. There was, to be sure, a more frightening prospect to spur them. More than even the leading GM badge, was the success of Plymouth in 1940, whose percentage gains for that year, when projected ahead into 1941, would have easily moved Plymouth into second place in the annual sales race.

The 1941 Ford was a brand new car in almost every respect, and the changes it embodied point up both design strengths as well as some of the weaknesses evident during the Thirties. The basic mechanical components of the car were virtually unchanged, a tribute to the rugged V-8 engine, the fine transmission, and the virtually unbreakable torque tube drive layout. All Fords of the Thirties have proven themselves to be superb, tough vehicles under the most arduous conditions, and this is the heritage of Ford products. Entering the Forties with the largest Ford yet and heralding styling that would stand virtually pat through the 1948 model year, the 1941's came in body styles largely carried over from 1940 but now were available in three separate trim lines: Super Deluxe, Deluxe and Special. One new body configuration, available only as a Super Deluxe, was the Sedan-Coupe.

The Ford was enlarged considerably in almost every dimension over the 1940 versions; wheelbase was up to 114 ins., and a much stronger frame mounted a body of expanded size. Average car weights were up some 300 lbs. Interior dimensions were greatly extended, and with the body now virtually overlapping the runningboards—which were revealed now by only a thin rubber strip—the front seat, for example, was 7 ins. wider than the previous year's. Fords now competed dimensionally with its chief competitors; Chevrolet and Plymouth.

Ford engineers worked hard at further refinements of silence, ride and interior comfort. The last efforts at civilizing the transverse springs were taken. They were lengthened, were set farther apart on a springbase now up to 125 ins., were softened with a lower 175-lb. deflection rate, and were mounted on shackles with an outward angle. Shock absorbers were softened. Body mountings were improved in order to reduce the transfer of road noise and to reduce body-wracking.

The end result was a car with a new solid feel, greater insulation from road noise, and the familiar Ford mechanical sounds hardly evident. It was a car much more like its principal competitors, but in the process it lost many of the characteristics of the Ford in the Thirties. As an example, the transmission ratios were changed to accommodate the new weight. Ford advertising proudly proclaimed: "New transmission ratios give faster getaway through first and second." In truth, the 1941 transmission simply used the ratios of the 1940 60 hp which gave a second gear of 1.773:1 and a low of 3.114:1, which had formerly been 1.604 and 2.82 respectively. Thus, the new Ford lost some of its superb high-speed capacity in second and low gear. But Plymouth and Chevrolet owners could now feel more at home in the Ford.

The 60-hp engine had not been a success in American use and perhaps it was prophetic that the engine was initially used in Europe where smaller cars and differing road conditions were more suited to its size. Though the 60 continued in production long after World War II on the Continent, the engine was phased out in Detroit in 1940. It was replaced by the little 4-cyl. Model N of 119.5 cu. ins. with an initial 30 hp for 1941. The new Four owed nothing to the Model B or C and was an altogether modern engine designed for stop-and-go delivery use. Despite its 30-hp rating, the Model N had a power and torque output remarkably similar to the 60-hp V-8 in the 500-to-1000 rev range which revealed at once the weakness of the 60 in commerical use. The Model N in truck use was short-lived, a 40-hp version for 1942 being the last offered.

The 1941 Ford was stronger in almost every way than its predecessor and sold well, despite Ford's greatest labor turmoils in years, culminating in a strike on April 1, 1941 which lasted two weeks. Ford dealers in 1941 were more often in short supply than at any other time in the previous decade. The growing war in Europe stimulated the American economy and farsighted people bought new cars.

The Ford faced even stronger competition from Chevrolet, whose 1941 car rightly deserves a central pedestal in the Chevrolet hall of fame. A total of 928,477 of them were built and they easily established Chevrolet's quality image through the rest of the dec-

Mr. Ford was an advocate of plastic materials, notably the soy-bean derivative, for its wide-spread use would be of economic value to farmers. Here he shows off the inherent strength of the soy bean-based synthetic on the deck lid of his personal sedan.

The 1941 Ford was by far the largest offered so far, and the Convertible was a favorite. Wheelbase was up to 114 ins., springbase to 125 ins. and interior widths were increased by as much as 7 ins. over the 1940 versions. A 6-cyl. inline engine arrived in 1941, the first in 35 years.

ade. Plymouth also sold well in that fateful boom year before the war.

When the final figures were in, Ford's passenger car production of 600,814 was only about 75,000 ahead of Plymouth. It was a near thing.

Though the 1941 Ford marks the turning point of the company into the new decade and was rightly described by the dealers as a revolutionary car, it has never enjoyed the esteem of collectors when compared to, say, its immediate predecessor of 1940. This is because the engineers designed a car for 1941 which would have more appeal to the central target of the market where Chevrolet reigned supreme. In doing so, the individuality of the Ford car was muted, as would be the case again in the next revolution of mid-1948. The conservatism of the Fords in the Thirties—which today are revered—nevertheless gave, by 1940, an embarrassment to some Ford designers and engineers. A critique of the decade's work may be seen in the 1941 Ford, with its bigger body.

The Fords of the Thirties were fun to drive. They were fast. Factory test data reported 74 mph for the 1932, increased to 84 mph in 1934. Top speed for the rest of the decade was about 86 mph. The ability of the Ford to sustain high speeds was due to full pressure lubrication, an advantage that Chevrolet was not able

Mercury paralleled the physical growth of the Ford; length, width and interior dimensions were up by large percentages. This is the bold frontal styling for the 1942 model year.

Plymouth made strong advances for 1941 and came out with perhaps its best lineup so far. Good looking, comfortable to drive and reasonably peppy, it set its own styling theme with which it would long dwell.

Mercury reflected new thinking, along with the rest of the industry, and had advanced far in its short lifetime. Like Ford, body weights had risen by nearly 300 lbs. for 1941, which improved ride and comfort. Tooling for both Ford and Mercury was now largely consolidated, and bodies were shared.

to match. Ford's light weight and the high-revving V-8 engine gave acceleration figures through the gears that were unbeatable by Chevrolet or Plymouth. The quick steering, especially before 1934, made the Ford controllable and responsive, and the much maligned transverse springs at least provided a taut ride.

The Ford was a car of personality and despite its anachronisms had a youthful image. The multiplicity of convertible types perhaps was part of that image but the sheer speed of the car was undoubtedly the most important factor. And one must not forget that in the Thirties, the personality of Mr. Ford was still very evident in the product. The Chevrolet loudly proclaimed corporate identity and even the Plymouth could really only echo the engineering of Walter P. Chrysler's senior cars. But a Ford was a Ford and was defiantly different. Perhaps this is why loyalty to the marque was of a high intensity in the Thirties; why today Ford enthusiasts are legion.

Material shortages caused by the war prevented the automobile industry's use of chrome-plated trim just prior to the entire industry shutdown. This unrestored 1942 Chevrolet is a rare survivor today.

Ford extensively reworked the 1941 front end for the 1942 model year, but the car's design was unchanged from the cowl back. The war halted production for Ford on Feb. 10, 1942, making '42's rare today.

It is the general opinion of car enthusiasts today, be they Chevrolet buffs or not, that the 1941 Chevy was far and away the very best model of this GM Division. Photo was made at a Vintage Chevrolet Club of America gathering where a record 24 restored Chevrolets vied for judging honors.

A MAN WHO WAS THERE

Looking Back with Emil Zoerlein

EDITOR'S NOTE: Emil Zoerlein worked in top-level Ford engineering from 1926 to 1959. Few men lasted as long with the company. Fewer still were in a direct working relationship with Henry Ford. Zoerlein was such a man.

Mr. Ford did not believe in job titles. Once, during the Thirties, he remarked, as he politely doffed the gray hat that he often wore, "The company's board of directors and the chariman of the board are right here, under this hat." To understand Zoerlein's words, as they relate to Ford in the Thirties, it is therefore imperative to realize two things: first, the temper of the times, and second, Mr. Ford, the man, because his memory obviously embodies Zoerlein's affection, and hence suggests the interviewer's impressions, be they repeated or not in earlier discussions. Enough can never be said, or learned, about those resolutions of history that were made more turbulent by the breaking storm of the Forties.

Mr. Ford would prove that he was a visionary, and a mass-production genius. To his recalcitrant soul, such words as "outmoded," "obsolete," or "uncomfortable," were tantamount to flashing a red cape before a bull. He had showed the nation its way, but he had never promised to take them anywhere, save in his Model T.

The Thirties would place the Ford Motor Co. on trial before its own success. Throughout all of this, Emil Zoerlein would gain a reputation as a man "who did the job right."

Emil Zoerlein, 70'ish, stocky, balding, yet fit; humble, yet proud and exacting, nevertheless spoke with admiration of the man he once knew—the man he called simply, "Mr. Ford." As he would say:

"Oh, I didn't call him, Henry. I called him Mr. Ford." Zoerlein would laugh, really more of a chuckle, because it was a good joke. You could sense it was something the two of them had shared; a sense of humor about it. But Zoerlein, good engineer that he was, also got quickly to a very big part of the man he called, "Mr. Ford."

"Mr. Ford had many, many ideas in his head, and was way ahead of the then-existing industry. He was very practical.

"The only shortcoming—I should say limitation—was that he wouldn't bring it out. And there were very few people that he would want to talk to. He abhored to talk with people who used three dollar-and-a-half words, and things of that sort. He wanted plain language, period.

"In many cases he would sit down and talk to you about something that he wanted, or that he would want—something that he had up in his head, and he would talk about it.

"He wouldn't come directly to the point. Then it was up to you to find out what he was really after. You started out going in one direction. And when you found that you were going in the right direction, fine. *If you didn't* go in the right direction, you found roadblocks in your way, here and there. You would have to have little things made up in shops, and so on. He was trying to feel you out. I think he wanted to teach you how his mind worked, and to teach you to be alert. He was a magnificent teacher. . . He taught me a lot."

Naturally, at this point, one wanted to know more about the mystical friendship that the two men clearly shared. One wondered about Zoerlein's beginnings with the giant manufacturing company. How had he done what most mortals had failed to do? How had he become a friend to Henry Ford?

"I am a German immigrant. I learned my trade there. The automobile is my trade." (He had served a four-year apprenticeship, studying mechanical and electrical engineering in Germany, and came to the United States in 1923.)

"I came to Detroit from New York in 1926. I had read a lot about Mr. Ford when I was a kid. . .and what he was doing and everything, so I wanted to get into Ford—period."

He and his young wife arrived in Detroit, and Zoerlein went to the Ford employment office, looking for a job.

"They said, 'We're down for inventory.' I was about 21 years old at the time. This was in February, and they said they would open up again in June. But I had to have a job, so I got a job with the Cadillac Motor Company, there in Detroit. In June, I was anxious to get out there, to Ford. There was a long line of people out there waiting, and I thought I'd get in line, too.

"My turn came to go in, and they interviewed me, and wondered what my capabilities were, and what my background was, and so forth. So naturally I said that I wanted to get into engineering at Dearborn.

"They looked at me in amazement. 'Why that's impossible!' (Zoerlein laughed a little, in his particular chuckle, at the thought of it.)

"So anyway, he said, 'We have openings for tool and die makers. Have any experience?' I said, sure. . .I spent four years of apprenticeship, plus college afterwards. So I took a job as a tool maker.

"They stuck me in a brand-new tool room, which was *beautiful*—beautiful machinery—as nice as I had ever seen before. I was there for awhile. Naturally, I was still digging away to get up to Dearborn. I had heard more about the engineering department, then, as time went on.

"I approached the superintendent of the tool room and asked if there was a possibility to be transferred to Dearborn. He looked at me in amazement. . .and his eyeballs practically fell out. 'What the! . . . *You want to get up to Dearborn?'*

"So I kept digging, and I approached the foreman who was under the superintendent. The foreman asked if I knew anybody up there. 'There's no chance to get up there if you don't know anybody,' he said. But then the foreman was transferred somewhere else, and I had a new one, by the name of Leslie Lowe, and I asked him. He said, 'Boy, you're biting off a big hunk!'. . . we got along very well . . . but he gave me a note to take down to the employment office. 'See what happens,' he told me. 'They occasionally borrow people from the Rouge Plant for Dearborn, when they get especially pushed for work. They take them up there and return them when the work is finished.'

"And he said, 'Maybe you can get a chance to get up there on a loan basis, and maybe you could get yourself known.' I took a note to the employment office, and I thought that the note would end in the rotary file, and that would be it.

"Well, lo and behold, a week later somebody came in the back door and said, 'Where's number 772?' That was my badge number. Each employee was assigned a badge. You weren't known by name, only by badge number. So I answered, Here! The man said, 'Pack your tool box and get up to Dearborn tomorrow.' I got up to Dearborn and was put into a sheetmetal shop, which I abhored . . . hated. Finally, I was connected with the designer—and the chief pilot, Harry Brooks, on the Flivver Ship." (The Flivver Ship was an airplane, a small, single-seat, low-wing monoplane that Mr. Ford was manufacturing on an experimental basis, until Brooks was killed during an extreme airborne test maneuver.)

"One day I was standing at my bench . . . using my file . . . making an instrument panel for the Flivver Ship.

"All of a sudden, somebody poked me in the ribs. It was Henry Ford! Mr. Ford, himself. It was the first time I had seen him within talking distance!

"I gulped. The first thing he said was: 'Where did you learn to file?' And I told him. 'Where did you come from?' I told him. 'What education have you had?' . . . 'What's your background?' He was not gruff, but friendly and to the point.

"I told him what my educational background was . . . and that didn't hold much water—the reason for which I found out later on. He said, 'Well, you're in the wrong place here, aren't you?' I said yes—and I tried to pull all my nerves together. I said I had been trying to do engineering from the Rouge plant . . . and I was told that I had to know somebody up here.

"Henry Ford said, 'Well, you know somebody now.'

And he turned around to walk away, calling over his shoulder, 'I'll see you tomorrow.' I watched him walk away.

"The next morning he came back. He had a job that he wanted me to do for him. It concerned a couple of models that were steam engines, broken down, and what have you. There were a number of people around who did that kind of work. This was just a test piece.

"So from then on, he stopped by—practically every day . . . and talked with me . . . and followed through, the work I did for him."

But then it was 1930. The decade had begun. The great wheels of Ford had begun slowing, with the phase-out of the Model A. To those who were in the middle of it, there was no time to analyze, only to perform. But something was up, something very secret.

"In 1930, Mr. Ford asked me to go over to Greenfield Village, to Edison's Fort Myers Machine Shop . . . Mr. Ford cautioned me, 'Whatever you see there, is absolutely secret. Don't tell anybody, not even Edsel.'

"When we first started out with the V-8 engine, there were two other people. And we three worked together. And I was elected to develop the ignition system. I was the dirty guy who put the ignition system where it was then." (Zoerlein laughed again.)

The interviewer absent-mindedly interrupted at this point, in order to clarify Zoerlein's title during the Thirties; something that for all practical purposes he already knew. Zoerlein answered in what may have been a characteristic answer—coming from Mr. Ford.

"During the Thirties, I didn't have a title. Nobody did. I just had the responsibility to work. That's what I did. When I retired, in 1959, things were all changed around. My title then was Manager of Engine Experimental Fabricating Department." (Zoerlein was then asked to return to the Thirties, and more specifically to this book, *Ford in the Thirties*.)

"In that building was developed the first V-8 engine having a monocast cylinder block. It was absolutely secret—all the way through. Not even Edsel Ford knew about it."

Henry Ford and Emil Zoerlein in December 1937.

Now, some of the questions became more pointed—and Zoerlein would answer, as the pattern of questions drifted from subject to subject.

Why were the exhaust passages run through the block?

"To Mr. Ford, there was a purpose behind running the exhaust passages through the block. When temperatures get down to zero and subzero, it's nice to get a warm engine—right quick. If you passed the exhaust ports through the water jacket, and then on, you got a quick warm-up.

"Mr. Ford also lived in Detroit, and in Detroit, the winters are cold . . . But Mr. Ford tried to get out of this overheating business by adding more radiator capacity, and more water flow through the block in order to get rid of the heat. He solved the problem after 1937, by putting the water pump in the cylinder block, which forced the water through the block, rather than sucking it through. Mr. Ford put the water pumps on the top of the block, initially, because it was the simplest way to do it.

"On the subject of thermostats . . . the reason they were not put in the V-8 before they were, was that they were not reliable. With the water pumps on the top of the block, the thermostats were rather difficult to control. With the water pumps on the top you're causing a partial vacuum . . . so your boiling point would be lower."

What was Mr. Ford's philosophy on the axles he used?

"Mr. Ford used quality steel for his axles, and he added an unusual safety factor. Let's say that you needed a one-inch diameter shaft, kikolated with let's say a 25 or a 50 percent safety factor. He said, 'Now double that! And make it an inch and a quarter, instead of one inch.' He definitely spent more money on axle manufacture than the competition."

Why did Mr. Ford stay with transverse springs? Was he trying to save money on manufacturing his product?

"It wasn't to save money. He absolutely did not go in for saving money on the product . . . Mr. Ford started out with the buggy springs, and he thought transverse springs were the best. Actually, when you look at the geometry, and the spring mount perches, you load diagonally down to the wheel—if they're arranged properly . . . You go directly from the body—from the top weight down to the wheel—to the tire. And you get less roll than you would get with four springs, *providing* that there are other things that enter into it on the four spring arrangement."

Why did Mr. Ford fire the whole engineering staff following the 1933 Briggs strike?

"Nobody was fired. We just closed up shop, because the banks were all closed. He didn't have any money. And he always had insisted that everybody be paid in cash. No checks. I didn't know the reason why he paid everybody in cash. It may have gone back to the days when he worked for someone else, and he was paid in cash, I don't know. There was never a time when he fired the whole engineering staff. I imagine he was capable of it — and other things similar . . . and I have heard of several . . . but to my knowledge, I know of just one other time when he did something like that, and I would not like to mention it.

"He wasn't that cruel. He was very much a humanitarian—*if you watched what he was striking out for.*

"But this thing about firing the whole engineering department—let's clarify it! You remember that there was a Depression in those days. Not only in Detroit, but in New York . . . and everyplace. The banks were closed. And, he didn't have any money to pay the people. So we were just strictly sent home—period.

"I was called back two days later—along with someone who worked with me there. We were there in this great big engineering department—all by ourselves.

"Mr. Ford was very much disturbed, too. And he talked to us, and said, 'Now you find something to do, here. And I'll see you from day to day' . . . and he was *MAD,* too . . . because all his money was tied up."

There were a lot of rumors that he had hidden a rather large amount of cash at his estate, and that nobody knew where it was.

"I knew where it was. It wasn't at his estate. It was in my office . . . I don't know how much . . . I just recall when it was removed.

"In my department was a conference table. There were chairs around it, and next to it, there were two safes . . . which we had bought. They were equipped with the latest safety locks and what have you. There were no guards there . . . I was there . . . (Zoerlein laughed). Of course, I wasn't there 24 hours around the clock. Nobody knew the money was there."

What are your thoughts, as you remember that the first Ford V-8 60 had huge mains of very narrow width?

"I don't know where that information came from. The first 60 had conventional main bearings. What someone must have been talking about was the 5-cylinder engine, where we had 5-inch diameter main bearings. . .But the 60 didn't have big main bearings. It had the conventional size main bearings, proportioned with the engine.

"Someone is confusing the 60 with the 5-cylinder engine in which Mr. Ford was very interested. A lot of time was spent on it. *They* had large main bearings . . . only the main bearings were large enough so that you could take the whole crankshaft and push it in from the rear. You had no caps on it. It was one piece, with the liners in it. And you could take that whole crankshaft and shove it in from the rear. I don't want to be accused here of making these statements which are not true."

In the late Thirties, why were the noticeable frustrations of the engineers something that could be hardly imagined?

"I wouldn't call it a noticeable frustration. For example, Mr. Ford was very well prepared to put a vertical distributor on, because I had models sitting all around . . . various versions. And he was all set to go . . . to take the distributor away from the front-end mounting. The front-end mounted distributor was built and mounted for a specific performance—to last for 50,000 miles, no less. But gradually, that concept lost favor, and they did everything possible to move the fan back, so finally we had to design a distributor that was only about 2½ inches long. And it had its shortcomings. We knew it.

"I personally told Mr. Sorensen about it. He was the one who pushed the fan back. And he said, 'Never mind — you let us worry about it' . . . and I felt right then that the distributor was going to be pushed off the front, so I started making models of vertically mounted distributors . . . and Mr. Ford was well aware of what was going on. (Zoerlein said that things never fell like bombshells to those engineers who had taken the foresight to be prepared.)

"Regarding the vertical distributor, it wasn't a bombshell when the decision was made. We were ready for it."

How many people complained of the severe struggling that preceded the introduction of the 1937 Ford?

"That is an exaggeration. The way it sounds is that everybody in the company from 1930 on up to the reorganization were a bunch of dumbbells. Somebody had to build this company . . . and make the money to continue building and selling dependable cars!

"There were no agonies . . . other than general

engineering problems that crop up anyplace—whether you design a washing machine or what have you. Mr. Ford always liked to say, 'If it works the first time, forget it. It's no good.'

"You have to go through pains. Analyze it. If it works the first time, it must be so darn silly, that you don't have to work hard on it. But any complicated piece of machinery. . .if it works the first time, watch out."

How did Mr. Ford decide to go ahead with hydraulic brakes?

"Well, here's what happened on that. Edsel Ford was much interested in hydraulic brakes . . . and Martin . . . and some other people. The usual procedure was that if we wanted to put something through, to get it built up . . . in that case we built up three or four chassis—some with hydraulic brakes, some with mechanical brakes—and we set them on the engineering department's floor, which was made of polished oak. And that particular section was right in front of my office.

"Mr. Edsel Ford had said to me, 'We're going to send up some chassis and set them up here. Maybe you can get there to look at them, and help us a bit.'

"So, they were sitting there, and he (Mr. Ford) walked by—because he came by my department practically every day when he was around—and one day he came around and asked me, 'What are those chassis out there for?' And I said, 'Oh yeah—we had some chassis built up, some mechanical brakes with several variations . . . and there's one out there with hydraulic brakes.' *'Hydraulic brakes?'* There was a long pause. And he looked at it . . . and didn't say much about it . . . and walked away. And that was the first breakthrough.

"The fact that he didn't *say* anything was an indication that he had softened up to the hydraulic brakes. I told Mr. Edsel Ford that he was there looking at it, and I think that the two of them got together, plus Sorensen, and Sheldrick, and the rest of the boys.

"Maybe Mr. Ford had had a bit of a phobia, in that he had wanted a direct connection between the pedal and the brake shoes. He didn't trust certain tendencies of the oil . . . leaking wheel cylinders, things of that nature.

"With his cable brakes, it wasn't the cable that caused the difficulties. It was a matter of metallurgy . . . the brake shoe material and the drum. There was an awful lot of work that went on in order to get the right drum material. Mr. Ford was one of the few who had pioneered the non-squeaking brake."

Do you feel that the flathead Ford V-8 was as good as anything on the market, for the price? And do you think that the passenger car bodies were as good or better than the competition?

"The V-8—yes! . . . in those days! Let's differentiate between what we knew then, and what we knew later on . . . what we learned.

"On the bodies—wind tunnel tests showed that Fords were as good or better than the competition. Not only that—but besides that—the amount of money that was expended every year for these annual changes is tremendous. On the one side there would be dipping sales . . . and on the other side, we would be coming along with new developments. He probably had reasons for what he did."

Have you had any sensitivity to reporters or authors in the past?

"Well, once Mr. Ford was putting on a show. There were antique cars down there, along with a duplicate of his first shop—which was built in the place. And along with the other cars there was a 2-cylinder steam car which was built in Lowell, Massachusetts . . . I don't know the name of the man who built it.

"I was there at the time, as a representative of the Ford Motor Company, and, these newspaper reporters came around and they asked various questions about the cars . . . and we came up to this particular steam car.

"One fella said . . . no, it was a girl . . . and she asked, 'Which is Mr. Ford's favorite car?' And I said, 'His favorite car is inside this building'—we had the original car in there. I was standing in front of the steamer when I answered.

"Out comes a newspaper the next day or so . . . and it read, 'Mr. Ford's favorite car is a steam car, built in Massachusetts', and so on.

"I got a telephone call from Mr. Ford's secretary, and she said, *'What are you telling those people down there?'*

"So there I was, in a mess!"

Can you remember any particular humorous thing that may have happened, during the Thirties?

"Well, there were many things. One that comes to mind concerns my laboratories, which consisted of three rooms, the last room being next to Mr. Ford's office. Naturally, in our laboratories, we had optical equipment, electronic equipment, mechanical equipment, and the whole thing.

"The last room on this side of the laboratory was the dance floor, where the children from Greenfield Village had their dancing lessons, and where Mr. Ford and certain selected people would come to have their weekly dance.

"Therefore, there was an orchestra, in most cases consisting of three people. My activity was right next to it. The ceilings were open, of course, and we could hear them plunking away, all day long. We might be tearing our hair out with some particular problem, and they would be striking up with some old-fashioned melody, or what have you.

"One time, Mr. Ford came in . . . in the middle of particularly hard problem. And I think he was aware of it.

"So Mr. Ford said, 'Come on down to the dance floor, and listen to Billy and the Boys play.'

"We went down there . . . and he had them strike up a waltz. Then he said to me, 'Now you show me how you can waltz.'

"Well, you can readily see how I felt . . . like a monkey on a stick. But, anyway, I joked around, and I didn't do it right, so he showed me how to waltz. Mr. Ford showed me how to waltz.

"There were just the two of us there . . . and the old-time orchestra."

1930 MODEL A

BODY TYPE	LIST PRICE	CURB WT. (lbs.)
Roadster	$ 435	2155
Roadster*	460	2230
Phaeton	440	2212
Standard Coupe	495	2257
Sports Coupe*	525	2283
Cabriolet*	625	2273
Tudor Sedan	495	2375
Fordor Sedan	600	2441
Town Sedan	660	2475
Town Car	1200	2525
Standard Sedan	600	2462
Roadster Deluxe*	520	2230
Phaeton Deluxe	625	2285
Coupe Deluxe	545	2265
Victoria	625	2265
Sedan Deluxe	640	2488
Station Wagon	695	NA

*with rumble seat

1930 MODEL A PRODUCTION FIGURES BY BODY STYLE

Phaeton....39,886
Deluxe Phaeton....4,365
Roadster....122,703
Deluxe Roadster....11,629
Standard Coupe....232,564
Sport Coupe....72,572
Business Coupe....110
Deluxe Coupe....29,777
Victoria Coupe....6,447
Tudor Sedan....425,144
Standard Fordor Sedan....53,958
Deluxe Fordor Sedan....13,710
Cabriolet....29,226
Sedan, 2-window....7,838
Town Sedan....122,534
Town Car....96
Taxi Cab....273
Station Wagon....3,799

1930 COLOR AVAILABILITY

Upper and lower body colors were available in varying combinations.

Upper Body	Code No.	Lower Body	Code No.
Chicle Drab	IM-91	Copra Drab	IM-440
Kewanee Green	IM-546	Elk Point Green	IM-543
Black	NA	Andalusite Blue	IM-121
Thorne Brown	IM-283	Thorne Brown	IM-283
Andalusite Blue	IM-121	Andalusite Blue	IM-121
Seal Brown	IM-118	Bronson Yellow	IM-545
Moleskin Brown Light	IM-544	Moleskin Brown Light	IM-544
		Ford Maroon	IM-1011

Body colors were pyroxylin lacquer.
All Model A fenders and valance panels were of black dipping enamel.

1931 MODEL A

BODY TYPE	LIST PRICE	CURB WT. (lbs.)
Roadster	$ 430	2155
Roadster*	455	2230
Phaeton	435	2212
Standard Coupe	490	2257
Sports Coupe*	500	2283
Cabriolet*	595	2273
Tudor Sedan	490	2467
Town Sedan	630	2475
Standard Sedan	590	2462
Roadster Deluxe*	475	2230
Phaeton Deluxe	580	2285
Coupe Deluxe	525	2265
Victoria	580	2372
Tudor Sedan Deluxe	525	2467
Sedan Deluxe	630	2488
Town Sedan Deluxe	630	2475
Convertible Sedan	640	NA
Station Wagon	625	NA

*with rumble seat

1931 MODEL A PRODUCTION FIGURES BY BODY STYLE

Phaeton....11,060
Deluxe Phaeton....2,875
Roadster....7,793
Deluxe Roadster....56,702
Standard Coupe....82,885
Sport Coupe....21,272
Deluxe Coupe....23,653
Victoria Coupe....36,830
Tudor Sedan....170,645
Deluxe Tudor Sedan....23,490
Standard Fordor Sedan....25,720
Deluxe Fordor Sedan....4,967
Cabriolet....13,706
Convertible Sedan....5,072
Town Sedan....65,447
Taxicab....7
Station Wagon....3,018

SPECIFICATIONS

1932 MODELS B AND 18

BODY TYPE	MODEL B (4-cyl.) LIST PRICE	MODEL B (4-cyl.) CURB WT. (lbs.)	MODEL 18 (V-8) LIST PRICE	MODEL 18 (V-8) CURB WT. (lbs.)
Roadster	$ 410	2095	$ 460	2203
Deluxe Roadster*	450	2150	500	2258
Phaeton	445	2185	495	2291
Deluxe Phaeton	495	2192	545	2300
Coupe	440	2220	490	2328
Sport Coupe*	485	2248	535	2356
Deluxe Coupe	525	2364	575	2423
Cabriolet*	560	2278	610	2386
Victoria Coupe	550	2310	600	2418
Tudor	450	2315	500	2423
Deluxe Tudor	500	2336	550	2444
Fordor	540	2462	590	2570
Deluxe Fordor	595	2460	645	2568
Convertible Sedan	600	2335	650	2443
Standard Coupe*	NA	NA	515	2370
Deluxe Coupe*	NA	NA	575	2423
Station Wagon	NA	NA	600	NA

*with rumble seat

MODELS B AND 18 PRODUCTION FIGURES BY BODY STYLE

Cabriolet	7,063
Convertible Sedan	1,142
Coupe	54,597
Fordor Sedan	36,649
Phaeton	2,705
Roadster	8,996
Station Wagon	334
Tudor Sedan	90,568
Victoria	8,870

1932 COLOR AVAILABILITY

Bodies	Code No.	Moldings	Code No.	Stripes
Ford Medium Maroon	M-1248	Black	NA	Gold
Brewster Green Medium	M-1017	Brewster Green Light	M-1247	Silver
Tunis Gray	NA	Old Chester Gray	M-1027	Tacoma Cream
Old Chester Gray	M-1027	Tunis Gray	NA	Tacoma Cream
Washington Blue	M-1246	Black	NA	Tacoma Cream
Brewster Green	NA	Brewster Green Medium	M-1017	Silver
		Brewster Green Light	NA	
Winterleaf Brown	NA	Winterleaf Brown Dark	NA	Tacoma Cream

1931 COLOR AVAILABILITY

Upper and lower body colors were available in varying combinations.

Upper Body	Code No.	Lower Body	Code No.
Black	NA	Lombard Blue	IM-1009
Thorne Brown	IM-283	Thorne Brown	IM-283
Elk Point Green	IM-543	Kewanee Green	IM-546
Copra Drab	IM-440	Chicle Drab	IM-91
Seal Brown	IM-118	Bronson Yellow	IM-545
Lombard Blue	IM-1009	Lombard Blue	IM-1009
Moleskin Brown	IM-544	Moleskin Brown	IM-544
Commercial Cars			
Blue Rock Green	IM-1012	Blue Rock Green	IM-1012
Molding Colors		Brewster Green Medium	IM-1017
Stone Deep Gray	IM-1015	Ford Maroon	IM-1011
Riviera Blue	IM-1013	Stone Brown	IM-1016
Elk Point Green	IM-543	Washington Blue Medium	IM-1014
Copra Drab	IM-440	Lombard Blue	IM-1009
		Kewanee Green	IM-546

Body colors were pyroxylin lacquer.
All Model A fenders and valance panels were of black dipping enamel.

FORD MODEL SPECIFICATIONS

1933 MODELS 46 AND 40

BODY TYPE	MODEL 46 (4-cyl.) LIST PRICE	MODEL 46 (4-cyl.) CURB WT. (lbs.)	MODEL 40 (V-8) LIST PRICE	MODEL 40 (V-8) CURB WT. (lbs.)
Roadster	$ 425	2183	$ 475	2337
Roadster*	450	2268	500	2422
Deluxe Roadster*	460	2278	510	2461
Phaeton	445	2281	495	2520
Deluxe Phaeton	495	2290	545	2529
Coupe	440	2335	490	2534
Deluxe Coupe	490	2299	540	2538
Coupe*	465	2384	515	2534
Deluxe Coupe*	515	2299	565	2538
Standard Coupe, 5-Window*	465	2335	NA	NA
Deluxe Coupe, 5-Window*	515	2384	NA	NA
Cabriolet*	535	2306	585	2545
Victoria	545	2356	595	2595
Tudor Sedan	450	2503	500	2621
Deluxe Tudor	500	2520	550	2625
Standard Fordor	510	2550	560	2675
Deluxe Fordor	560	2590	610	2684
Station Wagon	NA	NA	640	NA

*with rumble seat

1933 MODEL 40 AND 1934 MODEL 40A COMBINED PRODUCTION FIGURES BY BODY STYLE

(Totals of Standards and Deluxes where appropriate.)

Cabriolet..........24,299
Coupe, 5-window..........120,735
Fordor Sedan..........220,225
Phaeton..........8,365
Roadster..........11,187
Sedan Delivery..........11,741
Station Wagon..........4,562
Coupe, 3-window..........52,111
Tudor Sedan..........426,389
Victoria..........26,552

1933 COLOR AVAILABILITY

Bodies	Code No.	Stripes	Code No.	Deluxe Wheels
Black	--	Vermilion	M-1722	Aurora Red
Brewster Green Med.	M-1017	French Gray	NA	NA
Old Chester Gray	M-1027	Tacoma Cream	M-1224	Cream
Emperor Brown Med.	M-1295	Tacoma Cream	M-1224	NA
Duncan Blue	M-1296	French Gray	NA	NA
Coach Maroon Medium	NA	Vermilion	M-1722	Aurora Red

Black enamel was used for fenders and wheels.
Body colors were Pyroxylin Lacquer.

1935 MODEL 48

BODY TYPE	LIST PRICE	CURB WT. (lbs.)
Coupe, 5-Window	$ 495	2620
Tudor Sedan	510	2717
Fordor Sedan	575	2760
Deluxe Roadster*	550	2597
Deluxe Phaeton	580	2667
Deluxe Coupe, 3-Window	570	2647
Deluxe Coupe, 3-Window*	595	NA
Deluxe Coupe, 5-Window	560	2643
Deluxe Coupe, 5-Window*	585	NA
Deluxe Cabriolet*	625	2687
Deluxe Tudor Sedan	575	2737
Deluxe Tudor Touring Sedan	595	2772
Deluxe Fordor Sedan	635	2767
Deluxe Fordor Touring Sedan	655	2787
Deluxe Fordor Convertible Sedan	750	2827
Station Wagon	670	NA

*with rumble seat

MODEL 48 PRODUCTION FIGURES BY BODY STYLE

(Totals of Standards and Deluxes where appropriate.)

Cabriolet..........17,000
Convertible Sedan..........4,234
Coupe, 5-window..........111,542
Fordor Sedan..........124,984
Fordor Touring Sedan..........105,157
Phaeton..........6,073
Roadster..........4,896
Sedan Delivery..........8,308
Station Wagon..........4,536
Coupe, 3-window..........31,513
Tudor Sedan..........322,575
Tudor Touring Sedan..........87,326
Victoria..........235

1934 MODEL 40A

BODY TYPE	LIST PRICE	CURB WT. (lbs.)
Deluxe Roadster*	$ 525	2461
Deluxe Phaeton	550	2529
Coupe, 5-Window	505	2534
Coupe, 5-Window*	530	2582
Deluxe Coupe, 3-Window	545	2538
Deluxe Coupe, 3-Window*	570	2538
Cabriolet*	590	2545
Victoria	600	2595
Tudor Sedan	520	2621
Deluxe Tudor	560	2625
Fordor Sedan	575	2675
Deluxe Fordor	615	2684
Station Wagon	660	NA

*with rumble seat

1934 COLOR AVAILABILITY

Standard Bodies	Code No.	Wheels	Stripes	Code No.	Fenders
Black	--	Black	Tacoma Cream	M-1224	Black
Dearborn Blue	M-1723	Black	Tacoma Cream	M-1224	Black
Cordoba Gray	M-1730	Black	Tacoma Cream	M-1224	Cordoba Gray
Vineyard Green	M-1731	Black	French Gray	--	Vineyard Green
Deluxe 3-window Coupe and Fordor Bodies					
Black	--	Tacoma Cream	Tacoma Cream	M-1224	Black
Dearborn Blue	M-1723	Tacoma Cream	Tacoma Cream	M-1224	Dearborn Blue
Cordoba Gray	M-1730	Cordoba Gray	Tacoma Cream	M-1224	Cordoba Gray
Vineyard Green	M-1731	Apple Green	Apple Green	M-1225	Vineyard Green
Roadster, Phaeton, 5-window Coupe, Tudor Bodies					
Black	--	Tacoma Cream	Tacoma Cream	M-1224	Black
Cordoba Gray	M-1730	Cordoba Gray	Straw	--	Cordoba Gray
Vineyard Green	M-1731	Vineyard Green	Silver	--	Vineyard Green
Coach Maroon	--	Black	English Coach Vermilion	--	Coach Maroon
Commercial Bodies					
Vermilion	M-1722	Medium Cream	none	--	Medium Cream
Emperor Brown Medium	M-1295	Ford Medium Maroon	none	--	Ford Medium Maroon

1935 COLOR AVAILABILITY

Pass. Bodies	Code No.	Stripes	Wheels
Black	——	Apple Green	Apple Green
Cordoba Gray	M-173OA	Poppy Red	Poppy Red
Light Gunmetal	M-1738	Apple Green	Apple Green
Dearborn Blue	M-1723	Poppy Red	Poppy Red
Vineyard Green	M-1731	Apple Green	Apple Green
Commercial Bodies			
Vermillion	M-1722	none	Black
Tacoma Cream	M-1224	none	Black

FORD MODEL SPECIFICATIONS

1936 MODEL 68

BODY TYPE	LIST PRICE	CURB WT. (lbs.)
Coupe, 5-Window	$ 510	2652
Coupe, 5-Window*	535	NA
Tudor Sedan	520	2746
Tudor Trunk Sedan	545	NA
Fordor Sedan	580	2776
Fordor Trunk Sedan	605	NA
Deluxe Roadster*	560	2616
Deluxe Phaeton	590	2686
Deluxe Coupe, 3-Window	570	2656
Deluxe Coupe, 3-Window*	595	NA
Deluxe Coupe, 5-Window	555	2666
Deluxe Coupe, 5-Window*	580	NA
Deluxe Cabriolet*	625	2716
Deluxe Club Cabriolet*	675	2661
Delux Tudor Sedan	565	2756
Deluxe Tudor Touring Sedan	590	2786
Deluxe Fordor Sedan	625	2776
Deluxe Fordor Touring Sedan	650	2816
Deluxe Convertible Sedan	760	2862
Deluxe Convertible Trunk Sedan	780	2892
Station Wagon	670	NA

*with rumble seat

MODEL 68 PRODUCTION FIGURES BY BODY STYLE

(Totals of Standards and Deluxes where appropriate)

Coupe, 5-window..........................108,472
Tudor Sedan..................................486,310
Fordor Sedan (all).........................273,804
Roadster..3,862
Phaeton..5,555
Cabriolet..14,068
Convertible Sedan.............................5,601
Station Wagon....................................7,044
Club Cabriolet....................................4,616
Coupe, 3-window..............................21,446
Sedan Delivery...................................7,801

1936 COLOR AVAILABILITY

Pass. Bodies	Code No.	Stripes	Code No.	Wheels
Black	—	Apple Green	M-1225	Black
Gull Gray	NA	Poppy Red	NA	Gunmetal Gray
Gray Vineyard Green	NA	Silver	NA	Gray Vineyard Green
Washington Blue	M-1747	Tacoma Cream	M-1224	Washington Blue
Cordoba Tan	M-1748	Poppy Red	NA	Cordoba Tan
Spring Pass. Bodies				
Bambalina Blue	NA	Silver	NA	Bambalina Blue
Armory Green	NA	Silver	NA	Armory Green
Light Fast Maroon	NA	Gold	NA	Light Fast Maroon
Desert Sand	NA	Poppy Red	NA	Desert Sand

1937 MODELS 74 AND 78

BODY TYPE	LIST PRICE	CURB WT. (lbs.)
MODEL 74 (60 hp V-8)		
Coupe	$ 529	2382
Sedan Tudor	579	2513
Tudor Touring Sedan	604	2523
Sedan Fordor	639	2543
Fordor Touring Sedan	664	2553
Station Wagon (curtains)	744	2799
Station Wagon (glass)	764	2884
MODEL 78 (85 hp V-8)		
Coupe	585	2608
Sedan Tudor	610	2728
Tudor Touring Sedan	635	2760
Sedan Fordor	670	2761
Fordor Touring Sedan	695	2778
Station Wagon (curtains)	754	3018
Roadster*	693	NA
Phaeton	748	NA
Coupe	658	2618
Club Coupe	718	2728
Coupe Convertible*	718	NA
Cabriolet Club	758	NA
Sedan Tudor	673	2768
Tudor Touring Sedan	698	2791
Sedan Fordor	733	2783
Fordor Touring Sedan	758	2808
Sedan Convertible	858	2974
Station Wagon (glass	774	3105

*with rumble seat

MODEL 78 PRODUCTION FIGURES BY BODY STYLE

(Totals of Standards and Deluxes where appropriate.)

Cabriolet	18,684
Convertible Sedan	5,601
Coupe	134,122
Convertible Sedan	4,378
Fordor Sedan	71,947
Fordor Touring Sedan	144,218
Phaeton	3,723
Roadster	1,250
Sedan Delivery	8,948
Station Wagon	9,304
Tudor Sedan	342,119
Tudor Touring Sedan	212,227

1937 COLOR AVAILABILITY

Bodies, Fenders and Wheels	Code No.
Washington Blue	M-1747
Bright Vineyard Green	M-1751
Bright Coach Maroon	M-1758
Autumn Brown	M-1759
Gull Gray	M-1760
Desert Sand	NA
Black	M-1724
Spring Colors	
Silver Wing Gray	M-1764
Dalmatian Green	M-1762
Turquoise Blue	M-1761
Adobe Tan	M-1769

FORD MODEL SPECIFICATIONS

1938 MODELS 81A AND 82A

BODY TYPE	LIST PRICE	CURB WT. (lbs.)
MODEL 81A (60 hp V-8)		
Coupe	$ 595	2452
Tudor Sedan	640	2553
Fordor Sedan	685	2579
MODEL 82A (85 hp V-8)		
Coupe	625	2678
Tudor Sedan	665	2777
Fordor Sedan	710	2800
Deluxe Phaeton	820	2851
Deluxe Coupe	685	2709
Deluxe Club Coupe	745	2791
Conv. Deluxe Coupe	770	NA
Conv. Club Coupe	800	NA
Deluxe Tudor Sedan	725	2845
Deluxe Fordor Sedan	770	2876
Deluxe Conv. Sedan	900	2986
Deluxe Station Wagon	825	NA

MODEL 81-A PRODUCTION FIGURES BY BODY STYLE

(Totals of Standards and Deluxes where appropriate.)

Club Coupe	7,171
Convertible Club Coupe	6,080
Convertible Coupe	4,702
Convertible Sedan	2,743
Coupe	57,014
Fordor Sedan	122,307
Phaeton	1,169
Sedan Delivery	3,986
Station Wagon	6,944
Tudor Sedan	207,764

1938 COLOR AVAILABILITY

Pass. Bodies	Code No.
Washington Blue	M-1747
Bright Vineyard Green	M-1751
Bright Coach Maroon	M-1758
Gull Gray	M-1760
Comm. Bodies	
Vermilion Red	M-1722
Wren Tan Dark	M-1771
Demonstration Trucks	
Perch Yellow	MX-70868
Dartmouth Green	M-1772

1939 MODELS 91A AND 92A

BODY TYPE	LIST PRICE	CURB WT. (lbs.)
MODEL 91A (60 hp V-8)		
Coupe	$ 580	2463
Tudor Sedan	620	2608
Fordor Sedan	665	2623
MODEL 92A (85 hp V-8)		
Coupe	620	2710
Tudor Sedan	660	2830
Fordor Sedan	705	2850
Station Wagon	815	3080
Deluxe Coupe	680	2752
Deluxe Conv. Coupe*	765	2840
Deluxe Tudor Sedan	720	2867
Deluxe Fordor Sedan	765	2898
Deluxe Conv. Sedan	895	NA
Deluxe Station Wagon	920	3095

*with rumble seat

MODEL 91-A PRODUCTION FIGURES BY BODY STYLE

(Totals of Standards and Deluxes where appropriate)

Fordor Sedan	90,551
Tudor Sedan	144,333
Coupe	37,326
Sport Convertible	10,422
Convertible Sedan	3,561
Sedan Delivery	4,281
Station Wagon	9,432

1939 COLOR AVAILABILITY

Bodies	Code No.
Coach Maroon	M-1758
Gull Gray	M-1760
Dartmouth Green	M-1772
Mercury Blue Iridescent	M-1774*
Jefferson Blue	M-1775
Folkstone Gray	M-1776
Tropical Green	M-1780*
Claret Maroon	M-1785*
Cloud Mist Gray	M-1787

*Mercury only

1940 MODELS O1A AND O2A

BODY TYPE	LIST PRICE	CURB WT. (lbs.)
MODEL O2A (60 hp V-8)		
Coupe	$ 620	2519
Business Coupe 4	640	2549
Tudor Sedan	661	2669
Fordor Sedan	707	2696
MODEL O1A (85 hp V-8)		
Coupe	661	2763
Business Coupe	681	2801
Tudor Sedan	702	2909
Fordor Sedan	748	2936
Station Wagon	876	3232
Deluxe Coupe	722	2791
Deluxe Business Coupe	743	2831
Deluxe Conv. Club Coupe	850	2956
Deluxe Tudor Sedan	763	2964
Deluxe Fordor Sedan	809	2966
Deluxe Station Wagon	950	3262

MODEL 01-A PRODUCTION FIGURES BY BODY STYLE

(Totals of Standards and Deluxes where appropriate.)

Business Coupe	36,968
Convertible Coupe	23,704
Coupe	61,612
Fordor Sedan	117,301
Sedan Delivery	5,531
Station Wagon	13,199

1940 COLOR AVAILABILITY

Bodies	Code No.
Folkstone Gray	M-1776
Cloud Mist Gray	M-1787
Mandarin Maroon	M-1796
Sahara Tan	M-1797*
Como Blue Iridescent	M-1798*
Lyon Blue	M-1799
Yosemite Green	M-1800
Acadia Green	M-3903
Garnet Maroon	M-3905
Cotswold Gray Iridescent	M-3906

*Mercury only

V-8 ENGINE EVOLUTION

1932 (MODEL 18): The first flathead V-8 featured a 90-degree block of cast alloy iron, gear-driven cam with fabric cam gear, solid lifters and side valves. The bore and stroke were 3 1/16 x 3¾, giving a displacement of 221 cu. ins. Compression ratio was 5.5:1, with peak horsepower of 65 @ 3400 rpm. The cylinder heads had 21 studs, with water pumps mounted at the front of each head, and used 18mm plugs. Valve diameters (intake and exhaust): 1.54 ins., stems, .312-in. No valve seat inserts were used. Rods were 7 ins. center-to-center, with full-floating rod bearings (insert-type) spinning on 2-in.-diameter crankpins. The forged crank was counter-balanced with three 2-in.-diameter poured main bearings. Weight: 525 lbs.

1933 (MODEL 40): Change to aluminum cylinder heads of 6.3:1 compression, peak power raised to 75 hp @ 3800 rpm.

1934 (MODEL 40A): No changes except adoption of famous Stromberg 48 2-barrel carburetor to replace single-throat Detroit Lubricator carb. Venturis were 1.03-ins., and .048-in. main jets were standard. Horsepower was raised to 85 @ 3800.

1936 (MODEL 68): Steel pistons on mid-year models replaced aluminum pistons previously used. No horsepower change.

1937 (MODEL 78): Forerunner of modern line of flathead V-8's. Aluminum heads redesigned, moving water outlet to center of head and water pumps to upper front of block. New combustion chamber shape and use of domed pistons to reduce knock by giving better quench area. This dropped compression to 6.12:1. Famous Stromberg 97 carb was substituted for the 48, using smaller .97-in. venturis and .045-in. main jets. Forged crank featured enlarged mains of 2.4 ins. and insert bearings to replace the former poured babbitt type. Horsepower remained the same, engine became known as the V-8-85.
Compression was 6.1:1 for the Ford and 6.3:1 for the Merc, due to different displacements. Block unchanged. New crank: same stroke (3¾), 2.5-in. mains. Ford held 2-in. rod diameter, but Merc was 2.14. Rods unchanged, domed steel pistons used. New ratings were 85 hp @ 3800 for the Ford, and 95 hp @ 3600 for the Mercury. Water pumps lowered.

1938 (MODEL 81A): No changes other than change to 14mm plugs.

1939 (FORD 91A, MERCURY 99A): When the Mercury automobile was born, the entire V-8 engine was redesigned so that it could be used in both cars. Ford retained 3 1/16-in. bore, while Merc went to 3 3/16 ins. for 239 cu. ins. Heads changed to 24-stud design (extra studs for better sealing).

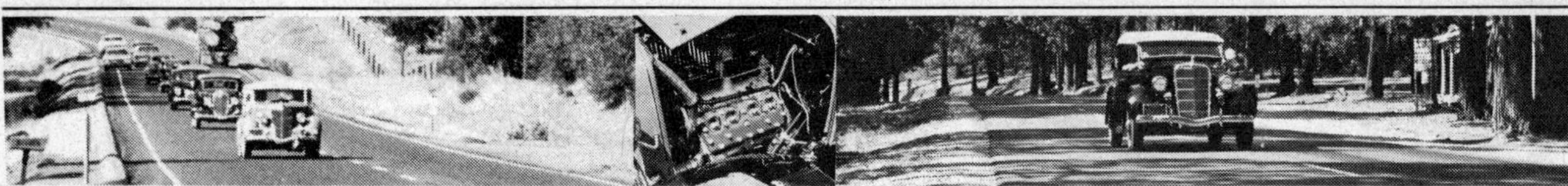

FORD V-8's OF THE THIRTIES IN RETROSPECT

1932 Ford makes the announcement, and production starts on the first of them. The favorite of restorers, it is fast becoming the most expensive of the flathead V-8's. The Phaeton, Convertible Sedan, and Roadster Pickup are the scarcest of the year's offerings.

1933 Ford enters the styling race and continues to improve the V-8 engine. 1933 Fords are rarely seen today, possibly because the '33 underwent more production changes than any other year, and that makes it hard to restore authentically. Oddball of the year is the Victoria.

1934 Ford continues with a good thing in an effort to save on production costs and pass the savings on to the customer. Improvements in styling makes everyone forget the '33. Truly beautiful evolution, and the 4-cyl. models are finally dropped as the V-8 proves itself. Restoration is high buck; the most popular models seem to be the Phaetons and Coupes.

1935 Ford enters the yearly styling cycle completely, the Convertible Sedan re-appears in a new form and Ford dealers begin pushing accessories. Many sedans are still roaming the streets today, and the '35 is an excellent choice for a first restoration.

1936 What can you say? Ford makes a styling hit and the '36's popularity is still going strong even today. Almost as much in demand as the '32, even the commercial offerings are nice to look at. Abundance of information makes restoration easy, scarcity of parts and accessories makes it increasingly hard.

1937 Streamlining enters the picture and Ford puts the headlights in the fenders instead of on them. An interesting new model is the four-place Club Coupe, forerunner of modern-day Coupes. Last year for the Roadster. Many '37's are still around at reasonable prices and they are good bets for the future.

1938 Marks the first major differentiation between Standard and Deluxe models, as Ford tries to appeal to a wider market. Last year for the Phaeton. All open models are scarce. Inexpensive parts, comparatively speaking, make the '38 a restorer's dream, but many aren't bitten by the looks. Last year also for mechanical brakes and the 21-stud engine.

1939 Ford makes a comeback with improved engine, styling and hydraulic brakes. The era closes for open cars as 1939 is the last year for the rumble seat and the Convertible Sedan. Strangely, Ford offers no four-place convertible this year, a style it had offered since late 1936. A nice-looking car and easy to drive, not a bad choice for investment. Last year for the floor shift.

1940 Ford realizes its mistake and brings back the convertible, to the everlasting joy of restorers everywhere. Good looks make the '40 a sales leader, and the fantastic survival rate is probably for the same reason. The Deluxe's die-cast grille is the most vulnerable part of the car.

OPPOSITE: Henry Ford; through the courtesy of Ford Archives, Greenfield Village, Detroit, Michigan.